AN EXPLORATION

OF

EXMOOR

AND THE

HILL COUNTRY OF WEST SOMERSET

WITH NOTES ON ITS ARCHÆOLOGY

BY

JOHN LLOYD WARDEN PAGE

MEMBER OF THE SOMERSETSHIRE ARCHÆOLOGICAL AND NATURAL HISTORY
SOCIETY; AUTHOR OF 'AN EXPLORATION OF DARTMOOR AND ITS
ANTIQUITIES'

With Map and Illustrations

LONDON
SEELEY AND CO., LIMITED
ESSEX STREET, STRAND
1890

CONTENTS

CHAPTER XV

THE SEAWARD SIDE

APPENDIX

ABBREVIATIONS

The references to the Principal Works quoted in the following
pages are abbreviated as follows .

Hon. J. Fortescue's 'Records of Staghunt-
ing on Exmoor' ..   ..   Stag-hunting.
Murray's 'Handbook to Wilts, Dorset and
Somerset'   ...   .   Murray.
'Proceedings of the Somersetshire Archæ-
ological Society'   ...   .   Proc. Som. Arch. Soc.
Savage's 'History of the Hundred of Car-
hampton'   .   ..   ...   Savage.

LIST OF ILLUSTRATIONS

PREFACE

So far as can be ascertained, no attempt has yet been made to describe in anything like detail the hill country of West Somerset. Now and again a book, generally a small one, has been given to the world, just sufficient to call the attention of the lover of scenery to the beautiful spots that exist between the Devonshire borders and the undulating line of Quantock; but that no volume treating of the *whole* district between Lynton and Cothelstone has made its appearance seems certain. It has, therefore, occurred to me that an account of a region every day becoming better known may not be altogether unwelcome.

As in a former work, for whose favourable reception I thank both critics and public, I have endeavoured to make my remarks on matters archæological in as popular a form as is consistent with what I fear many think a very dry subject. Archæologists themselves, however, may be of opinion that they have cause for complaint in that there is not enough of that anti-quarian leaven in which their souls take such delight.

To them I would reply that this book is topical first
and archæological afterwards : it is written not so much
for those addicted to the study of the past as for the
world at large ; and its pages are not, I would submit,
suitable for the histories of manors, of feudal tenures and
customs, for extracts from Domesday, and the thousand
and one other matters that come within the purview
of a work of purely archæological tendency. These
may be found in the pages of Collinson the County
Historian, in the proceedings of the Somersetshire
Archæological Society, and in other works dealing
with the records, facts, and traditions of earlier ages.

There being so few works upon the country described
in the following pages, I have to acknowledge little
assistance from brother authors. It would, however,
be both ungrateful and ungenerous not to mention the
Hon. John Fortescue's work upon Staghunting, whence
I have drawn much interesting information on the chase
of the red deer. In this connection, too, I would acknowledge with thanks the services of Mr. Arthur Heal,
the lately retired huntsman of the Devon and Somerset
Staghounds, who not only perused the fourth chapter
but added thereto certain observations which from
a man of his great knowledge are of considerable value.
I would also express my indebtedness to Mr. Thomas
Andrew, F.G.S., for his revision of the pages relating to
geology ; nor must I forget to thank Miss Alice King for
contributing to the article on folklore in the appendix.

I cannot be blind to the fact that in a work of this character there must be sins both of omission and commission. To my readers I would quote that dictum of Captain Cuttle, ' When found, make a note of.' In other words, I ask them to be kind enough to bring to my notice any omissions, any errors they may detect. There must be many an entertaining legend, for instance, that has not reached my ear, and which would be gratefully welcomed should the time come, as I trust it may, for another edition.

JOHN LL. WARDEN PAGE.

WILLITON, SOMERSET.
May, 1890.

EXMOOR

AND THE

HILL COUNTRY OF WEST SOMERSET

CHAPTER I

GENERAL FEATURES OF THE HILL COUNTRY

View from Dunkery Beacon—Rivers and Streams—Exmoor—
Roman coins at Exe Head—Its extent—Exmoor Forest—The
Perambulation—Foresters—Sale of the Forest—Scenery—Eleva-
tion—Absence of heather—Rivers of Exmoor—Fishing records
—The Barle—Pinkworthy Pond—The Chains—Moles Chamber
and its story—Roads—Climate—Minerals—The Brendon Hills—
The Quantock Hills.

THE western portion of the county of Somerset consists of very broken and hilly ground, covering an area
some thirty miles in length by fifteen in breadth. It is
bounded on the north by the Bristol Channel, on the
east by the Quantock Hills, and on the south and west
by Devonshire. The largest and most mountainous
tract is that occupying the extreme west—the wild
expanse of Exmoor. From its loftiest point, Dunkery
Beacon, the whole country to be treated of in this work

is spread out as on a map, and we will therefore imagine ourselves by the pile of stones which forms its summit, surveying the prospect beneath. To describe this panorama in detail is not our present intention; but merely to present to the eye of the reader—as far as may be—the configuration of the district which we are about to explore.

Immediately around and far to the west are the rolling steppes of Exmoor, channelled by many a deep combe, each the bed of a torrent. Along the northern slopes spread the gray waters of the Channel, into which the moorlands sink with great abruptness. From here the grand escarpment is not visible: it is indeed only properly seen from the sea, and no one who has sailed along these seaward hills will ever forget that magnificent coastline. Right out of the 'foam-laced margin' tower the great downs, here wooded nearly to their summits, eleven, twelve, thirteen hundred feet above; there bold and bare, the wind-shorn turf sprinkled with stony *screes* or sparsely shaded by storm-bowed oak. And, with the single exception of the break caused by Porlock Bay, the rampart continues from the huge Foreland of Countisbury to Minehead.

But it is not all Moor. Between Dunkery and Porlock are the deep, wooded glens of the Horner and its tributaries, while the vale dividing its steepes from the North Hill—as the short range running from Bossington to Minehead is called—is fertile and smiling, four miles across, and dotted with hamlet and homestead. From about the middle of this valley, another short range, that of Grabhurst, stretches nearly parallel with the

North Hill to the ancient and picturesque town of
Dunster. A long valley winds southward from this town
to Wheddon Cross, in Cutcombe, dividing the Moor
proper from the outlying hills of Croydon and Rodhuish,
and the straight, almost level, ridge of Brendon, reaching towards the Quantocks, which, separated from it
by a wide depression, rise in quiet beauty against the
eastern horizon, some fifteen miles away.

Allusion has been made to the grandeur of the coast-
line from our western limits to Minehead. But from
this quaint combination of ancient seaport and modern
watering-place the scenery changes. As far as Blue
Anchor, about three miles eastward, the shore is flat
and sandy—at low tide, indeed, not without a suspicion
of mud as well; there is no cliff, the narrow strip of
country between it and Dunster being flat as a fen, and,
in winter, nearly as marshy. From Blue Anchor the
coast again rises in those alabaster-veined cliffs so
familiar to the geologist. These trend away to Watchet,
thence to become a low red or gray wall, ending altogether where the Doniford brook spreads over the
shingly beach at the foot of the Quantock Hills.
Behind these cliffs the country undulates southward,
now rising, now falling, to meet the Brendon Hills.

It will thus be seen that this district has but little
level ground; in fact, with the exception of the plain
fringing Blue Anchor Bay, I am not aware of half a
dozen square miles without a hill between Glenthorne
and Quantoxhead, between Minehead and Dulverton.
With its purple moorlands, green valleys, undulating
pastures and waving woods, it presents such a prospect

as may well have been in the mind of that poet who conjured the traveller setting out for foreign lands to tarry awhile, and first visit the scenes of his native isle.

Although there are numerous streams, but two rivers, worthy of the name, water our district. These are the Exe and Barle, draining the southern half of Exmoor. The northern slopes supply streams of smaller size, which will be mentioned, more in detail, later. Eastward of the Moor we have the Avill* flowing down the valley of the same name (the high land about Wheddon Cross being the watershed between it and the Exe) to the sandy flats beyond Dunster, and the brooks of Washford and Doniford; the former rising in the Brendon Hills, entering the sea at Watchet; the latter, which takes its source near Willet and drains the valley of Stogumber, joining the channel as mentioned above a little to the east of that port. All these streams are clear, all rapid. More than one is rocky, too : a circumstance that adds not a little to the charm of the mountain flood.

Not only is Dunkery the highest part of Exmoor, but Exmoor is head and shoulders above the hills adjacent. A wild open moorland it is, little cultivated, bleak and lonely. The central part is dreary enough : no tor, as upon Dartmoor, breaks its sombre lines ; no tree, save in some sheltered combe, softens its stern aspect. But on its borders will be found some of the finest scenery in England ; dark, narrow valleys crowded thick with trees, lit by the white flash of an impetuous torrent dashing headlong over mossy

* Called at Dunster the *Laun*.

boulders, at one moment caressing, at the next sub-merging, the thickets of fern that fringe its course.

As little of commercial value can be made out of Exmoor, there are neither towns nor villages really upon it. At one time there were mines; but they have long ceased working, a fact that no lover of scenery will deplore. Not even chemical works or powder mills, those common accessories of waste land, disfigure the landscape. The villages—small, old-world, picturesque —stand at irregular distances about the skirts of the Moor, as if dreading its cold blasts and chilling mists; and the traveller will find little beyond a shepherd's cot between Oare and Simonsbath. He will not be troubled greatly, either, by contact with his fellow-man; for, though several roads have been cut across the waste, the population is too scanty to make much of a show upon them, and a human being about every four miles is as much as he can expect. If he be of tendency eremitical, or, like a poet of the Quantocks, one whc ' haunts lonely places,' we may commend him to the central district, where he will find no road at all, and may wander undisturbed over leagues of country the wildest of the wild, with no living object to disturb his meditations, unless it be a wild pony or wilder red deer. For Exmoor and the neighbouring hills are the last habitat of this beautiful creature.

Yet in spite of its barrenness it is not without beauty, a grim beauty perchance, and of a kind that in the heart of the Moor may, to some folk, become monotonous, but that still has its attractions. The great, round hills and dark, sullen ridges, in their very grandeur of desolation, cánnot fail to speak in tones very moving to him who loves the moorland. The wild heath beneath, the wild sky above—far up, but which seems at times so near —inspire a feeling of freedom to which the dweller in the lowlands is a stranger; while the keen mountain air, filling the lungs with the faint scent of the heather, the stronger perfume of the furze, or anon with the salt breath of the sea, induces an exhilaration of spirits of which even the most jaded is sensible.

And then the view. It may be questioned whether any highlands in England command the immensely varied prospect obtainable from this cradle of the Exe and Barle. Nearly the whole of the county of Somerset, quite half of Devon, a slice of Dorset, even a bit of Cornwall, lie beneath the eye; an expanse of salt water, from Avonmouth to Lundy, and far beyond into the wild Atlantic, stretches away right and left, while northwards the view is but blocked by the lofty mountains of central Wales. A panorama which is without equal south of the Scottish Border.

Of its history little can be said. Of course it was a British fastness—the beacons on Dunkery and other hills, and the barrows which here and there break the long line of heath, speak to us of an early people; but it seems to have been but sparsely inhabited, certainly not to the extent of its distant sister, Dartmoor. There are few, if any, hut circles; and none of those enclosures of 'standing stones' that render so interesting the wild tract between Tavy and Teign. Roman coins have been found near Exe Head, not very far from their reputed camp of Showlsborough

Castle; though what the conquerors of the world wanted in so desolate a spot is not apparent. Perhaps they utilized the old British trackway, which is said to have run from the Parret over the Quantocks and Brendons and up the Exe Valley to Barnstaple. Perhaps they ' prospected '—as was certainly the case upon the Brendon Hills—for minerals ; or, peradventure, and this is equally probable, the coins belonged to some native, who may have received them from a legionary in the camp ; though, of course, there is no actual reason for assuming that the position of the camp had aught to do with the presence of these coins, Roman money, as is well known, being current in Britain for a considerable period.

Where this wild tract begins, and where it ends, is rather difficult to determine. According to Sir Henry de la Beche, ' it extends from the valley of Stogumber and Crowcombe, separating it from the Quantock Hills on the east, to the Hangman Hills on the Bristol Channel, near Combe Martin, on the west. Near the latter place this high land forms a point whence it sweeps to the south-east by a curved line, passing by Parracombe, Chapman Barrows, Span Head, and the North Molton Ridge. Its southern boundary ranges from, thence by Molland Down, Dulverton Common and Haddon Down, to Heydon Down and Main Down near Wiveliscombe, whence the high land trends away to the Stogumber and Crowcombe Valley above mentioned.' So writes the eminent geologist, and, as far as geological formation and the natural ' lay ' of the land is concerned, he is doubtless right.

Local opinion, however, would bound Exmoor on the east by the valley dividing Dunkery from the heathery slopes of Croydon Hill.

A portion of the waste, consisting of about 20,000 acres, has from time immemorial been termed the Forest. When it first became such is doubtful; but, in all probability, it was 'afforested' soon after the Norman Conquest, together with Dartmoor, the New Forest and other wild tracts of country. Whatever acreage of woodland it may have borne in a former day, it is bare enough now. I do not think that the Forest, in its wooded sense, was ever of great extent. Doubtless what little timber it bore was cut down for fuel. As an open chase or hunting-ground it was used, and probably very few more trees than are at present to be found in its combes clothed the sheltered places of the wilderness.

To ascertain the limits of these forests, 'perambulations' were made, which were afterwards confirmed by Act of Parliament. The first and only recorded perambulation of Exmoor took place by Royal Commission in the twenty-sixth year of the reign of Edward I.,* when the bounds were decided, and, done into modern English, were broadly as follows: Beginning at what is now known as County Gate, where the road from Porlock to Lynton passes through the wall dividing Somerset from Devon, the line ran to Fistones, 'where,' says Mr. Fortescue in 'Staghunting,' 'Deddycombe cot stood, and where Culbone parish crosses the main road at its junction with Oare,' and thence by the

* *Vide* Appendix.

head of Lillycombe to Wear Water. From Wear Water it continued over Middle Hill to Blackbarrow and Alderman's Barrow (which is, in the opinion of the writer above quoted, the same as the *Osmundbergh* of the perambulation), thence following a south-westerly line to Orchard Corner. Near this it crossed the Exe, and ran to Redstone, on the road from Exford to Simonsbath, and from that point to a small stream running into Reddecombe, and on to Shutscombe. Deresmarke, the next point mentioned, ' is,' says Mr. Fortescue, ' apparently a thing of the past, but Stone-chiste is doubtless the spot where Withypoole joins at one corner the parishes of Exmoor and Exford.'

The next point was the Barle at Sheardon Hutch, whence the boundary ran to Willingford Water-crossing on the Dunn's Brook, thence following the existing county boundary to the starting-point.

Besides the Foresters appointed by the Crown to preserve the King's rights, there was one chosen by the interested parties as guardians of the woods, commons, and pannage held by Barons, Knights and Freeholders within the forest. The first of these Foresters was one William de Wrotham, in whose representatives, the De Peches, the office remained till 1337, when Matthew de Peche sold it to Sir Richard D'Amori, Knight, who twenty-one years later is supposed to have parted with it to Roger Mortimer, Earl of March. It is said to have continued in the possession of his descendants and of the Dukes of York until it came to the Crown in the reign of Edward IV.*

* Phelps' ' History of Somerset,' p. 40.

In 1815 the Forest was put up for auction, and sold to Mr. John Knight, a Worcestershire gentleman, who constructed round the whole a ring fence, enclosing, I am told, an area fifty-two miles in circumference. Such part of his purchase as was then represented by the Forest—for he bought up the interests of divers other holders—was, in 1856, made the present parish of Exmoor.

So much for the history—and very scant history it is—of Exmoor Forest. Now for the physical features of the land. Dunkery, being the highest part of the Moor, would, it may well be supposed, afford the best panorama of its surface. But this is not so. As a general outlook for the whole of the district hereafter to be described, it is indeed *facile princeps*, but, standing as it does almost on the western edge of the Moor, the person who views Exmoor from the Beacon, will, while acquiring a good idea of border scenery, scarcely obtain the best picture of the interior of the waste—the old Forest. To see Exmoor in its native wildness, he should take his stand on the high ground about Pinkworthy Pond, or midway between it and Hoar Oak Hill. From either of these points he will gain a very fair view of the Forest, and this is what he will see :

A bare, rolling waste of moorland stretching away into the eastern distance, like the ocean 'heaving in long swells.' Here and there a larger wave rises towards the sky, the sloping wall of some combe deeper than its fellows. There is one of these combes at his very feet; and a fine mountain glen it is. On either hand the bald downs tower to a height of a couple of hundred feet or more, scored here and there by little 'goyals' or gullies, down which sparkle tiny runnels, each lending its volume to swell the transparent torrent hurrying through the bottom to join a larger stream in the valley beyond. He will hear the voice of the waters, but nothing beside, unless, indeed, he move; when perchance a black cock will start up with loud whirr from the coarse grass, or a curlew vanish across the ravine, uttering its melancholy cry. No dwelling is within sight, though the knowledge that a shepherd's hut lies *perdu* in one of the folds, a mile or two away, will prevent that feeling of utter loneliness inspired by the desolation of the granite moorland five-and-thirty miles away to the southward.

Peaks, whether rocky or grass-grown, there are none; neither is there a hill of any considerable elevation with truly mountainous outline, unless we except Dunkery, rising purple a dozen miles ahead. But for all that the tableland is lofty: yon coach-road to Porlock runs at a level from 1,200 to 1,400 feet above the sea; those five tumuli that give name to a hill southward* are 1,619 feet high, and Chapman Barrows, to the west, reach an elevation but a few feet less.

But there is little heather; outside the ring fence there is plenty, but within 'Sir Frederick's' domain coarse grass flourishes, intruded upon by few clumps of the dark wiry shrub with its graceful waxen flower. Yet the Forest wants not for colouring; there is plenty

* Span Head or *Five Barrows*. For elevations, *vide infra,* p. 310.

of tall bracken, its vivid green in spring, its golden
brown in autumn, lighting up the dingy grass almost
as much as the occasional scarlet of the whortleberry,
which may be found in greater or less quantity on
every hillside.   There are, too, the usual emerald,
and brown, and red patches of bog, fringed with
nodding cotton grass; so that the Forest, though
heatherless, is not colourless. And if there be any
who think that the absence of heath must perforce
render a moorland region devoid of colour, let him
look across this wild expanse on a day of sun and
wind, when the cloud shadows are marching from hill
to hill, from valley to valley, and he will confess that
the presence of purple bloom is very far from being a
sine quâ non in the matter of artistic requirement.

   But why, if there be heather outside the Forest
bounds, should there be none within? The owner, says
Mr. Fortescue, holds that originally all the uncultivated districts of these parts were moorlands of rough
grass, and that the Forest alone remains in this condition, because, owing to the fact of its being Crown
property, it was untilled; and that the efforts which
were made to cultivate certain parts of the adjacent
moorlands resulted, where the land was exhausted, in
the production of heather—which he has indeed proved
to be the fact. *Per contra*, Mr. Fortescue points out
that, although Winsford Hill—a part of the Moor undoubtedly once brought under cultivation—is covered
with heather, so also is Dunkery, a hill very unlikely
to have been cultivated; and points, too, to the great
chain of heather from Dunkery to Martinhoe, including

the tract of Brendon Common, whereof the name, Brown Down, seems to indicate the presence of heather from the beginning of things.

Like all other highlands, Exmoor is the 'mother of manie rivers.' These have already been generally referred to, but a more particular description is perhaps necessary. The most important is the Exe—the most important, but not the largest—for its big brother, the Barle, pours into it near Dulverton a flood considerably greater than its own. The Exe rises in the Chains, a dreary bog in the westernmost corner of the Moor; the Barle, within a few miles, in the neighbourhood of Moles Chamber. Besides the Barle, the Exe receives, near Exton, the Quarme Water, which has its source in some wet ground on Dunkery, and the Haddeo, draining the western spurs of the Brendon Hills. The principal tributary of the Barle is Sheardon Water. After a rapid course southward the Exe, as is well known, empties itself into the English Channel at Exmouth.

From the northern watershed one or two short-lived streams find their way to the Bristol Channel. Chief of these is the Lyn, which, before reaching Lynmouth, receives the following tributaries: the Wear Water (really the head-waters of the river itself), the Chalk Water and Badgworthy Water, all rising near Alderman's Barrow, and the Farley and Combe Park Waters and West Lyn, from the Chains. The last three have almost their entire course in Devonshire, Badgworthy Water being, for half its length, the county boundary. In the eastern part of the Moor we have the wooded Horner, with its feeders the Chetsford and East Waters, which, after passing by the pleasant village of Bossington, falls into Porlock Bay. These are the principal rivulets, the remainder being mere torrents.

All swarm with fish. I remember meeting at the inn at Simonsbath a pair of anglers whose records are, I fancy, not often beaten : one could account for 149 trout taken from the Barle; another had killed 157 in Badgworthy Water—a pretty good day's work. Yet, even this was capped by a late Vicar of Stoke Pero, who, I am informed, between sunrise and dark lessened the population of the Oare waters by no less than 370! After this, the feat of a personal acquaintance, who, with a drive of thirty-eight miles thrown in, slew ninety-seven, sinks into comparative insignificance.

The scenery of these moorland streams is very varied and beautiful. Let us take the Barle. From its source to Simonsbath, it races down a bare, wild valley—a shining flood, so clear, that, except in sharp stickles, every stone that forms its bed may be detected as through glass. At Simonsbath it meets with its first woodland, skirting the plantations which render this little settlement so picturesque, and, what is more important, so secure from the blasts of the Moor. Thence it flows in ever-widening stream through a deep and again bare valley to the abrupt hill of Cow Castle, round which it sweeps, and presently, receiving from the south the Sheardon Water, passes in more sedate fashion beneath the arches of Landacre Bridge, where it may be said to leave the moorlands. And now covers fringe it, on one side or the other, for the

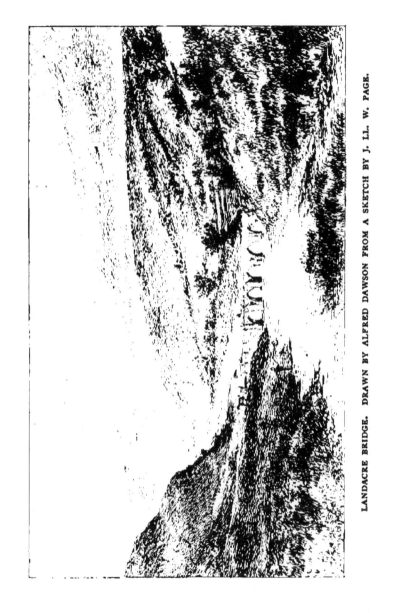

LANDACRE BRIDGE.   DRAWN BY ALFRED DAWSON FROM A SKETCH BY J. LL. W. PAGE.

remainder of its journey. Flowing past Withypoole, village of anglers, it reaches the ancient slab bridge, known as Torr or Tarr steps ; thence it winds through towering woods beneath Hawkridge and the old hill-fort of Mouncey Castle to Dulverton.

And this passage of the Barle may be taken as typical of that of most other Exmoor streams, except the Lyn and the Horner, which are shrouded by glorious woods the greater part of their course. But these streams are, or should be, too well known to need description here. The country about Porlock, and that loveliest of all lovely ravines, unsurpassed Waters-meet, are they not near to civilization ? while the way of the Barle is known only to those who have fished his waters, or, in search of the picturesque, wandered far into the moorlands.

These mountain rivers rise with extraordinary rapidity. He who in summer sees them, dawdling along with scarcely enough current to submerge their pebbles, their boulders bleaching in the sun, will scarcely recognise them in winter, as they pour down to the lowlands a flood of water against which nothing can stand. Of this very Barle, Leland quaintly says that ‘ the water in somer most communely rennith flat upon stones easy to be passid over, but when Raynes cum and storms of Wintre it ragith and ys depe.’

Exmoor owns but one sheet of water, and that artificial. This is Pinkworthy Pond,* a deep tarn near the Chains, formed by an embankment built across the

---

* On the Moor always called *Pinkerry*, and so Badgworthy Water is invariably *Badgery*.

head of a small combe. Yet its appearance is natural enough, and the little rough headlands projecting into the dark water give it a picturesque look. Unfortunately, however, the prospect from it is uninteresting.

There are no *dangerous* bogs; but some very nasty ones exist, notably the Chains, so often execrated by the stag-hunter. This was the spot excepted by the late master, Mr. Fenwick Bisset, in his comparison between hunting and legislating, a comparison very much to the disparagement of the latter. 'I assure you,' he said to a company of farmers, at a hunt dinner, 'that I would far sooner be anywhere on Exmoor, except on the Chains in the thickest fog, than in the House of Commons.'* Accordingly Exmoor does not furnish the exciting (if sometimes rather apocryphal) bog stories supplied by its more grim neighbour, Dartmoor. The only loss of life recorded—save in 'Lorna Doone'—and there are doubts even about that, is placed to the credit of Moles Chamber, in which a farmer is said to have perished, many years since, on his way home from Barnstaple market. The unbelieving, however, trace the name to the river Mole, a tributary of the Taw, which takes its source hereabouts. These will, probably, be strengthened in their theory when they hear that two other versions of the 'Farmer Mole' story pass current; one to the effect that both he and his horse were engulfed while hunting, the other that he 'rode into it in spite of the warnings and entreaties of his friends.' But neither marketer, Nimrod,

* 'Staghunting,' p. 83.

or lunatic will again incur danger in the morass, for it is now drained.

With the exception of the highways from Porlock to Lynton and Dulverton *viâ* Exford, there were, until the times of Mr. Knight, no regular highways over Exmoor. But the enterprising purchaser of the Forest made roads from Simonsbath to Exford in the one direction, and Lynton in another; connections between Simonsbath and South Molton on the south and Challacombe in the west. Thus two good main roads traverse the wild part of the moor; one from Dulverton over Winsford Hill through Simonsbath to Lynton, with a branch to South Molton; the other from Porlock over Lucott Hill to Exford, where it joins the highway first named. A third road crosses Landacre Bridge to North Molton, passing between North Molton Ridge and Molland Down. All three, through at least half of their distance, open up wild scenery; the wildest, perhaps, being that from Simonsbath to Lynton, where the road ascends to a considerable elevation and runs mile after mile over bare moor. The way, too, across Lucott Hill is wild enough, when one gets beyond the ugly enclosures to the north of Exford, and the view both of land and sea, as it descends towards Whitestones and Porlock Hill, is unrivalled in the west.

Like other elevated tracts, Exmoor does not enjoy a dry atmosphere; in fact the amount of wet weather endured by the moorfolk is best expressed by their saying, which has almost passed into a proverb—'it always rains on Exmoor.' Dunkery is their weather-glass, and directly the clouds begin to lower upon the

2

Beacon, they make up their minds for rain. Says a
local doggrel, possessing more truth than rhyme :

'When Dunkery's top cannot be seen
Horner will have a flooded stream.'

Having regard to its nearness to the sea, it would indeed be matter for wonder were the atmospheric conditions otherwise. To the Atlantic, also, must be credited
the chilling mists which sometimes enwrap its wastes
for days together. But the air is moorland air, nevertheless, and what *that* means, no one who has visited
these or any other uplands needs to be told. It is as
bracing as a showerbath; as exhilarating as champagne.

Speaking broadly, the geological formation of the
hills is Devonian; of the valleys, new red sandstone.
On this head more will be said presently; just now, it
need only be remarked that the Moor is, as is so often
the case with this formation, wanting in rock, without
which the finest hill must lose much of its charm.
Occasionally, a protruding crag will thrust its gray
head from the slope or brow of a combe—and there are
boulders enough and to spare on Dunkery—but rock,
or the want of it, is without doubt the weak point of the
scenery of these Moors of Western Somerset. The
only mineral at all plentiful is iron; though on the
outskirts—*e.g.* in the seaward range stretching from
Porlock Bay to Minehead, and in the neighbourhood of
South Molton, copper is also found, though not in sufficient quantities to pay for the working. Of these iron
mines, great hopes were at one time entertained, and
when, in 1851, the agent of Mr. Knight sent his specimen of Exmoor carbonate of iron to the Great Exhibi-
tion, there were many who thought that the Moor

had a great future before it. Perhaps it has ; but such companies as the Dowlais and Ulverstone do not withdraw their capital without reason. The last mines to cease operations were those on the Brendon Hills, really no longer a part of the Moor, and only mentioned here because Sir Henry de la Beche has seen fit to include them within his Exmoor boundary.

The reader will now think that Exmoor has been sufficiently enlarged upon, and that something is due to the other ranges that go to make up the hill country of West Somerset. These are, as he will have already noted, the Brendons and Quantocks. The former range is a long, straight, broad-backed ridge, in length about twelve miles, running parallel with the coast, from which it is divided by the vales of Williton and Monksilver. It is mostly under cultivation, and its tableland, cut into pretty equal portions by a road that follows roughly an old trackway, hereafter to be mentioned, rises at the one end from the valleys about Cutcombe, and dips at the other into the valley below the Quantocks. Many wooded combes run into the slopes, beautiful enough, but lacking the wild grandeur of most of the glens of Exmoor. The belt of heather, which, in anything but an unbroken line, forms the crown of the westernmost portion, would be almost monotonous in its dead level, were it not that now and again a fine barrow marks the surface. And at the eastern extremity there are the ruins, or perhaps, rather, the commencement of a big camp, which has given rise to no little learned surmise. The name is both Celtic and Saxon, *Bryn* and *Dun* both meaning the same—a hill. Of the

2—2

far more interesting and irregular line of the Quantocks, we shall here say little; a full description of their breezy slopes, not, like the Brendons, disfigured with hedges, but rising in bold outline, either bare or partly clothed with trees; their many combes, each with its foreground of woodland, each with its background of brown or purple moor; their villages, their antiquities, appears as we draw towards the end of our pilgrimage. Here it is enough to say that the range in its dozen miles comprises scenery of a kind, second to none on Exmoor, and far superior to the tamer delights of Brendon. Yet in elevation these beautiful hills have to yield the palm to both, the highest point being but 1,261 feet above sea level, a height which the Brendons, at their western extremity, exceed by 22 feet; though no one but an Ordnance surveyor would ever dream of giving Willsneck an altitude less than that of Elworthy Barrows.

With reference to the origin of their name, a tale, passing strange—and passing improbable, too—is told: There is a tradition that Cæsar, standing upon one of the loftiest summits, was so impressed by the panorama that he cried ' *Quantum ab hoc !*' It is scarcely necessary to tell the reader, that of Cæsar's presence in Somersetshire at all there is not one scrap of evidence. Possibly the etymology may be traced to *gwantog*, full of openings, or to *cantoche*, the water headlands, either of which accurately describe the peculiar features and situations of these combe-pierced seaward hills. But who shall venture with confidence on the thorny paths of the origin of place-names ?

CHAPTER II

CULTIVATION : GEOLOGY : FOLKLORE

Sterility of the hills—Sheep on Exmoor—Ponies—Farms—Wood carving — Plaster decoration — Geology — minerals — Primeval Forests — *Elephas primigenius* — Peasantry — Signposts and Parsons—Betty Muxworthy's prayer—Folklore—King's Evil—Charming Wens—Touching a corpse—The split ash—Boneshave —Overlooking—A divining loaf—Customs on Midsummer and Christmas Eve—Ghosts : Master Lucott, and Mrs. Leakey.

ALTHOUGH many hundreds of acres on the outskirts of Exmoor, the Brendons and the Quantocks have been brought under cultivation, it cannot be said that the main body of either—except perhaps the Brendons—has taken kindly to the spade of the agriculturist. The late Mr. Knight did his very best to open up both the mineral, and, as he believed, the agricultural possibilities of his territory; but, while lack of quantity in ore has extinguished mining hopes, lack of quality in soil, stormy winds and chilly mists have been too much for farming efforts. The gaunt walls of the unfinished mansion at Simonsbath are a sufficient commentary on the hopelessness of improving the wild Forest.

But Exmoor is a grand sheepwalk. I am told that the Forest wall encloses no less than nine thousand sheep, and it is no very rare thing to come upon a

shepherd's cot in the most unlikely situation.   There
is one, for instance, in the remote Doone Valley, as it
is now called,* (overlooking the scattered stones which
are said to mark the sites of the houses of those dread
freebooters painted in such vivid colours by the pen of
Blackmore,) and others, dropped as it were from the
skies, in one or other of the secluded combes.   And if
we except peat cutting—an industry not favoured, by
the way, of hunters, as the ruts are a constant source
of danger to horses—there is no other industry upon
the moor proper.   One or two farms, it is true, have
been reclaimed from the waste in places, notably about
Simonsbath ; but a great deal of the new cultivation is
represented by fields good for little beyond coarse
pasturage, enclosed by stone and turf hedges topped
with beech.   The most important piece of reclamation
is of older date than the reign of Mr. Knight.   This is
the tract of country between Exe and Barle ; and even
in the midst of that, Winsford Hill rears a bold brow,
mantled thick with heather, and having an area of a
good many square miles.   No ; Exmoor is best left
alone : 'the peat and heather in hill and dale,' says a
writer in *Chambers' Journal*, 'seem to defy the hand of
man ; and his little efforts to rob them of their natural
grandeur and obdurate ruggedness are quite futile.'

There are still a good many ponies both within and
without the Forest.   But crossing, particularly with
Arabs, has not tended to improve the breed ; and a

---

* 'The Doone Valley,' writes Mr. Bisset—'a new name.   It *used
to be* the combe between Haccombe and Withycombe ridge.'   'Stag-
hunting,' p. 251.

good 'Exmoor' is not so easily procured, even at Bampton fair—that great mart for the steeds of the moorland—as was the case fifty years ago. Nowadays it is to the care of the Acland family that we are indebted for pure 'Exmoors;' indeed the Holnicote pony has long been famous for possessing all the attributes which go to make up this sturdy and wonderfully staying little animal.

With regard to the Brendons, the Quantocks and the other hills comprised in our district, to the remarks already made little need be added. The former range has probably been cultivated nearly to its summit—if a tableland can have a summit—for a couple of centuries at least, while the beautiful ' Hilles ' that ' renne in crestes from Quantok-Hedde toward Tauntoun' are almost as wild as they were when Leland wrote his ' Itinerary.'

Some of the farm-houses are very picturesque, and many show traces of having seen better days. They are, indeed, old manor-houses ; or dwellings, at one time occupied by the gentry, which have, from one cause or another, fallen from their former estate. Between the Quantocks, on the east, and the Devonshire borders, on the west, there must be at least thirty of these ancient houses. They are nearly all of the Tudor period. Some have chapels or oratories still remaining; a good example occurs at Lower Marsh, near Dunster, a mediæval abode, with a tiny chapel over the porch, still retaining its piscina. About Exmoor, as might have been expected, these old houses are not so plentiful; but in the country between

Minehead and Stowey they are very numerous, and the President of the Somerset Archæological Society announced, in the last opening address, that in a strip of country parallel with the Bristol Channel, about fourteen miles long and three wide, he could easily count twenty-one, though not all were farms. Attention was at the same time directed to the fact that wood was often used in the place of stone, not only in the farms, but in houses of higher degree. The presence of timber is indeed very marked. Archways, many of them two or three centuries old, are constructed with solid beams of oak, and even the tracery of windows is carved out of the same material. From this it is, I think, safe to assume that, throughout this country, in the days of old the workers in wood excelled the workers in stone, and the exquisite carving in some of the churches, notably the screens and bench ends, lends strength to the theory. Among the many buildings—for almost every village has one where this woodwork is to be seen—occupying a prominent position, may be mentioned the farmhouse of Bratton Court, the tannery at Minehead, and a cottage at Lynch, near Porlock.

The highly ornamented plaster overmantels and ceilings are another feature, and these are common both in mansion and cottage; more common, of course, in the former than in the latter. I know of a ceiling, in a cottage at Sampford Brett, as elegant as any in buildings more pretentious. One is puzzled to account for the presence of these decorations in what are now cottages. It has been suggested to me that they were, perhaps, dwellings for younger sons. It is certainly difficult otherwise to explain the elaboration of some of these artistic patterns.

The fertility of the farms, of course, depends in a great measure on their situation. Few in England enjoy a soil more productive than that of those homesteads which are dotted about in the valley between Quantock and Brendon, or the rich marsh lands of Carhampton and Dunster. This new red sandstone is a famous fertilizer. But in the higher lands, matters are not so flourishing, though even here there are distinct grades. There is, for instance, the stone rag, where grass does well enough; while on the stone rush, which produces a hard inferior soil, subject to drought, crops are scanty. And here, perhaps, it may not be altogether out of place to say a few words on the geology of this part of Somerset.

The highlands are, as has been said, Devonian; so called by Murchison and Sedgwick because of their development in Devonshire. The Exmoor section is surrounded in the valleys on the east and north-east by new red sandstone, occurring chiefly along the route of the railway from Taunton to Minehead, though patches of this deposit are to be found extending as far as Porlock. The Quantock hills, however, are entirely surrounded with these new red deposits. Fringing the shore, from Blue Anchor to Catsford, are deposits of Lias, and at Doniford they are remarkable for their fossil ammonites, some of them from two to three feet in diameter. With regard to these cliffs of Blue Anchor, they furnish, as Mr. Ussher, F.G.S., remarked

in my hearing, an excellent illustration of the composi-
tion and relation of the Keuper marls of the Trias, the
lower or planorbic beds of the Lower Lias and the intervening black shales of the Rhætic or Penarth beds.

The geological literature of North Devon and West
Somerset has been carefully summarized by Mr. Etheridge, F.R.S. The Devonian 'consists of a succession of
sandstones, conglomerates and flagstones, alternating
with subordinate layers of sandy shale and beds of con-
cretionary limestones. The whole system is more or less
coloured by peroxide of iron, the shades varying from
dull rusty gray to bright red, fawn or creamy yellow,
the shales being in some instances curiously mottled.'
Mr. Etheridge also states that the Middle Devonian
or Ilfracombe beds have yielded seventy-three known
forms of fossil, of which twenty come from the Lower
Devonian or Lynton beds, but only three forms from the
lower ;* while twenty-eight from the Middle Devonian
beds are found in the Carboniferous beds generally.
Evidently molluscs, corals and crinoids flourished
abundantly in the waters of the sea covering this area
in the Devonian period ; the remains of encrinites, or
the rock lily, as it is frequently termed, are often met
with, particularly in the Quantocks.

But it may be asked, how were these hills upheaved?
During the Devonian period, the crest of the earth
became fractured in various parts, and mountain

---

* *Vide* 'Geological Transactions,' 1880, p. 263. Paper by Professor Hull, read March 10, 1880. There appears to be something
wanting here ; but the professor is quoting direct from Mr. Etheridge.

ranges and deep sea troughs were formed by the tilting up of the masses. To this cause the almost perpendicular strata of the Exmoor and Quantock ranges probably owe their origin, rather than to volcanic agencies, which so disturbed the area immediately to the south of Exmoor in the Carboniferous period.

That distinguished scientist, Sir A. C. Ramsay, F.R.S., was clearly of opinion that England and Wales had been planed across by marine denudation. It may not be amiss, therefore, to draw attention to the fact, that the main level of Exmoor, in its present height above the sea, corresponds with the main level of Dartmoor at the base of its several tors, suggesting the probability that here, after allowing for the water-worn furrows, we have the floor of the Post-carboniferous period from which the building of the British Isles really commenced.

Mr. W. H. Huddlestone, F.G.S., in his recent Presidential address to the Devonshire Association at Tavistock, characterized as well founded the claim of the Devonian to recognition as one of the great geological systems. In North Devon (in which he would include Exmoor), he said, there was a fossiliferous series interposed between beds which were held to be the equivalent of the lower and upper old red sandstones. It was these fossiliferous beds which forged the link that was missing, whilst the character of their fauna justified their being regarded as the headquarters of a separate system. These central beds constituted the backbone of the Devonian system, of which the upper and lower old red sandstones were integral parts.

As regards minerals, setting aside the lead mines of

. Combemartin as beyond our district, iron ore is or was
obtained in the Brendon Hills. It is to the low price
of iron and the expense of getting it to the market,
rather than to the paucity of the mineral itself, that the
stoppage of the works is to be attributed. Red
hæmatite iron has also been worked from the lower
new red sandstone beds in the neighbourhood of
Porlock, and was formerly extensively shipped from
Porlock to Wales. At Luccombe, indeed, it was so
near the surface as to be actually quarried. Copper,
too, has been found, but in small quantities. There is
an abandoned copper mine on the slopes of the
Quantocks, near Doddington. To the minerals of
Exmoor reference has already been made.

It may surprise some to learn that the beds of the
Exmoor district are geologically of similar formation to
those of the Cornish mining areas, which is Devonian.
Why then are they not so metalliferous? Probably
because of the absence of granite bosses. Mr. T.
Andrew, F.G.S., to whom I am indebted for several
suggestions in this chapter, referring to the fact that
the mineral veins of West Somerset are neither so
numerous nor so large as those of Cornwall, writes
to me thus: 'whether this is to be accounted for by
the absence of granite bosses, must remain an open
question; but it is noteworthy that the mines of Devon
and Cornwall are chiefly around the granite, and
most productive where the granite joins the slate.'

Roofing slates are found at Treborough, although
neither in quality nor quantity equal to those of the
Delabole quarries. Lime exists at Watchet and

Doniford; but is chiefly used for agricultural purposes. Exmoor is poorly supplied with lime: there are but patches between Dulverton and South Molton, at Combemartin, Exford and Withycombe. A very excellent silicious sandstone, slightly coloured with iron oxide, has been found at Williton. It is admirably adapted for building purposes, and is manifestly superior to the oolitic stone of the Bath district.

It only remains to be added that the stumps of a primeval forest, still visible at low tide, point to the day when the land extended much further seaward than now. One portion is in Porlock Bay, another between Blue Anchor and Minehead, a third in the neighbourhood of Lilstock and St. Audries. In the first and last the flint flakes of the aborigines of West Somerset have been found. Of recent years a curious discovery has been made in the foreshore off the mouth of the Doniford Brook, consisting of the gigantic tusks and teeth of the mammoth—*elephas primigenius*—once doubtless the inhabitant of the submerged forest. These were dug out, and are now deposited, with other interesting relics of a bygone day, at St. Audries House. Another fine fossil tooth of the elephant, found at or near the same spot, is in the collection of Mr. Spencer G. Percival, of Henbury, Clifton. It is thirteen inches in length and six in extreme width, and weighs more than eleven pounds.*

The peasantry of all these hills are characterized by their straightforward pleasant manner, which, though

* *Somerset County Gazette*, Sept. 9, 1882.

seldom wanting in 'honour to whom honour is due,' as
seldom, on the other hand, descends to servility. Like
all moorland folk, they possess a ready wit; not a very
coruscating wit, perhaps, but still quite sufficient to
open the eyes of the stranger who tries a joke at their
expense. Nor is sarcasm unknown. A gentleman,
only the other day, told me of a friend who had met
with an instance. The said friend had managed to
lose his way—no difficult thing on Exmoor. He
applied to an old fellow, who, after giving him some
rather complicated instructions, directed him, when he
came to a parson, to turn, as the case may be, to the
right or left. 'A parson?' said our wanderer, 'what
on earth do you mean?' The old gentleman looked
wondrous cunning, and intimated that he meant a
finger-post. 'And why do you call them *parsons?*'
queried our traveller. I dare not try to reproduce the
Exmoor spelling and pronunciation, but the peasant,
with, we may imagine, a heavy wink, replied ' Because
they be *supposed* to shew 'ee the right way.'

A good many of the characteristics of the Exmoor
peasantry are portrayed by the writer of 'Lorna
Doone.' There are plenty of the school of John Fry
and Betty Muxworthy still to be found. The latter
eccentricity was indeed 'drawn from the life,' and
known to many. She boasted that one prayer alone
had been sufficient for her throughout her earthly
pilgrimage. It was:

> 'Matthew, Mark, Luke, and John,
> ˎ Bless the bed that I lie on.'

The Folklore of the district is not, I think, either so

plentiful, or so varied, as that of the country further south. About Dartmoor clings enough of legend and superstition to satisfy the most exacting searcher after such matters; but this is hardly the case in West Somerset, and the peasantry of Exmoor and its neighbourhood appear reticent in imparting the little they do possess. There seems to be a lurking suspicion that they are being 'drawn' for the sole purpose of being laughed at; and this is, very naturally, productive of a disinclination to reveal anything beyond one or two superstitions which are so common, and, indeed, so thoroughly believed in, that incredulity, however derisive, will have little effect upon the narrator.

Chief of these is the belief in the efficacy of the charm known as 'touching for the King's evil.' In other parts of the country a seventh son is alone supposed to be able to effect a cure; but, in our part of the world, a ninth son has done wonders. While there is at Withypoole at this moment a seventh son, a bright intelligent lad, who is said to have healed many, there is, or was, at Winsford a *ninth* whose attentions are equally efficacious. At a pinch, too, a seventh, or I suppose, a ninth *daughter* will do. I have met several who have avowed that they or their friends had been cured by these simple means ; but why the touch of one hand is superior to that of another, and why a seventh or ninth child can alone remove the complaint, they could not tell. Great is the power of faith. Perhaps, too, like Rory O'More, they believe that 'there is luck in odd numbers.' At any rate the fact remains, that, in spite of the omnipresent School Board, the services of

the individual who can claim to be the seventh or ninth
of a family are almost as much in requisition as ever.
But he, or she, must perform the operation fasting ;
fasting, too, must the patient be ; for this, an old lady
tells me, is a *sine quâ non* for success.   Further, it
appears that the 'toucher' must make no charge for
his services, though a *present* would not be refused.

Nor is 'king's evil' the only malady curable by the
human touch.   A woman informed me, recently, that
her father-in-law, now some time dead, enjoyed a high
repute for charming wens.   He would visit the patient
before breakfast on nine successive Mondays, strike
the excrescence nine times, thrice in three different
directions, and, if the sufferer had sufficient faith, the
wen would ultimately disappear.

The old mediæval custom of touching a corpse still
prevails.   At an inquest lately, held at or near South
Molton, each of the coroner's jury, as he filed past the
body, laid his fingers on the forehead.   This act, it was
believed, would free him from dreams of the deceased.

But there are one or two other cases of faith-healing
which should not be omitted.   The first is that of the
'split ash,' which still retains its efficacy as a cure for
congenital hernia.   In a recent letter Mr. F. T.
Elworthy furnishes me with an illustration.   He could,
he said, point out an ash, not yet healed, through
which two children were passed, with all solemnity, 'on
a Sunday morning before sunrise.'   But alas! only one
was cured.

Another is the 'boneshave' cure.   This is a very
old superstition, and, I believe, peculiar to Exmoor.

Whether it exists in the present day I am not certain, but that it still obtains in some remote spots is, I think, far from improbable. 'Boneshave' is sciatica. 'The patient must lie on his back, on the bank of a river or brook of water, with a straight staff by his side, between him and the water, and must have the following words repeated over him, viz. :

> 'Boneshave right ;
> Boneshave straight ;
> As the water runs by the stone
> Good for boneshave.'

They are not to be persuaded but that this ridiculous form of words seldom fails to give them a perfect cure.'*

'Overlooking' is also believed in, not only in the wilder districts, but even in populous places. Indeed, only the other day a case occurred as far east as Bridgwater, where a woman excused herself for an assault on the plea that she had been overlooked. But with the exception of overlooking, or the evil eye, as it is sometimes called, I do not think that much 'witchcraft' survives. It has not been defunct long, though; for not many years since the villagers of Withycombe, by no means an *ultima Thule* among hamlets, firmly believed that certain ancient dames had the power of turning themselves into white rabbits ! †

When last on Exmoor I learnt of a curious expedient there resorted to for the discovery of a drowned body. A loaf is procured, in the top of which a candle is

---

* See Note to 'An Exmoor Scolding' (1778), lately edited by F. T. Elworthy.

† For other instances of superstition, *vide* Appendix C., 'Superstition in West Somerset.'

stuck and lighted.　The loaf is then launched upon the water, and if it does not come to a standstill over the corpse, great is the disappointment of the believer.　I fancy that the candle is rather a modern innovation; for one or two moorfolk, of whom inquiry was made, said that, while they were aware of the efficacy, or supposed efficacy, of the loaf,* they had never heard of it in conjunction with tallow.　This method was resorted to as lately as 1888, during the search for the body of a farmer who had committed suicide in the dark waters of Pinkworthy Pond.　Upon this occasion, however, the loaf, like the sometimes erratic divining rod, stopped over the wrong spot.

There is a church where, on old Midsummer Eve, one or two people still go to watch for the spirits of those who are doomed to illness or death within the ensuing year.　A few years ago so many were affected (or afflicted) with this morbid curiosity, that a gate, studded with nails on the top, and still in existence, though no longer *in situ*, was erected to keep them out.　The watchers were in the habit of repairing to the porch, there to note the faces of the phantoms passing into the building.　Those who came out again would have an illness, while those who remained within would assuredly die.　A short time since a tailor was remonstrated with for his tardiness in completing a suit of clothes.　He testily replied that there was no

---

* Can it be that this curious superstition is in any way due to a misunderstanding of the verse in Ecclesiastes : ' Cast thy bread upon the waters : for thou shalt find it after many days '—the *it* being taken as something other than the bread ?

necessity for haste, as the customer would be dead
within a twelvemonth; thus letting out that he, at any
rate, had been out on Midsummer Eve. It need
scarcely be added that he has never heard the last of it.
I did not ascertain whether a watcher ever saw his
own ghost : if such were the case, the experience can
hardly have been a pleasant one.

A prettier superstition, and one once common, not
only in West Somerset, but elsewhere, is still cherished
by a few old folk, who will on Christmas Eve steal to
the cattle-shed to see the oxen bow the knee in worship
of the Infant Saviour.

And we have our share of ghost stories. Of these the
history of the Porlock ghost and the extraordinary
antics of Mrs. Leakey are the most notorious. The
first of these hobgoblins was a wicked boaster, named
Lucott, who, a week after his fleshly interment, was
seen in spirit at the Weir, conducting himself in a
manner more impudent even than is the custom of
ghosts. Twelve parsons were called upon to lay him,
but only eleven were found with sufficient courage to
attempt the task. Like the abbot in the ' Jackdaw of
Rheims,' they

'Cursed him by candle, by bell and by book'

in Porlock Church, but with no good result; in fact,
with no result at all; for, unlike the feathered thief, the
ghost had no feathers to lose. In short, it is said that
the pallid countenance of Master Lucott, who had been
watching the proceedings, grinned with excessive delight, and that he even advanced down the church upon

the holy men, who scattered in the utmost confusion. Finally, a twelfth parson was secured, in the person of the parish priest of St. Decuman, who dared the ghost to eat part of a consecrated wafer. This settled him. Obedient to the bold priest's commands, he mounted a horse, and rode by his side all the way to Doniford, beyond Watchet, where, after having in a last flash of his old spirit knocked out the eye of a man who was staring at him, Master Lucott consented, *bon gré, mal gré*, to enter a little box, which the parson then hurled into the sea.*

Mrs. Leakey was quite a different character. She is generally known as the whistling ghost, and was sufficiently famous to be mentioned by Sir Walter Scott in his notes to the second canto of 'Rokeby.' Early in the seventeenth century she appears to have resided at Minehead, where her only son was a well-to-do shipowner. Her disposition was so kindly and genial, that her friends were in the habit of anticipating her death with regret; upon which she would observe that her appearance in the spirit would not be so grateful a her presence in the flesh. Well, she died, and the parish register records her burial on the 5th of November, 1634; and now, for no explicable reason, she forthwith commenced to haunt her friends, not only by night but by day. Her kindliness seems to have died with her, for she became a perfect virago, commencing by kicking a doctor who declined—and small blame to him—to assist her over a stile. She next attacked her son's vessels,

---

* This story, with some embellishments, is very humorously told in the *West Somerset Free Press* of 27th July, 1889.

and, directly one of them approached the port, would mount to the masthead and blow a whistle, which, raising a terrible storm, wrecked the ship utterly. Having ruined her son, this amiable ghost proceeded to strangle his only child. Whether she, too, was eventually 'laid,' I cannot tell; but the note gives this further extraordinary information, that, on looking over the shoulder of her daughter-in-law, the latter ventured to address her, whereupon the ghost sent her to an Irish bishop notorious for his evil living, to threaten him with hanging unless he mended his ways; to which the prelate philosophically replied, that if he was born to be hanged, at any rate, he would not be drowned.

The whole story is absurd in the extreme; but it was otherwise regarded when Charles I. was king. It was thought a fit subject for an inquiry, and the Bishop of Bath and Wells, Paul Godwin, and Sir Robert Phelipps solemnly reported upon the evidence of Elizabeth Leakey, the daughter-in-law, as taken by 'Mr. Byam, a grave Minister neere Minehead'—of whom we shall have something to say later—of Mr. Heathfield, Curate of Minehead, and of two others, all of whom declared that they had seen, and some of whom asserted that they had conversed with the apparition. The triumvirate, however, in their report, scout the idea of an apparition, and, after giving their reasons for doubting the statements of the witnesses, conclude thus: 'And for these reasons wee are yet of opinion and doe beleive that there was never any such apparition at all, but that it is an imposture, devise, and fraud for some particular ends, but what they are wee know not.'

This report, which was endorsed by no less a person than Archbishop Laud, is among the State Papers in the Public Record Office,* and a copy (together with a copy of Mrs. Leakey's will and other interesting information) will be found in a local paper,† to which they were contributed by Mr. William George.

Yet there are still, I hear, believers in Mrs. Leakey, and perhaps a relic of her story survived in the 'evil spirit,' which a few years since flitted—perhaps, indeed, still flits—between Culver Cliff, at the back of Minehead Quay, and the Warren Point, and before whose imaginary presence I once saw two children flee, as for their lives.

* 'Report of Bishop Pierce of Bath and Wells, Paul Godwin, and Sir Robert Phelipps, respecting the asserted apparition at Minehead of "old Mrs. Leakey," late of that place, who had died there about two years before' (p. 276). The date assigned to this document is Feb. 24, 1637-8 (Calendar of State Papers, Domestic Series, Charles I., 1637-8). In it there is not one word about the 'Irish bishop' or of the 'whistling,' while the loss of the ships is merely attributed to witchcraft generally.

† The *West Somerset Free Press*, Dec. 7, 1889.

CHAPTER III

THE WILD RED DEER

The Red Deer—His principal Covers—Master Hugh Pollard—Mr.
Fenwick Bisset—'Brow, bay and trey'—Stags and hinds—
Hunting on the Quantocks—A Meet of the Devon and Somerset
Staghounds—The 'field'—The Harbourer—Tufting—The Chase
—Seeking a Substitute—Soiling—The Death—Famous Runs—
Dangers to Hounds—John Boyse—Dr. Collins—Tom Webber—
'Jack' Russell—Keeping Harriers by Proxy.

FEW rare animals are now to be met with in our hill
country, nor are strange birds more common.*   There
is, however, one rare beast, who makes his home in the
wooded country about the spurs of the moorland,
which has, perhaps, brought the district more pro-
minently before the notice both of Englishmen and
foreigners, than either the word painting of guide

---

* Polecats appear occasionally ; the Montagu's harrier (*cireus
cineraceus*) is sometimes seen ; a snowy owl has been shot of
recent years, and in 1884 a pelican was seen in the North Forest.
As Mr. Fortescue suggests, he had probably escaped from confinement. He adds that the moorfolk attributed his presence to the
firing at Tel-el-Kebir ! The ring ousel (*turdus torquatus*) is also
found, and an eagle was lately seen upon the Quantocks, where it
swooped down upon, and for some distance carried a little dog.
And some years since, a golden eagle was shot by Mr. Nicholas
Snow's keeper, and is now in his house at Oare.

book, or the alluring periods of coach placards. This is the *wild* red deer, no longer to be found in its natural state south of the Border, save in the highlands of West Somerset and North Devon, and whose pursuit stands far and above all other classes of venery. His principal covers are those which clothe the sides of the Barle, Exe, Lyn, Horner, Haddeo and Bray. And the chase of the red deer is so different from other hunting, that it may be well to devote a few pages to a short history of its rise and progress upon Exmoor and the Quantocks.

It is no new thing. Three hundred years ago, in the reign of Queen Elizabeth, one Hugh Pollard, Ranger of the Forest, kept a pack of staghounds at Simonsbath ; and the noble sport has thriven, more or less, ever since, under the mastership at first of the Ranger for the time being, and, for the last century, of some county gentlemen—Aclands, Bassetts, Fortescues, Chichesters —their names are well known to all men of West Somerset and Northern Devon, who owe a debt greater than many of them fancy to the gentlemen, who often at great labour, and always at great expense, have fostered this sport of sports. Among those who fought a stern fight against heavy odds, was a late Master—the last but one—Mr. Fenwick Bisset, who for the first few years of his command had a hard struggle, owing to lack of necessary funds. Yet for more than a quarter of a century he hunted this country, only resigning his office in 1881, in consequence of the effects of a bad fall. And when, three years later, he was borne to his last resting-place in Bagborough Church-

RED DEER.

yard, there were few who did not recognise that a prince among hunters was laid low. But to sing his praises—at any rate to the man living between Countisbury and Cothelstone—would be a work of supererogation indeed. Fortunately he lived long enough, not only to enjoy the fruit of his labours, but to bequeath to his successors one of the finest and best-kennelled packs that ever hunted over Exmoor.

Stag-hunting is a science. You may pursue your fox directly you see him; but with the red deer the case is very different. Not *any* deer will satisfy the laws of venery in this our hill-country. The animal must be 'warrantable '—that is, should have his 'rights,' consisting of three tines or points on his antlers, known as the 'brow, bay and trey.' However, bay, trey and two *points* on top will do *faute de mieux*. At three years of age he generally has his rights ; at six two points on 'top.' At any time after, he may (or may not) have three on top; but, as Mr. Fortescue remarks, 'it is impossible to tell a deer's age accurately by his horns alone.'*

* The following verbatim opinion of Mr. Arthur Heal, late huntsman of the Devon and Somerset staghounds, to whom I am indebted for several suggestions, will doubtless interest the reader :

'A deer must not necessarily have his "rights" and two on top to be warrantable. A deer with brow, trey, and two on top will do, and is considered warrantable, when no older deer is forthcoming. Usually, a deer with brow, and trey, and two on top would be four years old ; brow, bay and trey, and two on top, or brow, trey, and three on top, five years. An early calf, or those who have been luxuriantly fed, invariably have a full head or "royal," viz., brow, bay and trey, with three points on top, at six years ; although it may be more frequent at seven years for a "royal" head. The above is after thirty-five years' experience.'

Hence it will be seen that the deer must have at
least eight points in all before he is warrantable.   He
has usually more ; two and three on top are common
enough, and even six on top one side and seven on the
other are not unknown.   From which it will be seen
that it does not follow that each antler will have the
same number of points; and any huntsman will tell
you that it is as common to find a stag with two on
top one side and three on the other, as to find the
number even.

The season commences with the second week in
August, and lasts to about April.   The first two months
are devoted exclusively to hunting the *stag ;* the remainder of the season being given to the hinds—which
again may not be hunted at any age, not indeed till
they are at least three years old.   The Quantocks
enjoy but one week out of all this time—perhaps I
should say *enjoyed*, for in the season of 1889-90 deer
were so plentiful that the number of meets was multi-
plied twice or thrice.   Prior to 1865 they did not
possess even this distinction.   But it had long been a
desire of Mr. Bisset to include this range in the hunt-
ing-country ; deer-stocking, therefore, commenced there
in 1861, and the first stag was killed on the 29th
of August 1865.   Notwithstanding the number of
deer afforded by the Quantock covers in the present
season, deer are not nearly so numerous as some years
since.   In 1880, towards the end of Mr. Bisset's
mastership, a herd of eighty-two were seen running
before hounds, none of them being stags.   Since then,
the herd has been considerably reduced ; the following

year (Lord Ebrington's first season) saw no less than
101 deer brought to hand.

In order to understand all the art and mystery of
stag-hunting from start to finish, let us attend a
meet. Not an opening day, look you—which is
always, more or less, of a gigantic picnic—but a day
well into the season, when the excitable pedestrian is
not quite so much *en evidence*. How Mr. Bisset dis-
liked these first meets appear in his diary: 'Cloutsham
opening day,' he writes, 'is becoming seriously too
much of a rabble and fair.' Again: 'The Quantock
gathering on the opening day is becoming worse every
year; and the rough and rugged character of the
Horner country is here wanting to check the impetu-
osity of the tag-rag and bob-tail who come out for a
lark.' And no one who has been present upon the
event last named can quarrel with his words. I have
seen all sorts and conditions of men, women, and even
children, down to babies in arms, at this gathering,
getting under the horses' feet, and generally trying the
patience of those who have not so much 'come out for
a lark' as for good downright work. Some of them
learnt that day the rough side of the huntsman's
tongue. 'Out o' the way, you fools!' was the phrase
wherewith that veteran thus addressed the motley
assembly crowding too closely round a beaten stag to
see the *coup de grâce*. And who will blame him? Not
I, for one.

It is a fine autumn morning, and both horsemen and
carriage-folk have turned out in numbers. There is
the Master, alert and active, notwithstanding the fact

that his left sleeve lies empty, and that he controls his
powerful horse with his right arm alone. 'He must be
a good-plucked one to ride down the side of a combe
with only one hand on the reins,' mutters someone.
'Ay,' is the reply, ' hanged if I'd like to try some of 'em
with *two*.'

The huntsman and whip are busy riding round
the pack, of which about twenty couple are present
—magnificent fellows, standing from twenty-five to
twenty-six inches high, clean limbed and strong, and,
as a bystander critically remarks, 'fresh as paint.'
There are horsemen of every type; here a fresh-visaged
squire in good melton, white cords and irreproachable
tops; there a sporting parson, arrayed in a pleasing
mixture of garments clerical—and the reverse. Just
behind him a half-pay general, who knows more of the
fox than the stag, is asking questions of a legal Nimrod,
who was yesterday sitting as magistrates' clerk at a
town a dozen miles away. There are horse-dealers, too,
keen for a job, but not less keen on a good run; a
couple of barristers; the inevitable and, alas! sometimes
useful doctor; and a handful of young and well-dressed
nondescripts, half of whom have 'come down to see
what stag-hunting is like.' And there are farmers of
all shapes and sizes; some got up almost as well as
their squire, some in rough-and-ready homespun and
leggings. There is one—weighing about twenty stone—
actually in shirt sleeves, *flannel* shirt sleeves, who looks
like business, nevertheless, and means it, too, if he
doesn't kill his horse in the first forty minutes. And
away in a corner there, by the plantation, are one or

two of those dear old gentlemen whose hunting days are nearly over, but

> 'Who, void of ambition, still follow the chase,
>   Nor think that all sport is dependent on pace.'

And there is a fair sprinkling of ladies, too, some mounted, others seated in the vehicles that line the neighbouring road.

A man hunting with the Quorn or Pytchley would rather open his eyes at the personal appearance of this gathering. There is not a single 'chimney pot' visible, and only two or three beyond the Master, huntsman and whip have donned 'pink.' More than half the field are in tweed, and each appears to choose his head-gear, as he does his clothes, from motives of comfort. For stag-hunting, especially in August, is hard work, as anyone who has burst across Exmoor on a hot, still day knows full well, while the combes are hotter still. Few of those great, solemn-looking hounds will outlast their fourth season, while many will find their second too much.* The horses, more-over, have not that sleek, well-groomed appearance noticeable in up-country studs; the eye is not arrested either by their graceful motion or perfect form; but let a Midland hunter attempt to compete with an Exmoor pony, or one of the strong-limbed, surefooted beasts ridden by the majority of our field, and he would soon find himself a very bad second,

---

* 'Druid,' a favourite old hound, was an exception, seeing his tenth season before being 'put to rest.' It is water that plays such havoc with hounds, causing chills, rheumatism, and finally permanent lameness.—*Arthur Heal.*

if not hopelessly outdone. The horse that knows the country will go down the side of a combe almost as straight, if not so fast, as a rolling stone; while our glossy friend from Leicestershire or Northamptonshire will descend it, as he eyes it, askance, like the stag; for deer, unlike horses, always, except when hard pressed, take a hill sideways.

Presently the harbourer rides up. A most important functionary is the harbourer, for he it is who 'slots' the deer from its feeding-ground in the early morning to its lair, when it is considered ' harboured.' He tells the Master that he has harboured a real warrantable one down in the oak wood below; but he also brings the not-so-welcome intelligence that there are several hinds, and one or two male deer there as well, a sore temptation to the younger hounds to stray from their duty. This is, however, an exception to the general rule. For an *old* stag usually selects some quiet out-of-the-way place to lie in, generally knowing how and where to find a younger substitute. If there are more deer or hinds in company, the animal—*i.e.*, in hunting season —usually proves a young deer. There is a moment's conference between Master and Huntsman, and then we are in motion. The main body of the hunt follow their leader, but a few make for some point of vantage, and there keep wary watch. So do all the pedestrians who are not absolutely ignorant of stag-hunting, for they know well that this is their only chance of seeing the stag. At an adjacent farm the hounds are kennelled, and only five or six couples of ' tufters '—strongest and steadiest of the pack, not only able to outlast the run, but who will not be lured from their work by other deer—are permitted to enter the cover. And now begins a period of waiting. It may be long or short —I have waited five hours, and seen nothing but three hinds break cover—or the stag may elect to take to the open at once.

Time is killed in the usual manner. The men smoke, the ladies chatter, and much interest is shown in divers baskets dragged from underneath carriage seats. Many a tale of the chase is narrated; and one rider, who boasts of being present at the end of a long run, when the poor stag plunged over the cliffs on to the boulders below, is listened to with eager attention.

Suddenly there is a cry—not of man, but of hound. 'They have found!' exclaims an excited tourist. The contents of luncheon-basket, the stirring adventures of hunters, are alike disregarded. Ladies stand up in their respective vehicles; cavaliers, who have been walking their steeds up and down the road, press to the nearest view-point; and agile foot-passengers spring to the top of the hedge and gaze eagerly down the combe. 'There he goes!' someone shouts, as a brownish-red body bounds from among the trees and gallops up the hillside. 'There *she* goes!' echoes a sarcastic horse-man, as the whip turns back a couple of too-officious tufters, with (if we were near enough to hear it) a stern reproach, coupled with a command to mind their own business. It is only a hind; we must try again. Hardly, however, has she disappeared over the brow of the ridge when a chorus breaks from below. There is a faint crash, as of branches struck aside by some hard substance, and over the bank, with a magnificent leap, sails a stag, *the* stag. No mistake this time. Even the uninitiated can see that he carries a splendid head; while the sarcastic one, thrusting his field-glasses into their case, catches hold of his horse's head, and, murmuring ' Brow, bay and trey, and two or three on top,' plunges down a shady lane, and is seen no more.

And now begins the chase. The hounds are unkennelled and laid on, and, in a few minutes, their long thin line—for they do not run in a pack, but in single file—is seen streaming over the hill towards the dark moorlands. Horsemen gallop for places, and before the excited pedestrian has decided whether he will have any chance on foot, the whole cavalcade has vanished.

Away over the heather bounds the deer, and after him hurry hounds and field, the veteran huntsman* well ahead. There is a deep combe, a couple of miles to the right, dark and well wooded, and into this our quarry sinks. He is a wily old gentleman, and his game is to destroy his identity, if possible, by mingling with any other stags that may be in the cover, and divert the attention of the hounds to one of his brethren, or, ungallant fellow that he is, even one of his sisters. This is a very common trick: a stag has been known to oust another from his bed, where he was lying close, and coolly appropriate the same; while the hounds, catching sight of the unwilling substitute, force him, for his own safety to run for it. Indeed, among the many amusing tales of the selfishness exhibited by

* Arthur Heal. The above was written shortly before he surrendered his horn to the then whip, Anthony Huxtable.

the stag, there is one almost passing belief. Two stags were actually seen fighting right in front of the hounds, being unable to settle in any other manner which should be the victim.

But should our deer be successful in his search for a scapegoat, it does not by any means follow that he will be allowed to rest in peace in his ill-gotten security. If practicable, the hounds who have started after the substitute are called off; the line of our cunning friend is recovered; and once more he climbs the hillside for the open waste. And then commences a contest of wits between pursuer and pursued. Having got well away from the chase, and there being no more coverts for many a mile, our stag as he sweeps along, casts about in his mind what he will do. He remembers that there is a stream not far distant, and if he can but get out of sight of those villainous hounds, he will try what 'soiling' can do. And so he makes a sudden spurt, covering the next two miles at terrific speed, until upon reaching the brow of the descent, he stops and glances back.

There is nothing visible on the great, wide moor, and for a moment he hopes that his enemies have, in some unaccountable manner, lost him. But a sound from that last dip undeceives him—the music, not by any means music to *him*, of the hounds. With a snort he plunges down the declivity and enters the stream.

In another ten minutes the hounds are poking their noses in the tufts of fern and heather overhanging the banks, wading or swimming down the middle, or

snuffing suspiciously at the boulders. The huntsman
rides slowly along, his practised eye noting any splash
upon the rock that may indicate the passage of something larger than a trout. Presently he sees it, and at
the same moment a hound leaps upward, uttering a
joyous note. Alas! poor stag. Not tarrying for a
nearer approach he leaves the watery lair, where he has
been lying under a bank, nothing but nose and antler
tips above water; and, refreshed by his bath, once more
springs vigorously away from his foes.

Swiftly the cloud-shadows glide over the heather,
momentarily changing the waste from gray to purple;
swiftly the wild bird rushes overhead; but swifter than
either the hunted deer bounds desperately forward.
But only for a few miles now, he is getting done.
Presently his antlers sink further backwards, and the
breath comes quick and gasping from his panting lungs.
His pace slackens, his limbs quiver; while ever and
again he turns his frightened eye in the direction of
that long piebald line running mute to his destruction.
Oh for water, water! where he may slake his burning
thirst, and make a last fight under the bulwark of some
great rock, with his face to the foe. It comes. A wild
valley yawns beneath; part clad in ancient oak forest,
part purple with heather. Down the precipitous slope
he stumbles, his eye afire once more, as he sees the
' water-brook' his soul has so long desired. He is in it,
bathing his heated sides, and marvelling, in a dazed sort
of fashion, whether he may again outwit his foes. But
no; at the same moment the leading hounds rush over
the crest, and, catching sight of their prey, raise an

exulting cry. Now they are in the water, splashing pushing, leaping on one another's backs in their anxiety to reach the King of the Forest, who stands with up-lifted—not *levelled* head, reader—to receive them, giving now and again a lightning thrust with his horns. But the huntsman is ready. While the hounds are busy in front he and his assistant are keeping watch in the rear, waiting their opportunity, when the antlers shall be thrown back for a moment, to seize and press them down on the creature's back, ere administering the *coup de grâce*. For so immense is the power in the muscles of a stag's chest, that two men, who unwarily caught the horns in a wrong position, have been hurled several yards by the toss of his head. Presently the moment arrives : the grand head is borne backwards ; the knife gleams for a moment in the air, then is plunged to the bold, brave heart; and the wild red deer sinks with a sob in the water, no longer clear, but stained with his blood. The struggle is at an end.

Such is a brief sketch of a stag-hunt upon Exmoor. There are many details, however, that can find no place here. But the whole subject has been treated most exhaustively in a recent entertaining work, and to its pages the reader curious in such matters is referred for further particulars. From it we shall but cull one or two records of notable runs, and then pass from the stag to one or two of his 'mighty hunters.'

On September 28, 1855, a magnificent stag was roused in Huscombe Wood, Haddon. He ran for the Exe, where he beat the water for nearly two miles to

Grants, whence he made for High Cross, where, owing to bad scent, there was a long check. On Birch Down it was again taken up, and followed with difficulty to Hadbarrow. But before reaching this point most of the field had given up. The Haddeo was tried unsuccessfully; but the voice of the hounds presently proclaimed that, notwithstanding the gathering darkness, there was still hope; and, after many 'tries,' the stag was finally killed at Clammer *by candlelight.* 'Seven hours,' writes Mr. Bisset, 'from the lay-on, the last hour and a half in the water, and dark.' No wonder that there were 'eight only at the finish.'

Upon another occasion a stag ran from Hollowcombe, near Cloutsham, *vià* Larkbarrow, to the North Forest, where he routed out an unfortunate hind, which the hounds—being, it is presumed, too far from control to be persuaded to leave—ran at tremendous speed* right away to the stream below Brendon Church, whence she ultimately climbed to Countisbury. Here, being hard pressed by the hounds, she sprang over the cliffs between the Foreland and Glenthorne, and was dashed to pieces. Four hounds narrowly escaped sharing her fate; they were actually on her haunches, and were dragged over the edge, but a projecting ledge saved them.

But hounds do not always escape, although both 'hounds and deer have so fallen a height of fifty feet and landed below uninjured,' more than a few have perished on the boulders which form the foreshore of

---

* The time was sixty-five minutes from the lay-on, and the distance could not have been less than fifteen miles.

this part of the Bristol Channel.* And one at least
has been drowned swimming out to sea after an
escaping hind. Add to this an occasional fatal thrust
from the horn of a stag at bay, and it will be seen that
the lot of a staghound is not altogether happy.

And now for the famous Bratton run, which, in Arthur
Heal's phraseology—and I have his letter before me—
eclipses all previously on record. On Wednesday,
October 29, 1889, hounds met at Leworthy Post,
Bratton Fleming, North Devon. The weather was
most genial, and attracted an enormous concourse. A
stag from Knightacott Wood was roused and headed
through Twitchen Wood and over Chapman Barrows.
The pack being laid on streamed away in a breast-high
scent by Whistland Pound, to Furze Hill, Hoar Oak,
Cheriton Ridge, and Farley Water, where 'he beat
upwards for awhile, and then broke away, leaving
Brendon Two Gates on the right and skirting the
withy bed on Brendon Common, to Badgeworthy
Water. Thence he crossed the Manor Allotment,
Kittuck, Porlock, and Lucott Commons, and over Great
Hill to Chetsford Water. Now over Wilmotsham
Common, and along by Hole Wood into the Horner
Valley, by Stoke Church. In the Horner Water lead-
ing hounds held him at bay, but on the pack coming up
he broke away, and sank to Horner Mill, ascending to

* On August 18, 1884, a stag leapt over eighty feet of cliff at
Glenthorne, and was killed ; five of the hounds followed : one was
killed on the spot, two had to be killed where they lay, the fourth
was crippled for the remainder of his days, but the fifth was,
strange to say, soon hunting again.—'Stag-hunting,' p. 268.

Parsonage side and Luccombe Plantation, whence he crossed to Whytchanger, and, hounds once more coming upon him, he turned to Luccombe village, and was killed in the Rectory grounds, after being on foot two hours and twenty minutes. This distance was estimated at from twenty-five to twenty-six miles, and the pace thoughout was great, across a perfect line of country, never touching a covert between Bratton and Horner. Such, in almost his own words, is Arthur's account of this celebrated run, and thus the enthusiastic old huntsman concludes : ' There may have been plenty of runs of similar distance, or even longer; but, taking the distance and open country into consideration, it stands without a parallel. May Bratton coverts supply the Devon and Somerset with many such deer in the future !'

We have only space to mention one or two stag-hunting worthies. A famous one was John Boyse, a hundred years ago the sporting Vicar of Hawkridge, more often in at the death at the end of a long run than perhaps any of his contemporaries. . He kept a record of the chase, which has been freely used by another notable hunter, Dr. Collyns, of Dulverton, in the compilation of his now rare work, ' The Chase of the Wild Red Deer.' After forty-seven years of hunting, he died in 1864, at the ripe age of three-score and ten.

Another and more humble follower was Tom Webber, described by Mr. Bisset and others as ' the best and truest stag-hunter that ever cheered hound.' This worthy farmer died in 1863, and was buried in King's Brompton churchyard.

But there was another gentleman for whom, not only Mr. Bisset, but the whole field —is it too much to say the whole country-side ?— entertained a very warm regard. This was the late Vicar of Swimbridge, the celebrated 'Jack' Russell. We say celebrated, for is not his name known from one end of England to another, this famous hunting parson, who 'saw his first stag killed in 1814 under the mastership of the first Earl Fortescue, and his last in 1884, when the hounds were being hunted by Lord Ebrington, his great-grandson'? He is mentioned more than once in Mr. Bisset's diary, and on October 6, 1876, we find that the head of a stag killed upon that day, was, on the following first of May, ' given to the Rev. Jack Russell as a memento of his eightieth birthday and sixty-third hunting season.'

Nor did he confine himself to hunting red deer, as the following amusing story will prove : Towards the close of his life he started a pack of harriers, rather to the disgust of his bishop, who sent for him, and desired, as a personal favour, that this addition to his sporting enjoyments should be given up. Jack agreed, and they were clasping hands over the matter, when the following words caused the bishop to drop the old parson's hand with as much celerity as he had seized it : ' I won't deceive you—not for the world, my lord,' quoth Russell. ' I'll give up the pack, sure enough, *but Mrs. Russell will keep it instead of me.*'* What the bishop thought of this pack-keeping by proxy, I do not know ; but the following terse opinion as to the reverend

* Rev. S. Baring-Gould's ' Old Country Life.'

Nimrod's character, heard by the Rev. S. Baring-Gould from the mouth of one of his parishioners, shows sufficiently how he was regarded by those living about his home. 'As for old Jack Russell, up and down his backbone, he's as good a Christian, as worthy a pastor, and as true a gentleman as ever I seed.' He was the last and best of the old type of hunting parson.

CHAPTER IV

HISTORY AND ANTIQUITIES

THE district now called Somersetshire was in ancient
times inhabited by the Belgæ, a brave Gaulish people,
but of Celtic origin, who migrated hither out of Gaul
A.M. 3650, 313 years before the birth of Christ, and
repelled the Britons—the aboriginal inhabitants of the
country, whose *carneds* still crown some of our highest
mountains—to other parts of the island.'

So wrote Collinson nearly a hundred years ago, and
it is a question whether we know much more of the
early history of our county now than was known to
our ancestors a century since. Certainly we know
very little more of its western extremity. Whether
the Belgæ came over 313, or, as Phelps says, 350
years before the Christian era, matters little ; that they

did arrive somewhere about that period historians are pretty well agreed, and nine-tenths of the earthworks upon our hills are dubbed by common consent Belgic-British camps. The *carneds*—which modern men call *cairns*—may be aboriginal or Belgic, the question can only be determined—and not always then—by an examination of their contents.

That this country—wild, hilly, and in those days begirt with marshes and almost inaccessible forests—was a refuge for the savage Celt, long after Roman, Saxon, and Dane, had taken turns at subduing England, no one doubts. The highlands were scarcely of a nature to tempt either Roman noble or Saxon thane, while the semi-amphibious Norseman found nothing congenial in the open moorland, except perhaps its free air and sky. Thus the Britons were probably left in comparative peace, being made the subject of attack only when their predatory instincts led them to descend into the lowlands, and harry some English homestead.

Their names are everywhere. There is Dunkery, *dun creagh* or *cerrig*, the rough hill; Triscombe, *tre-is-cwm*, the dwelling at the foot of the valley; Croydon, which has the same root and meaning as Dunkery; and Leather (*i.e.*, *lleddr*) Barrow, the steep barrow. There is Cutcombe, or *coed cwm*, the wooded valley; and Dulverton, which is *dôl ford ton*, the ford town at the (river's) bend. There is Dunster, *dun tor*, the towered hill; and Treborough, the place of the camp, or, perhaps, *tre berw*, the place of the waterfall, which is found in a glen hard by. Even Exmoor is partly Celtic: *ex* being but a corruption of *osc*, *uisg*, water. And occasionally, even now, in spite of the lapse of ages, and the number-less barrows opened, more substantial traces of their existence have been lit upon. Flint knives and other neolithic remains, and British cinerary urns, have been found on the Brendon Hills; and, within comparatively recent years, British weapons, and rare ones too, at the foot of the Quantocks. It is somewhat singular that, in spite of that Vandal of Vandals, the farmer, there are so very few hut circles *en evidence;* but still, among the hills behind Dunster, we may find the traces of a large stone enclosure, which fifty years ago contained a good many. And camps are plentiful. There is Danes-borough, on the Quantocks; Elworthy Barrows, on Brendon; one at least on Croydon; another—besides the so-called Roman earthwork—in Dunster Park; Mouncey, Brewers and Cow Castles, overlooking the Barle ; and Bury Castle, near Selworthy, all as ' Belgic-British ' as possible. North, south, east, and west, the Celt has unmistakably left his mark on this corner of Somerset.

Nor can we wonder. All this horn of Britain between the Severn and the English Channel re-mained unconquered, perhaps unassailed, until 556, when Ceawlin began to reign as king over the West Saxons. He it was who drove the Britons from their camp on Worle Hill. But even he only penetrated to the Axe, four miles further westward ; and it was not really till 926, when Athelstan, expelling the Welsh part of the population from Exeter, fixed their boun-dary at the Tamar, that Somerset generally became English.

And no doubt many *Wealhas*,* as the Sáxon scornfully called the poor Briton, haunted the wild hill
country for centuries after.   'From the Axe to the
Tamar,' writes Professor Freeman, 'and still more
from the Parret to the Tamar, the people are still
very largely of Welsh descent, though they have
spoken English for many ages.'

To the Briton came the Roman.   How much or
how little he affected the history of this particular
district we know not, perhaps never shall know.
Some have concluded—presumably from the presence
of certain coins—that a legion under Ostorius
occupied the country west of the Quantocks.   Hearne
quotes a manuscript to this effect : ' In the year 1666
two large earthen pitchers, full of Roman coins, each
weighing eighty pounds, were dug up, one in a ploughed
field in the parish of Laurence Lydiard, and the other
in Stogumber.'   This writer supposes that Ostorius,
after subduing the Cangi on the east of the Quantock
Hills,† marched westward, but was suddenly obliged to

---

* This word—the origin of *Welsh*—means *strangers*. *Wälsch*,
the German name for foreigners, is still the term applied by that
nation to the Italians.   In Alfred's will the counties of Somerset,
Dorset, Devon and Cornwall, all appear under the name Weal
cynne, or Welsh kind ; and an ordinance of Athelstan calls them
Wealhas, and their territory the Wylise.   And *vide* further R. J.
King's 'Dartmoor Forest and its Borders,' p. 41.

† I cannot find any sufficient reason for placing the Cangi here ;
unless, indeed, they were, as Baxter has supposed, ' a set of people
belonging to every tribe or nation of the Britons, who attended the
herds, and resided with them in different grazing grounds at different seasons of the year.'   The Triads certainly mention them as
chosen from the different tribes as herdsmen.   If they were a tribe

return to quell an insurrection among the Silures and Brigantes, and that the money was buried in these places for security. The coins are of Claudius, Nero, Domitian, Trajan, Antoninus, Septimius Severus, Aurelius, and of almost all the succeeding emperors. Others have thought that Kilton, near Putsham—where money of Diocletian, Maximus, Gallienus, and some of the thirty tyrants, have been found—and Stogumber were Roman stations, and Bicknoller, where also a number of coins have been unearthed, a treasury. Collinson, indeed, makes the original name of the village *bychan alwar*, the little treasury. Coins have been discovered, too, on Bagborough Hill; the Brendon Hills, at Dunster; and even as far away as Exe Head, in the most desolate part of Exmoor; perhaps here accounted for by the neighbourhood of Showlsborough Camp, said to be undoubtedly Roman. While touching on this subject, it may be well to mention that two other camps are claimed for the conquerors of the world, that of Ruborough, on the Quantocks, and Cæsar's Camp, in Dunster Park. Both will in due course be examined, and need at present no further remark. Many British camps were doubtless castra æstiva; and we are not, therefore, surprised to hear of coins, and other Roman relics, turning up in their vicinity. To rush to the conclusion that an

entirely distinct, such as the Durotriges or Damnonii, they are just as likely to have belonged to Wiltshire, or Flintshire, or Cheshire, or half a dozen other counties. It seems that *Cannington* has been the cause of locating them near the Quantocks. *Vide* Toulmin's ' Hist. of Taunton,' p. 11.

   * *Vide ante*, pp. 6 and 7.

earthwork is Roman *because* traces of their occupation may present themselves, is as unreasonable as it would be to suppose that a barrow marks the site of no grave because the opened *mound* discloses no deposit.

But other vestiges of a Roman occupation have been found on the Brendon Hills, in the shape of mining implements, in company, too, with considerable heaps of scoriæ, leaving no doubt that here, as elsewhere, they did their best to develop the mineral resources of the district. At present I do not know of any Roman masonry in West Somerset nearer than Taunton; but, perhaps, we shall some day unearth the tesselated pavement of a luxurious villa in the sunny valleys under the Quantocks, or in the pleasant vale of Avill.

In 445 the Romans left Britain, to be succeeded, fifty years later, by the Saxons. The Saxon history of West Somerset, though more ample than that of the first five centuries, has yet a long gap, which can only be filled by general statements. A Saxon palace is said by Camden to have stood at Porlock: Dunster possessed another. But the first event to which authenticity can be attached is the defeat of the Danes by the Ealdormen Eanwulf and Osric, and Ealstan, Bishop of Sherborne, in 845. This is said by the chronicler to have occurred at the mouth of the Pedridan, or Parret, but tradition places it a little to the west, in the parish of Stogursey.

Twenty-six years later (871) Alfred sat upon the throne of England. His relations with Somersetshire were of a very intimate character. Everyone knows the story of the retreat to Athelney—the burning of the cakes—the fight of Ethandune, the conversion of Guthrum. But few are aware that the greatest Saxon king had any connection with the country bordering on our district. Bishop Clifford is of opinion that the hollow below Cannington Park quarries is the spot where the 'heathen men' joined battle with the English under Alfred; and at first, indeed, defeated them. A few of the English, however, threw themselves into a fort—now no longer existing—and ultimately beat their opponents, killing their chieftain Hubba. Asser, Alfred's friend and biographer, under date 878, tells us the story:

'That same year,' he says, 'a brother of Halfden and Inguar, with three-and-twenty ships, bearing the legion of Demetia, where he had wintered, after he had made great slaughter of the Christians of those parts, set sail for Devon, and there, with twelve hundred men, rashly doing, he was in the end defeated and slain by the king's officers before the Castle Cynwit. For within the enclosure of this same castle many of the king's officers, with their men, had taken refuge together. Now when the pagans saw that the castle was destitute of provisions, and without means of defence of any kind, save that it had walls after our fashion, they did not attempt to carry it by assault; but, as the nature of the ground rendered it very safe on all sides except towards the east, they began to lay siege to it, thinking that those men, driven by hunger and thirst, would soon be compelled to surrender, for there was no water nigh to the castle. The Christians waited not to be reduced to such extremities; but, inspired by Heaven, and deeming it far preferable to earn either death or victory, suddenly rushed down upon the pagans, and, assailing their enemies like wild boars, put to the sword the greater part of them, together with their king.'

What really happened seems to have been this: A portion of the Danish force was on the further bank of the river, and, the tide being low, could not cross to assist their fellows. This the Saxons perceived, and accordingly fell upon the division laying siege to their earthworks, retreating to the hills before the rising tide enabled the remainder of the army to effect a transit.

Near the seashore in the parish of Stogursey is a tumulus, which more than one local antiquary thinks may be Hubba's grave. An excavation, however, even if disclosing Danish remains, can hardly determine the question whether Cannington Park was the scene of the battle of Cynwit or Cynuit, because, as before mentioned, tradition points to this neighbourhood as the *locale* of the fight of 845. It should be mentioned, too, that there are not wanting antiquaries who claim quite another spot as the sepulchre of the 'brother of Halfden and Inguar.'

Richard de Hoveden says that Hubba was buried at Cynwich (wherever that may have been); and near *Combwich*, on the Parret, is a tumulus, by some considered more likely to be his grave than the mound at Stogursey; and Upper Cock Farm, in the same neighbourhood, they presume to be a corruption of Ubba-coc, Ubba's heap. The theory, to say the least, is ingenious.

Now for the other side of the question. That all should agree that the Danes were defeated at or near Cannington presupposes a unanimity, which, fortunately for English history, is unknown among those interested in the study of the past. Bishop Clifford's theory about Cannington Park has been strongly combated by a fellow-member of the Somersetshire Archæological Society, and the following, gathered from a local paper,* sufficiently propounds Mr. Sloper's reasons for denying our neighbourhood the glory of the fight. He does not consider Bishop Clifford's opinion, as to the site of the battle of Cynuit, substantiated either by fact or by the Anglo-Saxon Chronicle, Florence of Worcester or Gaimar. The Chronicle places Cynuit in Devon,† and he therefore placed the position of the fort at Countisbury, where its rampart still remains ; and he thought Ubbaslowe, or Ubba's burial-place, to be nothing but a 'mump' or 'batch,' common in marsh land as a refuge for cattle in time of flood. Wherever this battle was fought, I take it to have been the one in which the Danes lost their famous banner, the 'Raven.' 'And the same winter the brother of Hinguar, and of Halfdene, came with twenty-three ships to Devonshire, in Wessex : and he was there slain, and with him eight hundred and forty men of his army: and there was taken the war-flag which they called the "Raven.‡"'

* The *Somerset Express* of August 11, 1877, kindly lent me by Sir Alexander Acland Hood.

† *Sed quære* whether this proves anything, for in Alfred's time surely all the country west of the Parret *was* Devon.

‡ Anglo-Sax. Chron., p. 356. Hume places the battle at the

The next important event was an invasion by the Lidwiccas, under the earls Ohtor and Rhoald. Again we have recourse to the Chronicle, where, under 918, it is thus told:

'In this year a great fleet came over hither from the south, from the Lidwiccas, and with it two earls, Ohtor and Rhoald, and they went west about till they arrived within the mouth of the Severn, and they spoiled the North Welsh everywhere by the sea-coast where they then pleased. And in Archenfield they took Bishop Cameleac,* and led him with them to their ships; and then King Edward ransomed him afterwards with forty pounds.

'Then after that the whole army landed, and would have gone once more to plunder about Archenfield. Then met them the men of Hereford and of Gloucester, and of the nearest towns, and fought against them and put them to flight, and slew the Earl Rhoald, and a brother of Ohtor, the other earl, and many of the army, and drove them into an enclosure, and there beset them about, until they delivered hostages to them that they would depart from King Edward's dominion. And the king had so ordered it that his forces sat down against them on the south side of Severn-mouth, from the Welsh coast westward to the mouth of the Avon eastward; so that on that side they durst not anywhere attempt the land. Then, nevertheless, they stole away by night on some two occasions: once, to the east of Watchet, and another time to Porlock. But they

mouth of the Taw. 'Hist. of England,' 1796, vol. i., p. 52. I believe there is a rock called *Hubbastone* in the estuary of that river.
    * Of Llandaff.

were beaten on either occasion, so that few of them got away, except those alone who there swam out to the ships. And then they sat down, out on the island of Bradanrelice,* until such time as they were quite destitute of food; and many men died of hunger, because they could not obtain any food. Then they went thence to Deomod,† and then out to Ireland.'

The Lidwiccas came from Brittany, and were probably some of the people planted there by Rollo the Ganger, who, tired of inaction, again betook themselves to a roving life. At their second repulse the English were, according to Evans, commanded by Ælle, governor of Bristol Castle. This man is, traditionally, said to have achieved many conquests over the pirates, and was evidently a person of some note. A curious ballad, written in 1468, by Thomas Rowlle, a Carmelite monk, father-confessor to William Canynge, founder of St. Mary Redcliffe, is copied in Mrs. Boger's 'Myths, Scenes and Worthies of Somerset.' It is entitled 'A song to Ælle, Lord of the Castle of Brystowe in daies of yore,' and its quaintness will, perhaps, excuse the quotation of the first three verses:

'O THOU (or whate remaynes of thee),
     Ælle, the darlynge of futuritye !
Lette thys mie songe bolde as thie courage bee,
     As everlastynge to posteritye !

* 'Some copies of the Chronicle have "*Bradanreolice*," *Broad* or Flat Holm, and some "*Steapanreolice*," which speaks for itself. I suppose the name *Reolic* is a Welsh name. In the life of Gildas the Welsh historian, the two Holms are called Ronech and Echin.'—E. A. Freeman's 'Old English History.'
† South Wales.

Whanne Dacyas sonnes, with hair of blood-red hue,
Lyke kynge-coppes brastynge with the mornynge dewe.

'Arraung'd in drear arraye
    Upon the lethale daye,
Spredde farre and wyde on Watchet's shore ;
    Thenne dydst thou brondeous stonde,
    And with thie burlye honde,
Bespryngedde all the mees wythe gore ;

'Drawn by thyne aulace fell,
    Down to the depthes of hell
Thousands of Dacyans went ;
    Brystowans, menne of might,
    Ydared the blodie fyghte,
And acted deedes full quent,'

and so on, for another three stanzas:

In 988 more pirates entered the Bristol Channel.
' This year was Watchet ravaged, and Goda, the Devon-
shire thane, slain, and with him much slaughter made.'
This appears to have been the only occasion that the
Danes fought a pitched battle in this part of Somerset.
Now where was this battle fought ?

There is, in the parish of Nettlecombe, a high
rounded field called Knap Dane. Adjacent enclosures
bear similar names; one is Brick Dane, another Furze
Dane. People in the locality say that large quantities
of human bones have been dug up here, and hold that
on this knoll the men of Somerset joined battle with the
pagans. One old man, indeed, told me that a sword
—date, fashion, and fate as usual unknown—had been
found here. There is no doubt, as will be shown later,
that this field *was* once crowned by an earthwork—in
fact there are very faint traces of something even now.

Whether Camden (or one of his numerous editors) got his information from the people, or the people from Camden, seems doubtful; but that antiquary refers in plainest terms to the spot. 'In a field called Knap Dane,' he says, 'in the parish of Nettlecombe, were found a vast quantity of human bones, supposed of the Danes who landed at Watchet, A.D. 918.' Why he should prefer the Lidwicca invasion, when the pirates are merely recorded as having landed to the *east* of Watchet (Knap Dane is due *south*) and being 'beaten,' to the invasions of 988 and 997, I do not understand. For myself, I am disposed to place the date at 988, both because there was apparently a pitched battle, and also because the words of the Chronicle referring to a later and last descent hardly bear out such an interpretation. We are simply told that in 997 they again landed at Watchet, and there 'wrought much evil by burning and by man-slaying.'*

Altogether the Danes seem to have had a fondness for Watchet, perhaps because one of King Ethelred's mints was there. It is rather curious that in this same year, immediately after sacking Watchet, they sailed round to South Devon, and, entering the Tamar and Tavy, sacked Lydford, where there was another mint. A coin bearing the impress of this mint is in the Taunton Museum.

But the scene of one of these battles (if more than one) with the Danes has been for so many years associated with a spot much nearer Watchet than Knap Dane, that some few remarks thereon are necessary.

* Anglo-Sax. Chron., p. 429.

A mile inland, close to Williton, is a field, or rather several fields, known as Battlegore, traditionally, as its name implies, the scene of a battle. In them are the remains of three large mounds, though one is now ploughed nearly level with the field, and another has been reduced one-half by a hedgerow. The largest is close to the road. From time immemorial the tale has been handed down that here the Danes fought with the Wessex men. A tradition, also unfortunately dating from time immemorial, states that much armour and many weapons have been discovered in these fields. But who found them, and what became of them, is as unknown as their period and fashion. The only weapon taken from the spot that I have seen is a remarkably fine bronze *celt* which would go some way to show that it was a British rather than a Danish battleground. Collinson refers to 'several cells composed of flat stones, and containing relics,' as having been found in these tumuli, to which he gives the name of *Grab-barrows*. From this it would appear that they were chambered tumuli. I venture to think, however, that he is mistaken, except perhaps with regard to the mound now nearly levelled, inasmuch as neither of the existing barrows have been properly explored.

Close to the barrow near the road are two enormous stones, the one lying on its side, the other leaning against the hedge, as well as a third and smaller block, nearly concealed by brambles. As there are no similar blocks in the vicinity, they must have been brought here for some definite purpose, perhaps to mark the grave of some notable chieftain. Or, perchance, they are, as certain antiquaries opine, the supports of a British cromlech. The local story is that they were cast there from the Quantocks by the devil and a giant, who had engaged in a throwing match. The print of Satan's hand still marks the leaning stone !*

There are four circumstances, then, which incline us to regard Battlegore rather as Celtic than Danish. The first is, that the spot is a dead level under rising ground—a spot that neither Saxon nor Norseman would select as a camping-ground; the second, the shape of the barrows, which are of the true British type; the third, the discovery of the celt; the fourth, the ruins or the supposed ruins of the cromlech. And yet the Ordnance surveyors, with a boldness that is rather surprising, print on their new map these words: 'Battle Gore, site of battle, A.D. 918.' There is this, and this only, to be said in favour of their statement: the fields are certainly south-east of Watchet, and at no great distance from Doniford, a point on the coast due east of that town, where the flat shore and banks, rather than cliffs, would favour a descent.

And now Porlock again comes in for 'war's alarms,' and those caused not by a foreign but by a domestic foe. Harold, son of Godwin, had, like his father, been outlawed, and had retired to Ireland. As he was lord of the manor of Dulverton, and very popular, he probably thought that in a descent upon West Somerset he would receive a certain amount of support; and the

* This stone was upright some forty or fifty years since. It was toppled against the hedge by some young men anxious to test the truth of the legend that it was immovable.

circumstance that his enemy, Algar, son of Leofric, Earl of Mercia (brother of the famous Hereward), then held Porlock, may perhaps have proved an additional temptation to his warlike soul. At any rate, in 1052 he sailed into the bay and effected a landing. But the people resisted, and it was only by hard fighting that he won his way. Nevertheless, his expedition was partially successful, and, after putting many to the sword, he 'took of cattle, and of men, and of property, as it suited him'—so says the Chronicle, but Savage adds that he set fire to the town as well. His authority for this statement he does not give. The fact is certainly not mentioned in the Chronicle.

More than once we find Harold making descents upon Somersetshire, but it is impossible to identify them with this part of the county. The next member of Earl Godwin's family who was connected, and that but in the slightest degree, with its history came not in war but in woe. In 1067 Gytha, the widowed wife of Godwin, the mother of dead Harold, embarked at Watchet for the Steep Holm, there, where the Armorican pirates had perished so miserably a century and a half before, to mourn the fallen fortunes of her house. Harold and his brother had perished on the field of Senlac. The Conqueror sat upon the throne of England, and so the once proud, ambitious countess, accompanied by other noble ladies who had lost their all, retired to this barren rock, where no Norman insult would be likely to reach her. What possible accommodation the islet could have afforded we are not told; perhaps the dwelling of Gildas the Wise, the earliest British historian, who is said to have here written his treatise 'De excidio Britanniæ,' afforded them shelter. But they 'there abode some time,' before again seeking an asylum at St. Omer.

From this time there is nothing very stirring for some centuries. The Norman came and built his castle of Dunster—so impregnable that Stephen retired from before it—upon the abrupt knoll of the Torre; but so far from the warlike world was De Moion's keep, that, with the exception of its connection with the cause of Queen Maud, we hear little of it till the days of the Stuarts, when it was for some time the theatre of military operations.

Many a West Somerset family suffered much in consequence of Monmouth's rebellion. Distant as was the battle-field—far away beyond the Quantocks, beyond indeed where the tapering spire of Bridgwater rises above the rich level pastures of central Somerset—the unfortunate 'love child' of King Charles II. wanted not for adherents from this remote corner of the county. Numbers flocked to his standard, and we all know the result. There was the carnage of Sedgemoor, and then the Bloody Assize of infamous Jeffreys, and the brutalities of Kirke and his 'lambs.' Five misguided patriots were executed at Minehead, three at Dunster—the tree on which they swung is still shown on the southern side of the road to Timberscombe—Dulverton, Stowey, and Stogumber; and two at Porlock and Cothelstone. Sedgemoor was the last battle fought on English ground, and since that day, two hundred years ago now, the land has had rest.

Such is a brief epitome of the history of Western Somerset. Of Stuart times I have made but passing mention. The story of Blake's advance from Taunton, of the unkind fate of Sir John Stawell, of Colonel Wyndham's defence of Dunster Castle, will be found more in detail as we reach the places of his attack. Our county took small part in the great Civil War compared with the Midland shires. There was the chief scene of military operations; there were fought the battles of Marston Moor, Edgehill, Naseby, and Worcester; thence came the most celebrated Royalists, the most famous Puritans. Let us pass, then, to the consideration of such relics of antiquity as our district can boast, ere setting forth on our travels, 'over hill, over dale,' for a personal inspection.

Most plentiful are barrows. Throughout the un-cultivated parts of the hill country, with the exception, indeed, of the Quantocks, where fewer are found, they mark nearly every prominent ridge. Most are un-doubtedly graves, but upon Exmoor some may have been thrown up as bounds of the Forest. Nearly all have been opened, generally imperfectly, the greater number probably under the powers of a license to search for treasure granted by, I believe, Edward II. The historian quoted at the commencement of this chapter has some remarks upon these lonely graves, which so nearly approach eloquence that I venture to present them. Referring to Exmoor he says: 'Here, upon this desolate spot, which perhaps never experienced the labours of the industrious husbandman, but has remained for a long succession of many thousand years,

the eye of reflection sees stand uninterrupted a number
of simple sepulchres of departed souls, whether of
warriors, priests or kings, it matters not ; their names
have long been buried with their persons in the dust
of oblivion, and their memories have perished with
their mouldering urns. A morsel of earth now damps
in silence the *éclat* of noisy warriors, and the green turf
serves as a sufficient shroud for kings.'

And here it may not be amiss to draw attention to
the reason why explorers of barrows so often meet
with no reward. *They do not excavate the ground beneath.*
Were it more generally known that, as a rule, the dead
man was interred beneath the natural surface of the
ground, and then an artificial mound raised over his
remains, results more satisfactory would, I feel confident, attend the labours of the searcher for antiquities.
But another cause may, I think, have at one time contributed to the abandonment of the excavation of these
tumuli ; and this will, perhaps, account for the slightly
disturbed condition of several, which, from appear-
ances, were dug into many years ago—I mean superstition.

For in former days a dread of opening these ' graves
of the giants,' as they were called—a dread that in this
prosaic nineteenth century will provoke a smile—existed among the less educated classes. The spirit it
was thought would avenge the violation of the body's
last resting-place, and trouble, illness, perhaps death,
would alone reward the adventurous explorer. A
curious instance of this popular feeling, and the extraordinary effect it had upon the violator, is recorded

by Westcote, in his 'View of Devonshire,' as having occurred on the very borderland of our district—namely, in the parish of Challacombe, 'next neighbour to Exmoor.'

'A daily labouring man, by the work of his hand and sweat of his brow, having gotten a little money, was desirous to have a place to rest himself in old age, and therefore bestowed it on some acres of waste land, and began to build a house thereon, near, or not far from, one of these barrows, named Broaken Barrow, whence he fetched stones and earth to farther his work; and having pierced into the bowels of the hillock, he found therein a little place, as it had been a large oven, fairly, strongly and closely walled up; which comforted him much, hoping that some good would befall him, that there might be some treasure there hidden to maintain him more liberally, and with less labour in his old years; wherewith encouraged, he plies his work earnestly until he had broken a hole through this wall, in the cavity whereof he espied an earthen pot, which caused him to multiply his strokes, until he might make the orifice thereof large enough to take out the pot, which his earnest desire made not long a-doing; but as he thrust in his arm, and fastened his hand thereon, suddenly he heard, or seemed to hear, the noise of the treading or trampling of horses, coming, as he thought, towards him; which caused him to forbear, and arise from the place, fearing the comers would take his purchase from him (for he assured himself it was treasure); but looking about every way to see what company this was, he saw neither horse nor man in view. To the pot again he goes, and had the like success a second time; and yet, looking all about, could ken nothing. At the third time he brings it away, and finds therein only a few ashes and bones, as if they had been of children, or the like. But the man, whether by the fear, which yet he denied, or other causes, which I cannot comprehend, in a very short time after lost senses both of sight and hearing, and in less than three months consuming, died. He was in all his lifetime accounted an honest man ; and he constantly reported this, divers times, to men of good quality ; with protestations to the truth thereof, even to his death.'

' It is at your choice,' Westcote goes on, ' to believe these stories or no; what truth soever there is in them, they are not unfit tales for winter nights when you roast crabs by the fire.'

Taken in connection with the above, the following more modern story will be interesting : At Castlehaven, near Bandon, County Cork, are seven large menhirs, none of which, says tradition, may be moved without bringing death on the person making the attempt. Last January a labourer was ordered to take up one, presumably for building purposes; the tradition was singularly fulfilled : the stone fell and crushed him to death.

Two principal British trackways traversed the district. The most important, crossing the Avon between Burghwalls and Stokeleigh camps, ran through the county to the Parret. Crossing that river at Combwich, it passed on to the fort on Cannington Park Hill—the fort said to be connected with the battle of Cynuit, and following the line of the present highway to Stowey, where it is still visible, climbed ' by a valley south of Over Stowey to the top of the Quantocks; descended and climbed Willett Hill and ran along the ridge of Brendon Hill, and thence into the valley of the Exe and to Barnstaple.'* The other stretched from Minehead to Neroche, a fine British camp six miles south of Taunton.

Earthworks, or as they are called nowadays, camps —to them allusion has already been made—are very numerous. Some overlook the long trackway whose course has just been described, notably Danesborough and Elworthy Barrows, two large fortifications, the first guarding the approach over the Quantocks, the latter—which for some reason was never finished—standing at the side of the way across the Brendon range. Nearly all are Celtic, the only exceptions being Ruborough, near the village of Broomfield, and ' Cæsar's Camp,' in Dunster Park, which have, as before stated, been looked upon as Roman. The first almost undoubtedly is so; but there is, I think, some doubt about the second. They are all on high ground, generally indeed on the top of a hill. Danesborough and ' Cæsar's Camp' in particular have situations noteworthy, both for elevation and the magnificence of the prospect which they command. Danesborough, indeed, stands over a thousand feet above the sea, from which it is a conspicuous object.

In his list of the chief British fortresses in Somersetshire, Murray, whilst mentioning few of the camps of

* Murray, p. 1.

West Somerset, includes Dunkery Beacon. What reason he, or anyone, can have for imagining this, the highest point of Exmoor, to be, or ever to have been, the site of a fortification I am at a loss to imagine. Beyond the beacon itself, and the ruined fire-hearths and scattered stones around; the hill, though not as smooth, is as devoid of anything approaching an earthwork as the lawn of a villa garden. Nor is there even any camp in the neighbourhood, save the small oval entrenchment in the wood behind Porlock; and this, tradition says, is Saxon, thrown up, it is supposed, at the time of Harold's descent.

Of primeval antiquities, by which are meant those rude circles of unhewn stone—the *lapides stantes* of ancient records—menhirs, avenues and the like, West Somerset can boast very few. Even such hut circles as were at one time to be seen, have almost totally disappeared. As these rough relics of our forefathers are, and apparently always were, so scarce in our hill country as compared with the numbers that still exist upon other moorlands, I can only suppose that the cause is to be found in the difference in geological formation. The granitic masses of Dartmoor and the Cornish peninsula, for instance, thickly strewn with fragments of rock, presented to Neolithic man materials ready to his hand, and hut basements and other stone remains are the result. Not so these moorlands of Somerset: except here and there, suitable stone upon the surface is not to be had; and so the aborigine would construct his hut of turf or 'cob,' roofed with rushes or wattle; and of course these have long since vanished, leaving no sign. Save for one small specimen at the back of Rodhuish hill, I know of no hut circle anywhere between the Quantocks and the County Wall, nor can I discover the person who, however long he may have known the county, has for many years encountered them. Nor are the so-called ' religious ' antiquities much more plentiful. Of ' sacred ' circles there are none. Of the three *Longstones* on Winsford Hill, two—both very small—are evidently rubbing posts for sheep. The third, however, may turn out to be important. I have lately had the good fortune to decipher something of the inscription, which the highest authority on Celtic monuments in the kingdom considers to represent the name of a Romanized Celtic chieftain of the fifth or sixth century ; whether the stone is monumental or cenotaphic, has not been at present determined ; the matter is now under the consideration of the gentleman above referred to, and until he can find time to visit the spot, I am unable to add much to the above information.

I am not aware of the existence of any other menhir within our district, with the exception of at all slab of slaty stone which may be found to the south of Chapman Barrows, about a mile within the county of Devon. The stones at Battlegore, near Williton, are, I believe, the only remains of a cromlech or dolmen, unless the Whitestones above Porlock Hill are the supporters of another such structure ; in both cases, perhaps, anything like certainty is out of the question.

As to the avenues or *parallelitha*—those strange parallel lines of upright stone, which have been variously regarded as commemorative of a battle, as Druid processional paths, or as approaches to graves—there appears to exist one solitary specimen, and that a mere fragment, consisting of but six small stones, extending some fifty feet, on a hill between Badgeworthy Water and Chalk Water; in fact, could any other use be assigned for it, I should hesitate to regard these lines of stone as an avenue at all.

With the exception of the foundations on Castle Mount at Stowey, there are no ruined castles in this part of West Somerset, for Stogursey is too far from the hill country to be included in this work. The Castle of Dunster, added to, and beautified, by several generations of Mohuns and Luttrells, has no remains of the original keep, and the old towers are in perfectly good preservation. Seated on a wooded knoll—and commanding from its terraces views of sea, mountain, valley and plain—it forms, with its surroundings, one of the most striking and beautiful pictures in a striking and beautiful country.

> ' Bold, rising on an insulated height,
> With deep encircling woods, all verdant, crowned,
> Thy castle, Dunster ! proudly meets our sight ;
> Though loftier mountains grandly girt thee round :
> And thou hast heard, in stormier times, the sound
> Of War's hoarse trumpet, and the cannon's roar ;
> Where now the timid deer treads o'er thy ground,
> And nought comes louder than the waves that pour
> When northern winds are high along thy level shore.'*

West Somerset formerly boasted of three religious houses: the Cistercian Abbey of St. Mary of Cleeve,

* Draper.

and the Priories of Barlynch near Dulverton, and
Dunster; a great part of the first still remains, consisting of a magnificent refectory, dormitory, common
room, chapter-house, part of the cloisters, and certain
offices.   The architecture is Early English and Perpendicular.   Barlynch, a small house founded in the
twelfth century, for Augustinian Canons, by William de
Say, only shows one or two crumbling walls, and will
not be further mentioned; while Dunster possesses
but a barn and dovecote.   But the churches are a
feature.   There are few that do not deserve a visit;
some are worthy of prolonged examination.   The style
is almost always Perpendicular, and one of them—that
of Bishop's Lydeard—has a tower considered by many
the finest specimen of this architecture in Somerset.
The most noted is the cruciform Priory Church of
Dunster. Among others may be mentioned St. Michael's
at Minehead, standing high on the hillside, above the
bay; St. Dubritius at Porlock, where are fine monuments: Luccombe, Selworthy, Exford, and Crowcombe
under the Quantocks.   The carving in wood found in
most of these churches has excited much admiration.
Where such magnificent screens, where such grace-
fully and, it must be added, sometimes grotesquely-cut
bench-ends, as in these gray old structures ? Thinking
on them, and their beauties, we had almost forgotten
a modern building, the very perfect Gothic church
standing in St. Audries' Park, on the site of the former
church of West Quantoxhead.

CHAPTER V

To approach a picturesque district by the unpicturesque
iron horse is the reverse of romantic. However, except
in very remote regions, coaching is a thing of the past,
and the visitor from a distance must put his romantic
ideas in his pocket and himself in a carriage of the
Great Western Railway. It is thus we approach
Dulverton.

The station lies nearly two miles from the town, with
which it is connected by a pleasant road passing
between wooded hills. Conspicuous on the right, high
above the meadows, through which sweeps the Barle,
is Pixton, the seat of the Earl of Carnarvon, a handsome
modern mansion backed by noble trees. Round a bend
in the road, and the little town comes into view. It
lies on a gentle slope on the north bank of the Barle,
here crossed by a picturesque bridge of five arches.

6—2

The river makes a great bend, and from this bend it is thought that the name of the town has originated. *Dôl* is Celtic for a bend, and adding to this *ford ton*, we have Dolfordton, the ford town at the bend (of the river).*

There is nothing of great interest in Dulverton. The church, standing at the top of the principal street, is a good Perpendicular building with well-carved battlements, but presents little that need detain us. With the exception of the tower, it was rebuilt five-and-thirty years since. It is better to climb the hill behind, whence a good view is obtained of the valley, with the river sweeping down from its Exmoor home through the woodlands, beneath the gray massive bridge, and on to the more open country. In fact Dulverton is the centre of a district famous for its walks and drives, and to its scenery, and above all its fishing—for the Barle swarms with trout—owes such notice as it has attracted from the outer world.

Happy is the country without a history. Perhaps happy, too, is the town. How happy then should Dulverton be : for, after diligent search, I cannot ascertain that it has been the scene of any stirring event ! It was held by Harold as a border manor of Exmoor in the days before the Conquest, at which time, as we have seen, he attempted the raid on Porlock, during his own and Godwin's banishment, a raid that

---

* Dr. Pring, 'Proc. Som. Arch. Soc.,' vol. xxix. He adds that *Dolfordton* in Dorsetshire is similarly situated, and notes that *Dolton* on the Taw is on a *bend*, but has no ford.

met with success, in spite of the fact that his unappreciative countrymen turned against him, and did their best to drive him into the sea.

The road to Exmoor leaves the street opposite the Lion Hotel, and, passing down a straggling lane at its entrance, but six or seven feet wide—and yet this is the coach road to Lynton and Barnstaple—winds along the river's brink for some distance. When a chapel standing on the opposite bank is reached, we turn up a long hill to the right, and climb to a quarry by the roadside. As we are afoot we may here diverge, and follow the course of the river. Passing through a gate on the left, just above the quarry, we emerge on a field through which a road leads to some hill farms. The field slopes steeply to the woodlands, at whose feet far beneath us flows a bright reach of the river, hemmed in for many a mile by lofty tree-clad hills. Away in the western distance a purple ridge or two marks the confines of the Moor.

Just before reaching the second farm, a shady lane descends sharp to the left, degenerating, where it comes out upon a wild hillside covered with bracken and low oak coppice, into a rough cart-track. Right ahead, rising out of the valley between us and the Barle, is a precipitous hill, a flattened cone clothed to the top with timber. It is a stiff pull to the summit, but our climb will not be for nothing; for it is encircled by the stone rampart of a hill fortress, which must in its day have been of great importance, as defending the approach to Exmoor. It is now known as Mouncey Castle, a corruption of Mounceaux, which is again a corruption of the name of the Monceaux family, who at one time held lands in this neighbourhood.

The rampart is in places very massive, and constructed of stones of far greater size than is usually the case.   It forms an irregular circle, and encloses a space of from three to four acres.   It is impossible to make accurate measurements, as the whole enclosure is thickly overgrown with bracken and trees.   The latter are covered with long gray lichen, which give them a peculiarly eldritch appearance, particularly in the gloaming, when,

'Bearded with moss and in garments green, indistinct in the twilight,

they induce a melancholy feeling, which is not lessened by the mournful voice of the river, two hundred feet beneath.

Except on the southern side the rampart averages about six feet in height. Just within it, where the ground falls rapidly towards the Barle, are the ruins of a small rectangular building about six feet square, covered with moss, and beautified by fern.   This may have been a guard chamber, though what it guarded is not very apparent, as there is no trace of an entrance. In a meadow to the south-east of the hill, and on the very brink of the river, is a large heap of stones, which popular legend connects with the camp.   What it was I cannot say : but there are indications of a rampart, and possibly it was an outpost of the camp above. Close at hand a black 'clam' bridges the river, indicating at once the position of the mound.

Mouncey Castle is the first of a chain of hill fortresses extending up the Barle. Across the river are Hawkridge Castle and Brewers Castle, while nine miles up beyond Landacre Bridge is Cow Castle. All these we shall visit in due course. That they are Belgic-British camps is scarcely open to doubt : both their position and configuration forbid us to entertain the theory that any one of them is of Roman construction.

There are the usual wild legends pertaining to Mouncey Castle. A neighbouring farmer announced his opinion that it was Druidical ! while another told me that the ground beneath was hollow, and that as a consequence people were afraid to dig there. There was a rumour, too, of a subterranean passage, but where it was supposed to lead was unknown.

Crossing by the clam, or ' clammer,' as my farmer called it, a lane is reached passing under Hawkridge Castle, situate on the top of a wooded hill opposite to, but not so lofty as Mouncey Castle. There are little or no traces of a rampart. About a quarter of a mile further on, where the lane, after crossing the bridge over the Dunn's Brook, commences to ascend towards Hawkridge village, is another camp, known as Brewers Castle. This is a circular fortress, similar to, but much smaller than Mouncey, whose wooded steeps can be seen through the trees across the Barle. The ramparts are not high, and the enclosure is much overgrown. In one place advantage has been taken of a crag of natural rock, which forms the highest part of the circumvallation.

Ascending the hill we soon come out upon a breezy common, across which a cart-track, in many places more a name than a reality, leads to Hawkridge, a tiny hamlet of some half-dozen houses. The little homely-looking church enjoys the local reputation of being the oldest in the district. The doorway has a Norman toothed arch, but the windows, though new, are decidedly Perpendicular. The tower, with a stair turret rising somewhat higher than is customary above the battlements, is low and sturdy, as befits the situation of a building exposed to every wind that blows. The view southward from the churchyard, though by no means grand, is in the early weeks of autumn wonderfully rich in colouring. On the hither side of the valley, the fields slope down a vivid green to meet the rich purple of the heathery spurs of Exmoor rising against the sky-line, the downs above Anstey and Molland.

A steep road descends the northern slope of the ridge to the Barle, along which it winds in a position certainly trying to the nerves of any carriage-folk who may follow its course. It is cut in the side of a steep wood, and literally overhangs the rushing river eddying 50 feet below. Not a shadow of wall or railing protects the vehicle, which in case of accident must inevitably be hurled into the flood, here quite strong enough to sweep it and its occupants to destruction. There is a somewhat similar spot on the road from South Molton to Simonsbath, where a carriage actually was precipitated into the Barle. But the stream at that spot is much smaller, and no injury beyond a broken collar-bone was the result. Still, even a collar-bone is better left *in statu quo*, and it is marvellous that, in the face of such an accident, this spot is left un-guarded.

A beautiful walk brings us to a spot where the river passes through a meadow hemmed in, as is the case throughout almost the whole of its lower waters, by wooded hills. The stream is here 120 feet wide, and for carriages fordable. Foot-passengers may cross by a very curious bridge, which, as a relic in all probability of Celtic antiquity, merits some attention.

Torr or Tarr Steps, as the old bridge is called, con-sists of large slabs of stone laid on roughly piled piers projecting about a yard on either side of the roadway. The average length of a slab is perhaps about 7 feet, the width 3 feet 6 inches; the longest being 8 feet 6 inches by 5 feet wide. In the centre they are laid singly; towards the ends the stones, being narrower, are placed side by side. The piers facing the current are pro-tected by sloping stones about 4 feet in length. There are no less than seventeen openings. The total length of the bridge, including the paved approaches, is 180 feet, and its height above the water, except in flood time, when it is submerged, is about 3 feet. There is not an atom of cement in the structure.

Those who know the 'clapper' bridges of Dartmoor will at once recognise their similarity to this curious erection. There is one over the river Cowsic near Bair-down Farm, which, in particular, bears a marked resem-blance, though its length is much less. These bridges are almost unhesitatingly dubbed Celtic by antiquaries, and I think there is little doubt but that the structure

before us spanned the 'silver Barle' at a very early
date in the history of Britain. It is the subject of more
than one absurd story. It is sometimes called the
Devil's Bridge, and the woman in the cottage above
told me that it had never been quite finished, the
apron of his satanic majesty giving way with the
weight of the stones, several of which might still be
seen in an adjoining plantation! Another version says
that he built it in one night, declaring that it was for
his exclusive use, and that he would destroy the first
creature crossing. An unfortunate cat attempted the
hazardous passage, and was at once torn in pieces.
This appears to have broken the spell, for a parson then
crossed in safety, interchanging compliments, more
forcible than polite, with the architect. 'The devil
called the parson a black crow, to which the parson
replied that he was not blacker than the devil.' I am
told that the late Rector of Hawkridge, Mr. Jekyll,
considered that a man named Tarr was the builder:
but at what period he lived I could not ascertain, nor,
do I think, could Mr. Jekyll. Various suggestions have
been hazarded to account for the name, but the likeliest
seems that of Mr. Langrishe, who derives it from Toher,
the English form of the Celtic Tochar, a causeway,
many of which exist in Ireland, such as Knocktopher,
anciently called Cnoc a tochar, the hill at the causeway.
But Ireland can boast none of such fine proportions as
Torr Steps.

A winding, up-hill lane conducts us in about two miles
to the first genuine piece of moorland—Winsford Hill.
Between the finger-post marking the cross-roads and the

TARR STEPS ON THE RIVER BARLE.

hedge on the right, and at the side of an old track—
I believe the former highway—is a rude standing stone
of hard slaty rock, known as the Longstone. It leans
considerably out of the perpendicular, and has met with
rough usage, a portion of the top having been broken
off. The height is 3 feet 7 inches, the breadth 14 inches,
and the thickness 7 inches. It is inscribed lengthwise
with characters, but of what age or date I am unable
to decide. That they have been there for many centuries, there can, I think, be no doubt, their worn appearance testifying to many an onslaught of the elements.
The aforesaid fracture, the work of a mischievous youth
but a few months back, has probably obliterated a part
of the second line, and although I was able to find the
splintered fragment, and fit it into its place, it availed me
not, as the surface had flaked off. I read the inscription
thus :

C V R Ā A C I

F P V S

The first word apparently stands for ' (son) *of Curatacus*,'
evidently the Latinized form of some British name. This
is the only interpretation I can offer.* The local legend
says that it marks a deposit of treasure ; but it is somewhat strange that there are no traces about the stone
indicating that a search has been made. There is little
view from it except the bare heath, with Dartmoor rising
on the southward horizon. Two other stones (also called

---

* The antiquary alluded to in my reference to this stone in
Chapter IV. has not yet been able to make his examination. If
practicable, the result will be given in the Appendix, but it is feared
that numerous engagements will postpone his visit for an indefinite
period.

Longstones) may be seen in the heather to the right of the Withypoole road, but they are merely rude slabs of slate about two feet high, in all probability erected as rubbing-stones for the accommodation of sheep.

Keeping along the road Moorwards—*i.e.*, towards Withypoole—we shall notice three tumuli on the highest part of the down. They are known, I cannot tell why, as Wambarrows. From them, and indeed from the road itself, there is a very extensive view. Dunkery upheaves to the northward, his lower slopes not improved by the cultivated (and uncultivated) enclosures creeping upwards. However good a thing cultivation may be, it must be confessed that it is ruinous to moorland scenery. A mountain of heather, even though not particularly bold in shape, is a grand and pleasing spectacle; but the same mountain with the heather grubbed up, and the slopes ruled into geometrical lines by ugly fences of turf and stone, becomes an abomination. However, Dunkery still rears his head many hundreds of feet above the barren-looking fields; and long may he continue to do so!

The view to the southward takes in the outlying downs about Hawkridge, and is bounded, as I have already remarked, on the far horizon by the chain of Dartmoor, oddly named Yes Tor, towering high above the range, which from this point has a very lofty and imposing appearance. The eastward prospect is wild moorland, through which the folds marking the course of the Barle can be traced nearly to its source. Westward the eye travels towards the Brendon Hills, and the wooded country between them and Dulverton. Winsford

Hill is the highest land off the main body of Exmoor, rising, it is said, 1,500 feet above the level of the sea, which on a clear day may be descried to the right of Dunkery.

Below the Barrows to the north the land sinks very abruptly into a yawning chasm or combe, which, from its circular shape, is known as the Devil's Punch Bowl. There is some water at the bottom. The road now descends to a gate, which prevents the cattle straying from the commons on to the highway. In the valley beneath lies Withypoole, apparently more famous for its 'foolish woman' than for anything else. I remember asking a man whom I met by the gate if there were anything to be seen in the hamlet. His answer, 'Nothing but a foolish woman, sir, who will be sure to see *you*,' was not exactly encouraging. Nevertheless I descended the steep hill, with its rocky floor, hoping that this village character would give me a wide berth. Not so : as the corner leading up the hill towards Simonsbath was turned, she addressed me—and a hasty retreat was the result.

But Withypoole has other attractions than the blandishments of idiots. The fishing here is splendid, and many a crafty Zebedee may be seen working the waters of the Barle. There is nothing particularly interesting about the village, it is true, but the scenery is pleasant, and the wild downs across the river form a fine contrast to the luscious-looking water-meadows below the white cottages. The appearance of the church is a decided blot on the landscape ; at the time of its restoration, the tower was partially demolished,

and then, because, as I was told, ' it were stronger than
they thought,' left a gaunt ruin. The idea of leaving
a church in such an incomplete state as this, merely to
save trouble, will not commend itself to anyone with
a sense of the fitness of things. Perhaps, however, its
re-erection is in distant—I fear very distant—contem-
plation ; and, if such be the case, the ugly appearance
of the building must be tolerated without complaint.

The peace of this quiet village was once rudely
broken upon by a stag-hunt. Mr. Fortescue, in his
book, ' Stag-hunting,' relates how the hounds once
chased their quarry through its street, while the Re-
vising Barrister was holding his Court. He does not
say whether this counsel learned in the law was a sports-
man, but what he does relate is, that barrister and court
rushed into the open air to see the pursuit, and did not
resume their labours till the hounds had vanished.

A lane ascends to the moorlands, soon degenerating
into some faint ruts, over which a finger-post marked
' Exmoor ' points vaguely. At first sight it seems
unnecessary to have such an indication at all, for the
moorlands are right ahead ; but, on inquiry, it will be
found that there is a ' method in its madness.' Exmoor
is the postal name for Simonsbath ; and, as it is becoming fashionable to drop the old name, probably,
before many years have fled, the little metropolis of
Exmoor will bear its name.

The walk along the upland for the next three miles
is not to be recommended, and far better entertain-
ment will be provided by the Barle, to whose banks we
descend by a steep hill. At the foot is picturesque

Landacre Bridge, with its five pointed arches, over
which the road proceeds to South Molton. It is on the
very confines of cultivation; a few fields, and these but
on the northern bank, separating it from the Moor.
Beyond the rough hedgerows, a fine breezy spur slopes
gently to the stream, covered in bracken, relieved by
occasional dashes of pink ling; on the left a low, rocky
promontory juts forward, and above it the bare downs
stretch away to the sky-line. The river courses merrily
down the valley, divided just below the bridge by an
island clad like the hills in fern.

We follow the northern bank for about a mile, over
fairly good, but occasionally boggy, ground, until a considerable stream, the Sheardon Water, peninsulating
Shear Down, comes in on the left. Near this point a
cart-track is reached, which leads to a wild valley, one
of the most romantic spots on the Barle; on each side
the bare hills descend abruptly, those across the stream
showing some scattered masses of rock. In the centre
of the valley rise three steep knolls, the highest perhaps
200 feet above the river. This is known as Cow Castle.
The crest is encircled by the rampart of a large hill
fortress, enclosing an area of 470 paces—*i.e.*, about 1,400
feet in circumference. The loftiest part of the rampart
is not less than 10 feet. Except where the declivitous
nature of the ground rendered such a precaution unnecessary, the rampart is protected by a fosse. The
shape of the camp is an irregular circle, in fact it is as
much square as round. The ground within slopes
upward to a high rocky brow overlooking the river.
Beneath this, the rampart, becoming unnecessary, is ill

defined, and in places disappears altogether. There are
no traces of hut circles in the neighbourhood that I
could discover, though a neighbouring antiquary tells
me he thinks they may be traced in some few stones
at the bottom, between the camp and the rocky conical
knoll to the south-east, not inappropriately named the
Calf. It is said, too, that there are pit dwellings on the
hill behind. These I investigated, but am of opinion
that they are quite modern excavations, probably abandoned attempts at 'prospecting' for minerals! On the
right is a narrow and rocky valley, down which comes
the rapid stream of the White Water. A short distance
up is a ruined cottage, an evil-looking place, under a
dark slate quarry. It is said to be haunted, nor can
we be surprised when we hear of the terrible crime
enacted there, or on the adjacent Moor.

Thirty years since the house was occupied by a
widower, named Burgess; he had but one child, a
daughter, who, it is said, was obnoxious to the woman
he wished to marry; so the unnatural father determined
on her destruction. The poor child was murdered and
buried upon the Moor.

Now it was customary for sheep-stealers to tempor-
arily inter the carcase of their prey, until a favourable
opportunity for its removal presented itself. Two men
wandering on the Moor came across the spot where
the child lay concealed, and thinking that a dead sheep
lay there, informed Burgess of the fact, and arranged,
with his assistance, to remove it under cover of
darkness. It need scarcely be said that the murderer
was before them. The corpse was exhumed, and

thrown down a disused mine shaft. Burgess then disappeared, and the child being missed, a search was
instituted, and in the grave of the supposed sheep, a
fragment of the child's frock, and some of her hair, detected. A mysterious light too is said to have hovered at
night over the shaft, perhaps caused by the exhalations
from the decomposing body, perhaps by the presence
of minerals. At any rate, as my informant said, 'the
Queen hearing of it, insisted on the shaft being examined,' and the body was of course discovered.
Burgess was apprehended in Wales, and ultimately
making a full confession, was executed at Taunton in
1858. Such is the gloomy story attaching to this glen,
and if few can be found to visit it after darkness has set
in, who shall blame them? In fact, without at the time
knowing aught of the tragedy, I experienced a distinct
feeling of depression as I climbed the track behind
the haunted ruin, through the rain of an autumn
evening.

A rough road conducts us to a farm whence a lane
leads into the high road to Simonsbath. The walk
is not interesting, for the wild glen down which the
river courses is no longer visible, and the expanse of
Moor threaded by the distant road monotonous in the
extreme. Long lines of beech hedge divide the un-
fruitful looking enclosures, excellent as a shelter from
an Exmoor storm, but very much detracting from the
wild beauty of the moorland. In the distance, near
this highway, we can almost discern the bog, known as
Cloven Rocks—*why*, I cannot explain, as there are no
rocks whatever—where the great John Ridd had his

7

terrible struggle with Carver Doone, which ended, the
reader will remember, in the outlaw meeting with an
awful death in the treacherous ground.   I must confess
that I do not attach any great amount of credence
either to the scene itself, or to the fact that it was
enacted at this spot.   Indeed a wet patch upon the side
of Dunkery has been--with just as much likelihood--
pointed out as the scene of the death-struggle so
graphically described by the author of the popular
Exmoor romance.*

A long hill descends into Simonsbath, passing the
neat little church and pretty vicarage, to the handful
of cottages that make up the metropolis of Exmoor.
There is an inn, with the singularly inappropriate
name of 'The William Rufus;' an old house—older
than it looks—the occasional residence of the lord
of Exmoor, Sir Frederick Knight, and the scene of one
of the numerous escapades of that notorious outlaw
Tom Faggus.   Two centuries ago it was an inn, and
here Tom put up one night, ignorant of the fact that
his foes were on the watch.   He was actually captured,
but, with that wonderful luck which usually attended
him, contrived to make his escape.   Behind rise the
grim ruins of the mansion commenced by Sir Frederick's father, like so many other Exmoor projects
doomed never to see completion.   There is a blacksmith's forge, presided over by a communicative Vulcan
(who is also postmaster and registrar of births and
deaths!), a school, and one or two other habitations,

---

* A tree close by is actually pointed out as the one from which
the giant tore the limb with which he smote the Doone Captain !

more or less embowered in trees—for Simonsbath is quite a Vallombrosa—and within doors you positively cannot, except in one or two spots, *see* Exmoor at all. The pastures are well drained, and the agent of the late Mr. Knight must be congratulated on the success which has attended his attempts to reclaim Simonsbath from the waste.

The place is popularly said to take its name from a deep pool in the Barle a hundred yards above the fern-clad bridge, formerly a primitive structure without parapets, but now widened and improved. This *Simon's bath* was the bathing-place of an outlaw, once the terror of Exmoor; but when he flourished no one seems to know. Some say that he rests in Simonsborough, a barrow on the Blackdown Hills; while a recent writer[*] thinks that he has no connection with the pool at all, but has simply given his name to the old bridle-path that crossed the Moor to Barnstaple. Another tradition, mentioned by Mr. C. S. Ward, M.A., connects the pool with King Sigmund, the dragon-slayer.

Standing upon the bridge, and looking down-stream, we have a glimpse of the wild hills descending abruptly to the river's brink. Behind, a road winds up the hillside under a firwood towards North and South Molton, opening up a fine view of the Barle valley far below, and passing on the way Span Head, one of the loftiest risings of the Moor, which, though uninteresting in itself, commands a magnificent view of the Northern coast of Devon from Morthoe to Bideford, and the mountains of Dartmoor. Several large tumuli

* Mr. Fortescue.

crown the ridge, conferring upon it the alternative name of Five Barrows—the name, indeed, by which to the moorfolk it is generally known. These barrows were in former times dubbed the Towers, and appear to have been thrown up rather as bounds than as sepulchral heaps.*

From Span Head—the county as well as the Forest boundary—we may cross more or less boggy moorlands, or follow the road, such as it is, to the deserted house at Moles Chamber, once a bog, but now drained. It is said to be the last resting-place of one Mole, who, returning long ago from Barnstaple market, stumbled upon it in the darkness and was engulfed in its black depths.† On rising ground to the west is Showlsborough Castle, 'the only undoubted Roman camp in this neighbourhood,' to quote the words used by a neighbouring rector. It is, roughly speaking, a square, surrounded on three sides—the north, east and about half the west—by a double vallum, a shallow fosse, some thirty feet in width, lying between. The outer vallum is not more than a yard high, the inner varies from about four to seven feet. On the south the ground falls suddenly. The only entrance is on the west. In the northeast corner is an opened mound, about eighty feet in

---

* 'A place callid the Spanne, and the Tourres; for ther be hillokkes of yerth cast up of auncient tyme for Markes and Limites betwixt Somersetshir and Devonshir, and here about is the Limes and Boundes of Exmoor Forest.'—LELAND. It is, I think, probable, that at any rate one of these barrows—by the way, there are *seven*, not five—is sepulchral. It is flat, and nearly encircled by a trench and low mound. Diameter, 66 feet.

† For other versions of this story, *vide ante*, p. 16.

circumference, possibly the *prætorium.* The dimensions
of the camp, within the area, are about 480 feet from
north to south, and 429 feet from east to west. Two
Roman swords at least—one I was told having a golden
hilt—have been dug up close by, and turf-cutters have
from time to time discovered other objects of interest.
There is a vague tradition, that the camp was once
held by King Alfred against the Danes.

The view is magnificent, better even than that from
loftier Span Head, as the bold crests of the Hangman
rise against sea and sky to the north-west. Dim on
the horizon behind is the pale line of Lundy, and even
a bit of the Welsh coast, somewhere about Tenby.
The ships in Bideford Bay seem almost beneath; and
there is, of course, the long rugged wall of Dartmoor
far away southward. Never shall I forget the view
from this old earthwork one spring evening, when the
sun was low over the blue promontory of Hartland.
The estuary of Torridge and Taw was one mass of gold,
in which the pale sand dunes of the Braunton Burrows
were merged and almost lost. Against the low hills
behind drifted the smoke of the once famous port of
Bideford. Below the spurs of the moorland rose a
single church tower, that of Challacombe; for in the
mists of coming night none of the other hamlets
' cradled in the dells' stood revealed.

CHAPTER VI

EXMOOR IN DEVONSHIRE

THE portion of Exmoor in Devonshire, as compared
with that in Somerset, is very small. Having regard to
this fact, it is somewhat surprising how very general is
the belief that the Moor is mostly in the former county.
With the exception of the hills of Showlsborough Castle
—the camp gives its name to the hill—and Chapman
Barrows, there are really no moorland eminences
worthy of special remark west of the County Wall.
Small, however, as is the Devonshire section of Exmoor,
it is far from uninteresting; and, as we have now
reached a point over the Somerset border, a favourable
opportunity occurs for exploring the hills and glens
lying between Challacombe, Brendon, and Lynton.

Challacombe, old Westcote's 'next neighbour to
Exmoor,' lies almost at the foot of Showlsborough

Castle, in the upper valley of the Bray, a clear stream which courses down the village on its journey southward towards the Taw. The village is not interesting, nor does the church, situated on a hill at some distance, call for much attention. The tower, which, according to the old clerk, a bit of an antiquary, contains Saxon work, is very beautifully adorned *inside*, with a variety of rare ferns. Among them may be noticed some graceful sprays of maiden-hair, not at all common in this part of the country. Under the arch is a handsome Early English font, supported by a central and several smaller columns. The nave and chancel were rebuilt in 1850.

In the churchyard is the grave of a somewhat celebrated local character, one Edward Webber; 'A very fine man,' said the clerk, 'who would wrestle till he burst his coat; and you know, sir, that a wrestling coat be mortal strong.' This athlete, a sort of modern 'Jan Ridd,' seems to have wrestled to some purpose, even with that great 'thrower,' Father Time, for his tomb-stone records his demise in his 102nd year. He died, I think, in 1847.

Superstition yet lives in this semi-moorland village. An old man cannot be persuaded but that every illness entailed by his failing years is the direct result of witchcraft.

There is no inn at Challacombe—at least, none with 'good accommodation for man,' and, I should think, but dubious quarters for beast. Shenstone, who believed that the traveller on 'life's weary round' found

'His chiefest comfort at an inn,'

would have certainly given Challacombe a wide berth;
but this, the nowadays' wayfarer need not do, for there
are the most comfortable of lodgings—to which I, as
the first lodger, can testify—at Home Farm. Doubtless there are many charms in a country hostelry, but
there are more, many more, at a genuine country farm.
How pleasant, after a long day's tramp, to sit with the
good farmer and his family round the great wide
chimney-place, and, to the faint puffings of church-
wardens—*pipes*, not parochial dignitaries—listen to the
disjointed sentences, rich with folklore and old-world
traditions, that fall from the lips of these children of
the soil! And then the fresh, sweet-smelling bedroom,
the floor adorned with wonderful home-worked mats
and the skins of sheep and badger, with its window
opening upon the brook, singing gaily

> 'In little sharps and trebles,'

just across the road. You retire to rest; but almost
before sleep has well had time to sit upon your eyelids
—at least, so it seems to *you*—there is a stir in the
barton below, and chanticleer (curse him not if he *does*
wake you) announces in cheery tones that

> 'The morn, in russet mantle clad,
> Walks o'er the dawn of yon high eastern hill.'

During some recent alterations at Home Farm, a
cannon-ball was unearthed—not the only one, I believe,
found in Challacombe. It is perfectly formed, and
evidently of no great age, certainly not older than
Stuart days. It seems probable that some skirmish
took place here during the Civil War, though I can find

no record of such an occurrence; and the villagers talk, but vaguely, of an old house—now a farm—where 'papers were signed in the war time.'

The valley of the Bray to the southward, where the red deer harbour in numbers, is not of the Moor, which has now died down into poor-looking fields, succeeded by more productive, though scarcely more interesting, enclosures; and there are no romantic combes, as among the slopes about Porlock, to arrest the gaze. So we turn northward to the more entertaining country to be found on the spurs of the waste west of the lonely mound of Woodbarrow.

We shall visit Woodbarrow itself later; but the mention of the tumulus reminds me that Westcote, in the chapter on remains in the parish of Challacombe, has a legend about it. A 'conjurer'* persuaded some men that he knew—it is presumed by a species of divination not vouchsafed to the ordinary mortal—that Woodbarrow contained a large brass vessel full of treasure. An arrangement as to sharing the plunder being arrived at, the excavation commenced. No sooner was an opening made, than a deadly faintness—the inevitable result, in former days, of such desecration — overcame the party. However, they plucked up courage, and persevered, only to find the

---

* Conjurers are still, to a limited extent, believed in upon Exmoor. 'The farmer who loses a colt goes to the conjurer to learn where the animal has strayed ; the mother, whose sailor-boy has not been heard of for years, finds consolation in what the dealer in magic reveals to her concerning him.'—Alice King : *The Argosy*, Jan. 1, 1870.

bottom of an earthen jar containing a trifling quantity of refuse. For some time after this event conjurers must have been at a discount in the neighbourhood of Challacombe.*

But to return to our travels. Leaving the village we cross a number of rough fields, and descend into the depths of a wild combe known as Pixy Rocks. Among the crags jutting here and there from the steep walls of this glen the Pixies dwelt in days gone by—perhaps the very Pixies who haunted Bratton Down not so very long since, and whose machinations could only be defeated by the 'pixy-led' traveller turning his glove inside out. It is a pleasant scramble up to the head of the combe, where rises the great grassy hill of Chapman Barrows. By tracing the stream to the right and ascending the slope whence it takes its source, we shall come upon a tall lean slab of slate, the Longstone. It stands in the middle of a bog, and being the only object that for some little distance breaks the monotony of the Moor, is rather impressive. The history of this lonely rock-pillar is unknown; but there it has been from a time 'whereof'—as the lawyers say —'the memory of man runneth not to the contrary.' The height is nine feet, the greatest breadth about two feet eight inches, but the thickness only a few inches. There is no trace of an inscription. Whether it is a specimen of the *maen hir* (the long stone) of antiquity,

* About a mile and a half north-west of Challacombe are the ruins of a house called Broken Barrow, close to the mound opened by the 'daily labouring man,' of whom Westcote speaks. This was probably his house. *Vide ante*, p. 76.

it is useless to inquire; it is, at any rate, possible, because near at hand are many vestiges of primitive man, in the shape of sepulchres.

For Chapman Barrows, as its name would imply, is plentifully dotted with tumuli, and tumuli of colossal proportions. There are about a dozen altogether, seven stretching in a straight line over the brow of the hill. Some are cut into by a fence (for even to this point, nearly 1,600 feet above the sea, cultivation has climbed), but more than one is still ten or twelve feet high, and 300 feet in girth at the base. Most have been opened, though, as usual, imperfectly. The Longstone, as seen from the top of the loftiest, presents a curious, and rather weird appearance: owing to its being broader in the middle than at top or bottom, it looks for all the world like a gigantic figure gazing towards the graves of a people perhaps contemporary with it. Indeed, I am inclined to think that Chapman is but a corruption of some older name; *man*, as is well known, is frequently used for *maen*, a stone;* though what the first syllable signifies I cannot tell.

The panorama of moorland seen from Chapman Barrows is impressive, but the view westward is less beautiful than that from Showlsborough Castle. The most prominent feature is the Hangman, in shape far more graceful than any hill upon Exmoor. Below is the village of Paracombe, on the coach road from Lynton to Barnstaple. It is worth while making the

---

* *E.g. Bairdown man*, a rock pillar on Dartmoor ; also *Coniston old man*, and the *man o' war* rock (*maen vawr*, the great stone), Scilly Islands.

two miles' descent to inspect the Celtic earthwork of Halwell Castle, crowning a spur to the south of the village, but the surrounding country can hardly be called attractive. The twelfth-century church, although still standing, has lately been superseded by a new building, erected in 1878.

Less than a mile east of Chapman Barrows is ' Sadler's Stone,' where once stood a boundary stone of Exmoor Forest. The spot is now marked by a gate in the wall, and the post fixing the limits in this direc-tion of the large parish of Lynton. From this point we shall in a short time reach Shallowford Farm, close to a stream, a feeder of the West Lyn, which comes down a rather fine combe, one of the last genuine moorland glens we shall for awhile encounter. Hence there is a fairly interesting walk by a rough road to Barbrook Mill and Lyn Bridge, below which the West Lyn begins to fall more rapidly towards the wonderful gorge where artists by the dozen congregate from May to October. Glen Lyn is a deep wooded ravine between the towering Lyn Cliff and the town of Lynton, through which the torrent comes down, like that of Lodore, in a 'succession of waterfalls.' In half a mile the stream falls no less than 400 feet.

The environs of Lynton, however, are better known than the country lying between Chapman Barrows and Brendon. So we will make our way across the commons in the direction of that most scattered of villages. Crossing the combe before mentioned, where the torrent may almost be taken in a man's stride, we soon reach Furzehill, a little hill-farm just above another tributary of the West Lyn. Here the entrance is very unsuitably decorated with a pair of pinnacles formerly on the tower of the demolished church at Combe Park. And now up a cart-road and into a dirty lane, the only communication between the hill-farmer and civilization. He does not seem, however, to mind either his abominably bad roads (save the mark!) or his isolation, except in winter, when he will tell you 'it be cruel bitter out over'—*out over* means Exmoor. But about summer he waxes almost enthu-siastic, and enlarges, with quite bucolic eloquence, on the beauties of his hills and glens. Notwithstanding their sometime poverty-stricken appearance, there is much of old-world interest about these cottages—they are little more—on the slopes of the border combes. Here 'the sower goes forth to sow his seed,' much as he did a century ago, for on Exmoor the 'patent Archi-medean drill,' whatever that may be, is as unknown as the steam plough and the threshing-machine. For the flail still resounds upon the granary floor : I heard the musical thud, thud, thud, quite recently ; but whether the sound would be as melodious to the machinist or the lowland farmer, with his chemical manure and prize turnips, may perhaps be doubted. On the left-hand side of this lane, in a field just above the Combe Park Water, is another of the numerous Celtic strong-holds of the West Country. It is small, being but 900 feet in circumference, and has the usual single rampart, from four to six feet high, surrounded by a fosse. There are entrances—whether original or not, I cannot determine—on the east and west.

A hill, 'like the side of a house,' descends to the stream, into which the lane dips before climbing an equally abrupt ascent to the small farm-hamlet of Cherriton. The foot-bridge, or clam, placed for the convenience of pedestrians is the most primitive I have ever crossed. The agile wayfarer may, with care, reach the further shore (distant, fortunately, but a score of feet) dryshod ; but woe to the aged, the careless, or the inebriate ! for our bridge consists but of a small and very uneven tree or branch, guarded only by one rude handrail.

From the hillside above, there is a pleasant peep up the valley towards the moorlands and down beneath the woods towards Combe Park. Across on the opposite brow is the earthwork, which, for want of a better name, I will call Furzehill Camp, and the long undulations of the wilderness, now well in our rear, beyond.

Below Cherriton is the combe of the Farley Water, its slopes beautifully wooded. The shortest way to Brendon is by Bridge Ball, at the foot of the descent, and then over the hill to the church; but those who love the picturesque should, instead of crossing, follow the road and stream to Ilford Bridges, where, under a single ivy-hung arch, the little Combe Park Water comes rushing down under the woodland to meet the Farley Water. Close by is the other bridge, a wooden clam, which we cross, and mount the long hill towards the church.

No man can climb this hill without frequent pauses to look back and down at the beautiful glen between

Combe Park Lodge and Watersmeet, where the united waters of Combe Park and Farley enter the Lyn stream. Between the trees glimpses may be caught of two roads: the upper climbing the hill westward to Lynton, the lower—and what a scene it opens! —winding along the waterside to Lynmouth, three miles distant.

Brendon church-town can scarcely be called a village at all. It is made up of church, school-house, parsonage and a few scattered farms. The most considerable part of the village is at and near Millslade, down in the deep valley of the Lyn, or, as it is here called, the Brendon Water, a mile or more from the church. The church of St. Brendon is indeed 'set on a hill,' the sturdy brown tower rising from a little grove three or four hundred feet above the rushing river. It is a picturesque feature in the landscape, and its re-erection in 1828 has done little to destroy its venerable appearance. The remainder of the church calls for no comment. It, too, has been rebuilt—according to a stone tablet let into the south wall in 1738. There is a sundial, bearing the date 1707, over the porch. Beneath the lych gate is a coffin stone.

Down the steep hill winds the road to the Rockford Inn, perched on the very edge of the river, here crossed by a clam. The road passes on up the valley to Millslade and Malmsmead Bridge, spanning the Badgworthy Water, the boundary between Devon and Somerset. It is a beautiful walk, the hills being wooded nearly the whole of the distance. At Millslade, 'where the Lyn stream runs so close to the forge that he dips

his horse-shoes in it '—at least so he did in the days of
the Doones—is the blacksmith's shop mentioned by
John Ridd. We will cross at the bridge hard by, and
then there is a choice of routes to Lynmouth : by a long
climb to the moorland village and church of Countisbury, or by the river path.

To describe in detail the beauties of this, perhaps, the
loveliest valley—or shall we say ravine ?—in the West of
England requires a more eloquent pen than mine.   Not
one yard in the whole four miles is tame.   On either
side of the rock-fretted river the precipitous hills rise
against the sky, here wooded, there bare, and marked
with patches of *screes*.   In one spot, where the river is
shut in by rugged cliffs, the dashing of the water
increases to a roar.   It is the voice of the cascade
tumbling over the rocks into a long pool.   A mile below
is another lovely scene, the meeting of the streams—
lovely Watersmeet.   And so the path winds downwards,
the hills increasing in height as Lynmouth draws nigh,
breaking out presently in the crags of the Tors Walk
on the right, and those of Hawkse'en and the Lyn cliff
on the left.   All too soon we reach the Lyndale Hotel,
and look up the shorter gorge where West Lyn comes
leaping and foaming down to join his bigger brother.

Attracted by the beauty of this walk we have almost
forgotten to climb to the so-called Roman Camp above
Watersmeet.   It is perched on the rugged ridge dividing
the river from the sea, 750 feet below.   The eastern
end of this ridge, where it slopes into a bare hollow,
is defended by an enormous rampart, thirty-five or forty
feet in height.   Nature probably formed the ramparts

of the remaining sides : on the north and south, the land, falling precipitously towards river and sea ; on the east, the rocky summit, crested with tors, slopes away towards Lynmouth. Midway down the seaward declivity, almost overhanging the ocean, runs the road, at no spot level, but presently dropping suddenly to Lynmouth at a gradient that has alarmed many a passenger by the coach, and will alarm many more.

The situation of Lynton and Lynmouth is, from an artistic point of view, as nearly perfect as can be imagined. The former lies on a high plateau beneath Hollarday Hill, the latter 400 feet and more below, along the banks of the Lyn. Probably no towns or villages in the West of England have received so much attention at the hands of both artist and author as these settlements above and beside the Lyn streams. And it is not too much to say that neither the pencil of the one or the pen of the other can easily exaggerate the romantic charm of their surroundings.

Crossing the Lyn by the Lyndale Hotel, we are at once in one of the most beautiful parts of the valley that even Southey could scarce find words to describe. Looking up there is a fine view of the gracious foldings of the hills with the river swirling down around—and in freshets, *over*—massive boulders mantled with moss and the stains of a thousand winters. Looking down is the irregular line of the street of this ' village port'— cottage, boarding-house, lodging, hotel, with a background of precipitous hill heavy with foliage. At the bottom of the street is the smallest of harbours ; a rough brown quay, at its head the picturesque Rhenish

8

tower, as much a feature of Lynmouth as the chapel above the pier is of busier Ilfracombe. For a ' modern antique' this watch-tower deserves nothing but praise, and no one would imagine that the warm-coloured stones of General Rawdon's gift were not so very long since yet unquarried.

At low tide the Lyn is the only water in the harbour, as the sea retires for some distance, laying bare a rather impracticable foreshore of boulders and pebbles, with here and there a strip of sand. But, unlike most estuaries, there is no mud, and the waters flow down past the tall posts that mark the channel as clear as when they left their moorland home. Whether the sea is at ebb or flood the spot is singularly beautiful, but there can be no doubt that it is at high water that Lynmouth presents its full attractions. The risen tide has dammed back for awhile the impetuous river, filling the harbour with clear water, in which the watch-tower, the rude walls of the pier, and even the heights above, are faithfully reproduced.

Neither town nor village—they must be taken together, for they are practically inseparable—have much history. The name of both—of course derived from the Lyn—is Saxon : *hlynna*, a torrent. Of the several families who have held the Manor since the Conqueror gave it to William de Chieure, I know of but one with an interesting story, that of De Whichehalse, Flemish Protestant refugees, who came to Lee in the sixteenth century, one of whom figures in ' Lorna Doone.' We shall presently have occasion to refer again to this family, and to the tragic end of its

LYNMOUTH.

members. With regard to Lynmouth, Westcote
appears to have been more impressed with the
'unworthy' haven and the legend of the departure of
the herrings than by the beauties of the scenery. In
his quaint language he tells us of this 'little inlet,
which in these last times God hath plentifully stored
with herrings (the king of fishes), which, shunning their
ancient place of repair in Ireland, come hither
abundantly in shoals, offering themselves (as I
may say) to the fishers' nets.' In consequence of this
plenty he goes on to inform us that fishermen 'soon
resorted thither with divers merchants, and so for five
or six years continued (to the great benefit and good of
the country) until the parson vexed the poor fishermen
for extraordinary unusual tithes, and then (as the
inhabitants report) the fish suddenly left the coast,
unwilling, as may be supposed, by losing their lives, to
cause contention.' The story may be commended—
for what it is worth—to the notice of the Anti-Tithe
agitators.

A lift or railway, just opened, connects Lynmouth with
the town above, rising at a gradient of 1 foot in 1¾ feet,
to a height of several hundred feet, showing at once the
steepness and elevation of the surrounding country. I
suppose we must commend the spirit of enterprise that
has thus managed to circumvent nature, and save the
toilsome though beautiful ascent to Lynton. But it must
be admitted that these modern conveniences, however
much they may add to the comfort of the visitor, certainly detract from the romance, if not the appearance,
of the place he is visiting. We ourselves prefer taking

8—2

the road, gaining thereby many a peep into Glen Lyn, though hearing rather than seeing the flood plunging downwards beneath the frowning Lyn Cliff.

I have already referred to this grand ravine, but no one who, by the aid of a silver key, has obtained admission and followed the path upwards to the Seven Falls, will think a few words more a work of super-erogation. Under the shadow of trees that on the hottest day keep the air cool and dark, past ferns whose fronds, owing perhaps to lack of sunlight as well as to excess of moisture, are of a green unusually brilliant, over rocky ridges, round rocky boulders rushes the West Lyn. Here for a moment the torrent tumbles headlong into a little 'bay,' or pool, but only to gather breath, as it were, for another dive down the resounding gorge. As a mass of falling water the Seven Falls, where the path comes to an end, bears the palm; but there are many spots equally beautiful between this noble cascade and the point where the torrent rushes into the arms of his brother hundreds of feet below.

I have been in most of the picturesque districts of Western England, but never have I met with such an *embarras de richesses* in the matter of scenery as about the town looking down upon the Lyn. It is positively difficult to make up 'what one is pleased to call one's mind'—as the cynic remarked—which point to attack first. As we have already seen something of the hills and glens towards the Somersetshire border, we will now turn west, and explore a species of country to which, as yet, we have been strangers; a rocky seafront and a crag-crested valley, which latter will remind those who know the county further south of the great mountain-moorland of Dartmoor.

The man who designed the North Walk deserves credit for a daring piece of, I had almost said engineering. For more than a mile this wonderful pathway is cut in the face of a sheer mountain declivity, in places indeed a precipice. Here and there *screes* and boulders, red and gray and orange, covered for the most part with lichen or tendrils of ground ivy, lend splashes of vivid colouring to the hillside. Above tower those singular rock masses, the natural bastions of the valley, lying just inside. The most prominent are the great Castle rock and the curious pile called 'Ragged Jack,' the two fortresses guarding the entrance to this well-named Valley of Rocks. In words the view is not easy to describe. At the top of the zigzag which ascends to the path from Lynmouth there is a noble panorama of bay, foreland, and tors. As we advance westward, turning corner after corner (not without some trepidation if the wind be high, for there is no railing, and the sea is under our very feet), an equally grand view of the bays and promontories towards High Veer opens out. Far below we may almost count the ant-like figures on the deck of the swift excursion steamer about to enter the bay with her complement of passengers. Then suddenly we turn beneath the Castle rock and enter the famous valley.

A smooth green hollow, traversed by the road to Lee Abbey, the Valley of Rocks owes its fame almost as much to the beautiful view of wood and bay to the west as to the curious tors that help to frame that lovely picture. The principal pile—in addition to those already mentioned—is the Devil's Cheesewring, a tall column of slabs, looking at first sight like one of the masses that rear their strange forms in the neighbourhood of Tol Pedn Penwith and Land's End. It has, or had, an evil reputation, for here was the rendezvous, if not the dwelling, of the witch Mabel Durham (the Mother Meldrum of Jan Ridd's acquaintance), a lady much respected—or feared—by the whole countryside. But the ever-increasing shoal of tourists has long scared away any ghost that may have haunted the gray rock; and as for the pixies, they dare not, except at night, raise their heads above the bracken.

Across the valley, nearly opposite, is a zigzag path, leading down to pretty Ring Cliff Cove and the caves beneath the Castle Rock. Further west are Lee Bay and Woodabay, both beautifully timbered. Above them is Lee Abbey, a handsome mansion, standing on the site of the old home of the De Whichehalses, of which, I believe, no part remains. Certainly the ivy-clad *ruins* are as much 'modern antique' as Lynmouth watch-tower. Within the grounds, and at the western horn of Ringcliff Cove, crowned by a tower, is Duty Point and the precipice known to this day as *Jennifred's Leap*. Jennifred de Whichehalse lived in the days of James II., and was, so the story goes, beloved of Lord Auberley, by whom she was deserted—some say betrayed as well. One night she was missing, and when morning dawned her mangled body, still wet from the tide, was found

THE VALLEY OF ROCKS, LYNTON.

upon the boulders beneath. She had thrown herself from the cliff. De Whichehalse brought the affair to the king's notice, but Auberley was too good a courtier, especially in those days of disaffection, for his master to heed the wrongs of a remote country gentleman. James turned a deaf ear to the fierce accusations of the poor father, and for ever alienated the allegiance of the lord of Lee Abbey. And so, when the great Western Rebellion came, De Whichehalse was found among the ranks of Monmouth. There Auberley met him face to face, and there vengeance overtook the perfidious lover. He fell before the sword of De Whichehalse. But the old man himself did not long survive. Soon after the horrors of Sedgemoor he set sail for Holland. The refugee, however, was fated never to reach that asylum of Monmouth's adherents : a storm arose, and all on board perished—a fitting end to one of the saddest of West Country stories.

CHAPTER VII

No one can be said to have seen Exmoor in its
native wildness who has not explored that desolate
tract, stretching from Moles Chamber to the great
valley of the Badgworthy Water, the westernmost
corner of Somersetshire. Here is utter desolation ;
here the almost ubiquitous beech hedge testifies but
seldom to the hand of man ; no ugly slate-faced cottage
mars the landscape ; no wretched sodden-looking
enclosure gives an air of pseudo-cultivation to the
great rolling steppes. Such shepherds' cots as necessity
demands are comfortably hidden in the combes ; nature
and solitude are joint rulers of the waste.

Let us attempt then to cross the moorlands towards

the Badgworthy Water, and the haunts of the wild
Doones. A track follows the fence known as the
County Wall, the boundary bank separating Devon
from Somerset; but this we shall not long pursue, turning to the right, towards the melancholy tarn of Pinkworthy Pond, and crossing the boggy but not dangerous
morass of 'The Chains.' The ground is horribly soft,
and the greatest care in treading upon the tufts of
coarse grass will scarce prevent an occasional plunge
over the ankles in a bog hole. The only prominent
hill hereabouts is Woodbarrow, a mere swelling in the
Moor marked by a solitary mound. All around are the
headwaters of the Exe, tiny runnels trickling through
the peat in every direction. Presently, in mounting a
dilapidated bank of turf, a gray gleam catches the eye,
and, hastening down a glacis of firmer ground, we find
ourselves upon the bank of the tarn.

Not a cheerful place certainly. At the head of a
shallow combe lies a sheet of water, possibly 600 feet
long, 200 wide and 40 deep, in shape an irregular
triangle. The aspect is quite natural; art, indeed has
had nothing to do with its formation, with the exception
of the construction of a massive embankment pierced
by a sluice, through which the surplus water rushes,
tumbling in a picturesque cascade down the rugged
side of the deepening glen. Here and there the banks,
steep and rocky and tufted with clumps of heather, cast
a pleasing reflection upon the clear waters. The tarn
forms, however, little attraction to the artist, for there
is no view at all. Dull, monotonous slopes of rough
bog grass rise on either hand to the sky line, shapeless

and almost colourless, save when a cloud-shadow sweeps across the surface.

Pinkworthy Pond is one of Mr. Knight's 'improvements.' It was constructed as a reservoir, I believe, to feed a contemplated canal, which, however, never got beyond the initial stages. What good purpose this canal was to have served I am unable to state. Perhaps it was thought that when Exmoor was once cultivated, commerce would visit the uplands, and the waterway be thronged with slow-moving barges, exchanging the produce of Exmoor for that of the lowlands. But alas! the wild waste declines to be 'improved ;' 'Pinkerry' Pond, as it is always called, lies a forlorn witness of a wisely-abandoned undertaking.

I fancy few moorfolk would be willing to pass the pond after nightfall. Bog-trotting at any time is disagreeable enough, but bog-trotting in the company of a possible ghost does not commend itself to the mind of even a moorman. And 'Pinkerry.' is haunted, though but by the unromantic wraith of a Devonshire farmer, who, crossed in love, committed suicide there but two years ago. He disappeared, and, after a few days, some hasty words he had uttered about 'Pinkerry Pond' being remembered, the pool near Woodbarrow was visited. There on the bank lay the hat and coat of the unfortunate lover. The pond was dragged without result ; the magic loaf set afloat proved a false indicator, and came to anchor over the wrong spot, perhaps because the candle was not inserted, though no flame would long remain alight in the breezes of Exmoor ; and ultimately a couple of divers were summoned from Cardiff. But the disturbed peat sediment at the bottom of the pond was too much even for them ; ' it was,' they said, ' like searching in a pool of ink.' So the water was let out; and, in a comparatively shallow spot, close to the shore, lay the body of the suicide. So tragical an event had not occurred upon Exmoor since Burgess murdered his child down by the White Water, and I am told hundreds of people flocked to the spot to watch the operations.

We turn our backs upon this depressing piece of water, and seek a more cheerful scene. Nor shall we be long in finding it. From the rising ground above the whole expanse of Exmoor bursts upon our view Dunkerry, prominent to the eastward, with the long swell of Black Barrow Down, where ' Uncle Caleb ' carried on his mysterious mining operations, prominent in the foreground. The scene is wild enough, though lacking in boldness, save where here and there a combe, more deeply cut than its fellows, furrows the face of the moorland. Such a one lies not far from us, in a north-easterly direction; a deep ravine, its sides scarred with gullies, down which pour miniature torrents, tributaries of the brook that dashes down the bottom filling the air with hoarse music.

Following this valley to its lower end, we find ourselves in another, a very fine and deep hollow in the hills, with steep and in places rocky slopes—the upper end of the combe of Farley Water. On an eminence at its head stand the ruins of a shepherd's cottage, and below is a solitary and forsaken sheepfold and a quantity of scattered stones. The grand appearance of this valley, combined with the sheepfold and loose stones, might well impress upon the traveller the conviction that he had reached the far-famed haunt of the Doones of Badgworthy. Alas! the Doone Valley has features far less romantic than those of the valley beneath us; and, though we will not anticipate, it is but fair to warn the reader not to build too much upon the exciting descriptions of Mr. Blackmore.

We are now in Devonshire, having crossed the boundary a short distance back. Mounting the hill across the Farley Water, we again follow the County Wall to Brendon Two Gates (there is but *one* now), where it crosses the high-road to Lynton. As we ascend the hill, we can, on looking back, see the stream we have just left, winding down the valley towards cultivation in the neighbourhood of the village of Brendon. Very soon the top of Hollarday Hill, above Lynton, comes into view, and then the Great Hangman, which we have noticed on many a previous occasion, raises its cone against the sea. By the way, the circumstance from which this fine hill has derived its unpleasing name is curious. It is said that a man, carrying a sheep across the hill by a noose attached to his neck, was strangled by the sudden tightening of the cord.

The head of the Doone Valley comes up close to Brendon Two Gates. To follow down this combe, a rather tame one, is not nearly so interesting a pilgrimage as the longer walk over the moor, striking the Badgworthy Water about two miles below the spot where the outlaws' fastness opens upon that stream,

which passes the very mouth of the glen. We maintain a direction due north-east across the moors until,
in about three miles, we find ourselves upon a bold
heathery brow, looking down into a grand valley, the
grandest of its kind upon Exmoor, watered by a wide
swift stream. This stream is the famous Badgworthy
Water, and the valley the principal and most picturesque approach to the smaller combe of 'Glen
Doone.'

Across the stream, approached by a clam, is a solitary
white cottage, along which, in gigantic letters, some
name is painted. As we descend the four or five hundred
feet of heather and screes which form the wall of this side
of the glen, we shall be able to decipher the legend—
'Lorna's Bower.'

I am afraid this cottage, with its misleading inscription, has much to answer for, especially as the cheery
old lady, who presides over the comfort of the wayfarer,
taking advantage of its hospitality, is apt to declare, in a
general sort of way, that this is the Doone Valley. As I
have already stated, it is nothing of the kind; and as for
'Lorna's Bower,' if it ever existed, it must be sought
above the 'Waterslide,' a mile or more up the stream.
The name was given in irony by the landlord, Mr.
Nicholas Snow, who, when asked to name the place, on
the occasion of its extension as a refreshment house,
suggested the romantic title which stares so boldly from
its whitewashed walls. In this sparsely-inhabited district the little half-farm, half-lodging house is a welcome
object, and its plain accommodation not to be despised
by the man who has wandered far over the moorlands.

And there is a venerable patriarch within, past his
fourscore and ten, who can still prate of Exmoor as it
was before the days of guide-books, and when coaches,
with names smacking strongly of Blackmore and Whyte-
Melville, were undreamt of altogether.*

And now for the Doone Valley. There are those
who say that 'Lorna Doone' should be studied before
Exmoor is visited. I say, see Exmoor first and read its
romance afterwards. Disillusion is never pleasant; and
those who expect to find the Doone Valley the wild
ravine painted by the glowing fancy of Blackmore, will
be more than disappointed. For that this haunt of
those terrible outlaws *is* disappointing, and very distinctly so, no one who has visited it after a perusal of
the Exmoor romance will deny; and I fear that the
literary license indulged in by its author has not always
met with that consideration which works of fiction are
supposed to deserve. Having thus prepared the reader
of 'Lorna Doone' for what he is *not* to expect, let us
follow the pathway which skirts the Badgworthy
Water, and approach the spot with philosophical re-
signation.

What a pity for the lovers of romance that the
Doones had not the good taste to dwell in this beautiful
glen! Here are rocks and heather, ancient oak wood
and modern fir plantation, glowing gorse and waving
bracken. Right up from the stream there rises a
rugged knoll, one mass of colour, and crowned with a
rock-pile for all the world like a Dartmoor Tor. Here
is a heap of moss-clad boulder, there a patch of whin-

* Since the above was written the old man has died.

Bridgewortthy Valley:

berry shrub covered with purple fruit. And down from his moorland home comes the shining river, at one moment sliding over a shelf of rock, at another tumbling helter-skelter over obstructing masses, again rippling in short reaches, where the trout may be seen in numbers sufficient to throw any properly-constituted angler into a fever. That Blackmore had this romantic spot in his mind when he described the Doone stronghold there can be little doubt, and but very little poetic exaggeration, added to a true picture of the valley, would represent the 'Glen Doone' of his pages.

The old woodland of gnarled oaks, known as Badgworthy Wood, is soon reached. I believe the Rev. John Russell, the 'Jack Russell' of world-wide notoriety, that genial Nimrod of Exmoor, held that it was a Druid grove, and fancied that he could discover traces of an altar in its shadowy recesses. It is to be feared that fancy was stronger than fact. There is nothing in Badgworthy Wood in the least resembling an altar, beyond the excrescences of natural rock which occasionally protrude through the undergrowth. An unbelieving age that is, alas! fast forgetting the sporting parson, will have none of Druidism without evidence of the most satisfactory character, and refuses to adopt slabs of rock, however convenient, as places that have, in a former time, run with the blood of the victims of Britain's white-robed priests.

On the northern flank of this wood, a lovely little stream comes rushing down a glen, over a succession of rocky slopes; this is the Waterslide, up which John Ridd is supposed to have scrambled during that adven-

turous loach-fishing expedition, which ended in his in-
troduction to Lorna.   As a matter of fact, he need not
have climbed it at all, as the banks are easily accessible, and the torrent is no more a glassy rush of water
than scores of others in the fair West Country.   It is
spanned, near its confluence with the Badgworthy
Water, by a 'clam' of boughs overlaid with turf, which
conducts the path onwards.

Beneath the steep hillside this path is followed for
another mile, gradually ascending; the valley, meanwhile, losing in depth, though gaining in wildness.
Presently we turn sharp to the right, past a little knoll,
and find ourselves in a shallow combe, nearly blocked
by some low eminences.   Above, on the slope, stands
an unpicturesque shepherd's cottage ; below, beneath
the hillocks, are some nearly undistinguishable ruins,
consisting of lines of stone, which, for the most part,
appear to mark the walls of enclosures.   The most
perfect building is represented but by the ruins of a tiny
hut, about twelve feet square, with walls nowhere exceeding four feet in height.   On the knoll commanding
the entrance to the valley are more ruins, perhaps those
of a lookout, with an incomplete enclosure uncommonly
like a sheepfold.   The Moor rises but a couple of
hundred feet at most on either side the combe, and
the slopes are of the easiest gradient.   A small brook,
concealed throughout part of its course by a beech
hedge, runs down the bottom, falling into the main
stream not far above the rough track climbing the hill
towards Porlock, the so-called warpath of the Doones.
Such is the valley visited every summer by many scores,

BADGEWORTHY WATER-SLIDE. DRAWN BY ALFRED DAWSON.

nay, hundreds of people who, with dispelled visions of precipices, passes, and what not, depart sadder and wiser men, rather unjustly blaming the author of a picturesque romance, because the real and the ideal do not exactly coincide.

Nothing will be gained by following up the valley, so we return the few steps traversed in our examination of the ' Doone houses,' and, crossing the brook, keep up the Badgworthy Water, amid scenery which every moment becomes of wilder description. In about a mile or a little more, a stream of nearly equal size comes in on the right, which we cross, and soon after, crossing the Badgworthy itself, make our way over the downs to the north-east. This will enable us to visit another fine moorland glen, that of the Chalk Water, which, though less grand than that watered by the stream we have just left, is still a fine specimen of the border combes of Exmoor.

Up the hill on the right runs a stone wall, while on our left hand is a rush-grown and boggy goyal. I am particular in giving these directions, as, in this object-less part of the Moor, they form useful landmarks. As we ascend, some dark stones come into view against the sky-line, forming an avenue which, short though it be, will, in a district peculiarly devoid of rude stone monuments, at once excite speculation. There are but six low slabs, having a height of about two feet, and set opposite each other at very nearly equal distances. The avenue is fifty-two feet long, and about twenty-one wide—a width far greater than any upon Dartmoor, where four feet is, as a rule, the utmost width

of these mysterious monuments.   There is nothing in
the vicinity to suggest sepulchral remains, unless one or
two very small rush-grown mounds mark the site of
ruined cairns.   Nor is there any indication that the
stones stretched for a greater distance than is now the
case.   I have examined the ground at both ends, and
can find no traces whatever.   Were it not for their
number, and the uniformity of distance between them,
I should be tempted to regard them as rubbing posts,
small though they are.

The head of the Chalk Water combe is·visible from
the top of the hill, and a narrow, but fairly-defined,
sheep-track follows the bright little stream to its confluence with the East Lyn, two miles below.   The
hills roll upward in fine heathery sweeps, dotted here
and there with sheep.   No tree softens the wildness of
the glen except an occasional thorn ; the whole valley
is wild in the extreme.

At Oareford, a farm and one or two cottages, a road
is once more reached, and we turn westward to visit
the humble little church where Lorna Doone was
married.   It is but twenty minutes' walk down the
pleasant wooded valley, and stands above the road, in a
grove of ash and sycamore.   There is nothing particularly interesting about the exterior.   The tower is low,
and the windows, square-headed and unadorned with
tracery, call for no comment, with the exception of one
on the south side, edged with stained glass, through
which the brute Carver Doone is said to have shot the
bride.   People who do not know that the chancel is a
comparatively recent addition, will wonder how he

OARE CHURCH.   DRAWN BY ALFRED DAWSON.

could have possibly hit her. It need scarcely be said that the story that her bloodstains still mark the altar is as mythical as it is romantic.

There are two curious panel-paintings fixed to the walls of the tower. On the north stands Moses, holding the Tables of the Law, and on the south, Aaron, in priestly garments, swinging a censer. The former is inscribed, ' Peter Spurryer, Warden, 1717 ;' the latter has the artist's name, ' Mervine Cooke, Painter.' Both are full length, and both are unspeakably ugly. In the church itself are sundry tablets to the Snow family, who have held land at Oare since the days of King Alfred, and one, with the three plumes in high relief, placed to commemorate the visit of the Prince of Wales in 1863. The grave of the 'gert Jan Ridd' will be sought for in vain, but a witness to his Samson-like strength may be seen in Mr. Snow's grounds hard by. Here is a mighty ash, whose lower limbs, bending curiously earthwards, are said to have been forced into that position by the mighty muscles of Lorna's lover.

We have taken a long round to reach Oare. From the cottage by the Badgworthy Water, something like nine miles has been traversed ; and yet, in a direct line over the hill, through the Deer Park, it is but some 1,200 yards ! But no one who has an eye for wild Nature will grudge the détour of the last three hours. Some of the most picturesque spots of Exmoor have been visited, and the traveller who desires to know the wilderness thoroughly, *must* wander far from the straight path.

The road goes on to Malmsmead Bridge, across the

Badgworthy Water, here, and for some miles, forming the boundary between Devon and Somerset. The romantic valley of the East Lyn has already been noticed, so we follow the lane to the right, opposite Mr. Snow's residence (according to Blackmore, anciently the farm of the Ridds), and, crossing the bridge over the river, mount the long hill to the Porlock Road.

The prospect which bursts upon the stranger, as he reaches the top of the ascent, is magnificent—so magnificent, indeed, that, high as we are above the sea, we must even climb higher still in order to obtain as perfect a view as possible of the panorama 1,000 feet and more below. A few yards westward, close to the Glenthorne Lodge, is County Gate or Cosgate, and through this we shall pass for a few yards into Devonshire, and ascend the rising ground to the left of the road. To throw ourselves upon the sweet-smelling heather, and study the glorious map of land and sea, is a welcome change after the arduous labours of the last few hours. Almost under us lies the Channel, stained a darker blue where cloud-shadows brood upon its surface, bounded on the north by the rugged hills of Wales and the varied line of its coast from Gower to Cardiff. There, on the extreme left, is the Worms Head, rearing its strange form from the waters, like some gigantic sea-serpent. There is the smoke of Landore, above Swansea, and the yellow sands that stretch to the Mumbles Light; while the white pillars of Nash mark the dangerous sands near Porthcawl. And so the eye travels eastward to the two rocky islets of the Holms, dim in the haze towards Weston, and the vague shapes of the Mendip Hills. Right under us, 900 feet below, lies Glenthorne, but a patch or two of roof visible.

There are traces of remains of a former day on the summit of the eminence, at our rear, in the shape of a very small circular enclosure, which may have been a kind of redoubt connected with the camp of Oldbarrow on the next hill to the west, or, what is just as likely, the remains of a sepulchral mound. Oldbarrow itself is so fine a specimen of the rude castrametation of our forefathers, and has been so badly treated by guide-books, that it will be well to describe it a little in detail here. It stands on the summit of a lofty hill, rising right out of the sea to a height of over 1,100 feet, though but little above the surrounding Moor. We first come upon a shallow fosse, encircling a vallum, 9 feet high, on the southern or landward side, but dwindling down to 6 feet, where the land slopes away seaward. Mounting this, a level about 57 feet wide is crossed, then another small fosse, and then a low vallum, having a height of but 3 feet. Another fosse and a third vallum follow. This, again, is higher on the south than on the north, reaching a height of 6 feet as we face moorwards, while it is but 4 feet high towards the Channel.

We have now reached the innermost part of the camp, which is 100 feet in diameter, and calls for no other remark, except that a very small and nearly obliterated mound—perhaps the chief's quarters—lies exactly in the centre. The shape of the whole camp is almost as much square as circular; in fact, it may be described as square, with rounded angles. This has caused some antiquaries to assume that it is Roman. Whether Roman or British, it is an unusually perfect specimen. With the exception of an opening, apparently original, through all the ramparts on the north, and an insignificant modern breach in the outer vallum on the south, both ramparts and fosse are in an extraordinary state of preservation, and lie one within the other with almost mathematical precision. It is somewhat remarkable to find an earthwork of this description with such low ramparts, though in this exposed situation they may well have disintegrated rapidly.

I shall not soon forget my visit to this old hill-fortress, for the atmospheric conditions were such as to mark the day indelibly upon the memory of anyone. Although the Moor was bathed in brilliant sunshine, and rejoiced in an atmosphere of wonderful clearness, the sea below, which, under ordinary circumstances, stretches a vast, gray-blue sheet for seventy miles, was totally invisible. Above was a firmament of intense blue; below, a field of cloud. Far as the eye could reach lay the great white billows shrouding, not only the coast of Wales, but even parts of the precipices below. The huge shape of the Foreland, two miles away to the left, rose mountainous from slow-moving banks of fog, which the sun lit up with an intensity painful to the eye. The North Hill beyond Porlock was peninsulated by the snowy vapour which hung, too, in uncertain wreaths about the tree-tops of Glenthorne. Up from the depths below came the hoarse whistling of steamers lost in worse than darkness, while I, perched upon the heather above, was in a blaze of light, and a heat of fierce intensity, probably refraction from the vapour. Presently a luminous arch appeared against the cloud-masses, the rare 'fog bow.' I had intended taking the cliff pathway along the steeps by Countisbury to Lynmouth, but the danger of attempting such a thoroughfare—none too safe at any time—covered, as was now the case, in thick vapour, was too apparent, and I returned by the road. The sensation produced by plunging suddenly from sparkling sunlight into dense fog, half-way down Countisbury Hill, was more peculiar than agreeable.

Those who do not object to a rough scramble, may descend to Glenthorne down the almost perpendicular hillside, a little to the east of County Gate. This will save over two-thirds of the distance, as the zigzag carriage drive covers a length of no less than three miles. The line of heather hereabouts ceases some 600 feet above sea level, and the hanging woods, which cover the cliffs for the next six miles, are soon reached. Glenthorne lies almost at the foot of the slopes, about 100 feet above the stony beach.

At the head of a rough path leading to the stables is a fountain, surmounted by a rude, but picturesque cross, which I at first took for an ancient monument; but, on finding that the arms were *bolted* into the shaft, I made inquiry, and ascertained that the present owner of Glenthorne had caused its erection. By the way, whilst alluding to Mr. Halliday, let me offer him my thanks—and those of every other lover of Nature —for the liberality he has always manifested in throwing open his wild and charming domain to all comers.

The house is a pretty Tudoresque mansion, pitched upon a tiny plateau, the only level spot for miles. On every side dark woods climb the giant hills, watered occasionally by diminutive streams, which tumble down to the beach over mossy rock half concealed by fern brakes. This is the land of ferns, and as we scramble along the rough cliff path towards Porlock we shall see the spaces between the tree stems covered thick with feathery fronds. What a walk it is! There is no view upwards, and but very little outwards, save where a break occurs in the woodlands, permitting a glimpse of the distant Welsh shore. But downwards, between the trunks, is many a peep of boulder beach, fretted by a line of foam; of heavy-looking coaster, delayed by the tide, riding at anchor; or of fleet steamer, hurrying towards Ilfracombe or Cardiff.

We have rambled more than four miles through these romantic woods ere we come upon 'a church and churchyard, situated in as extraordinary a spot as man, in his whimsicality, ever fixed on for a place of worship.' Culbone Church is placed upon a little level in a gorge between the hills, quite 400 feet above the sea, and so shut in that, during the winter months, the rays of the sun touch it not. The branches of the trees that project from the steep slopes, towering another 800 feet at least, to the Porlock road, almost brush the walls of this, the smallest church in England. A couple of cottages and a keeper's lodge, perched anyhow on the declivity, constitute the village; so that the building

CULBONE CHURCH.   DRAWN BY ALFRED DAWSON FROM A SKETCH BY J. LL. WARDEN PAGE.

small as it is, presents ample accommodation for the parishoners, even if we include the population of the one or two outlying farms. The dimensions are, length thirty-three feet, and breadth twelve, but, notwith-standing its Lilliputian proportions, the little church has its nave, chancel, screen, font, and even porch. Above the western end rises a truncated spire, similar to, but not so hideous as, that at Porlock. The style, as far as there is any, is Perpendicular. In the church-yard, which is less than a quarter of an acre, are the remains of a fourteenth-century cross, consisting of about a foot of the base, mounted on a rude octagonal calvary.

The modern name of the church and parish comes from the dedicatory saint, Culbone; but the ancient name was Kitnore, derived, says Savage, from the Anglo-Saxon *cyta*, a cavern, and *ore*, the seashore.

A more peaceful God's Acre than that of Culbone does not exist. On a cloudy day, when the voice of the birds in the surrounding woodland is hushed, the silence is only broken, and that but feebly, by the tinkling sound of the brook, that hurries down the ravine to the beach; and the outlook, such as it is, may be called beautiful, for the descending hills frame in their notching a strip of blue sea, bounded by the rugged mountains of Wales.

Culbone is traditionally said to be the scene of the following tragic occurrence: two lovers were riding through the woods, when the steed of the lady was startled by the sudden apparition of a red deer. It saved itself from destruction on the very edge of the cliff, but its rider, losing her balance, was precipitated on to the rocks below and dashed to pieces.

From Culbone to Ashley Combe the path becomes wide and firm, is indeed a carriage road, and there is an easy walk, mostly down hill, to the Earl of Lovelace's mansion, a modern house of no particular architectural pretensions, seated under a tremendous hill, and having a fine view of Porlock Bay and Hurlstone Point. Admirers of the poetry of Lord Byron may be interested to hear that the Ada of his poems—his daughter—was the first Lady Lovelace.

Almost beneath Ashley Combe is the port of Porlock—Porlock Weir. It is a humble little harbour enough, with the scantiest of trades, nothing larger than a coaster ever finding a berth therein. A hotel, largely patronized in summer time, and a handful of cottages, fringing the shore, make up the hamlet.

Nearer Porlock is West Porlock, a straggling village, which offers nothing to detain the traveller. A walk of another mile between hedgerows, with frequent glimpses of the bay and Hurlstone Point on the one hand, and the steep wooded spurs of Exmoor on the other, and we enter Porlock.

In consequence of our having elected to follow the romantic pathway by the cliff, we have seen little of the high-road, that runs across the Moor, from Lynton to Porlock. A *high* road it certainly is, the average level being somewhere about 1,200 feet above the sea, though in places it rises 200 feet higher. From County Gate to Porlock Hill, a distance of about six miles, the panoramas commanded by this elevated highway are

FORLOCK WEIR. DRAWN BY ALFRED DAWSON.

wonderfully grand. The whole expanse of Exmoor
lies on the right, the whole Bristol Channel on the left.
With the exception of one or two fir plantations, the
route is treeless, and heather is king. We shall not
meet with any great amount of traffic by the way,
beyond a carriage or two of folks on pleasure bent,
or the gaily-painted coaches sweeping merrily along the
almost level surface, thickly packed with tourists, who
are eager to know *which* is the Doone Valley, and
whether they can see Oare Church. As a matter of
fact they can discern the former but very imperfectly,
a mere crease in the moorlands, the depression pointed
out by the coachman being, as often as not, Badgworthy
Valley, while the latter is under the steep side of Oare
Hill. As we win the highest point of this hill, the view
eastward opens out—the greater part of Somerset, the
only bar to the panorama being the fine line of the
Quantocks. Fourteen hundred feet below is the sea;
Bossington Beacon towers across the Vale of Porlock,
ending in the rugged nose of Hurlstone Point, thrusting
itself into the bay, marked ever by a line of breakers;
Dunkery is prominent four miles to the right, descending in dark undulations towards Holnicote.

Near the spot where the road from Exford sinks
from the high downs of Lucott Hill to join our route,
are two massive stones, about four feet high, upstart-
ing from the heath. They are known as the White
Stones, why, I cannot say, as their hue is undeniably
dark. A local legend states that they were thrown by
the devil from Hurlstone Point, which took its name
from the occurrence. Another—and, shall we say,

'improved'—version of the story has it, that the devil
and a nameless giant were the throwers.   If so, they
were very nearly matched, for the blocks are but a few
feet apart.

There are two ways down to the plain beneath : one
branching to the left, near the White Stones, reaches
the low ground in a succession of zigzags, cut through
woods, a long, but most interesting descent; the other,
up which the coaches climb, making no bones of the
matter, plunges, with the exception of a bend or two,
straight down to Porlock.   The latter part is a most
nerve-shaking declivity, and 'as steep as Porlock Hill?'
is the West Country query when any especially stiff
piece of road is mentioned.

CHAPTER VIII

FROM PORLOCK OVER DUNKERY

' Porlock, thy verdant vale so fair to sight,
  Thy lofty hills, which fern and furze embrown,
  Thy waters, that roll musically down
  Thy woody glens, the traveller with delight
  Recalls to memory.'

SOUTHEY.

A LONG straggling street, with curious old-fashioned
cottages, many with tall round chimneys, instead of
windows, facing the street, a protection, says Savage,
against spies in the troublous times of the Stuarts, a
profusion of flowers wherever flowers will grow, such is
the ancient town of Porlock.   Behind, steep wooded
hills tower moorwards towards the range of Dunkery,
while seawards, a flat stretch of fertile land intervening,
the rugged headland of Bossington or Hurlstone Point
pushes itself into the waters of the Channel.   In summer
the quaint old place wakes several times daily to the
inspiriting sound of the horn of coaches bearing names

that remind one forcibly of *Lorna Doone* and *Katerfelto*; in winter it is the quietest of the quiet. Of Porlock in winter, as of Chagford, on the outskirts of Dartmoor, little can be said. It is reported that a traveller, approaching the latter and asking its name, was met by a doleful shake of the head, and the melancholy exclamation 'Chaggiford—O Lord!' From November to May the town under Exmoor is almost as shut out from the world as the old Stannary town beneath the shadow of Dartmoor.

But in the days of Saxon rule, as has already been shown, it was quite a famous place. Here was a palace of their kings, and on the hills yonder a chace, where they not only hunted the red deer, but wolves as well. In an earlier part of this work we have alluded to the Lidwiccas'* invasion of 918, when an attempt was made to land here, but the assailants were beaten off, as well as to the more serious raid of the following century, when Harold descended upon Porlock, only to find his countrymen rise against him, and that a bloody fight was necessary

In the end the sons of Godwin triumphed, and, sailing away laden with spoil, they joined their father, and, returning in force to London, the haughty Earl was pardoned, King Edward making a virtue of necessity. In a wood, rather more than a mile south of the church, the remains of a small oval camp mark, it is supposed, the earthwork thrown up by the invaders.

---

* '*Lidwiccians*—from *lid*, a ship, and *wiccian*, to watch : because they abode day and night in their ships : or, more properly, because they had no residence on land, but lived entirely on board ship.'—Savage, p. 90.

In ancient days there is some probability that Porlock was a seaport, and that, as was the case with
Glastonbury,

> 'The flood of the Severn sea
> Flowed over half the plain.'

According to most writers the name is derived from the
Anglo-Saxon *Port*, a harbour, and *luc* or *lucan*, to shut
up—the enclosed port. It is scarcely necessary to state
that no harbour exists there now. The sea has retired,
and Porlock Weir, two miles distant, is the port of
Porlock.

The Parish Church, dedicated to Saint Dubritius,* is
a structure of fair proportions, though not altogether
beautiful to the eye. It is spoilt, in fact, by an amazingly
hideous truncated spire covered with tiles. This spire,
which is octagonal, once rose to a considerable height,
but was destroyed by a storm in 1700. There is a nave,
chancel, and south aisle, divided from the nave by
octagonal pillars of appearance somewhat severe. The
general style is Perpendicular, but the east window and
double piscina are Early English. Against the north
wall of the chancel is fixed an old stone altar, or altar
tomb, handsomely carved. But the finest monument,
indeed, the principal object in the church, is the
canopied table monument, under the eastern arch in the
south side of the nave. It supports the recumbent
figures of John, fourth Baron Harington and Elizabeth

---

* 'Bishop of Llandaff and metropolitan of Caerleon, d. 522, a
fact indicating, like the dedication to St. Decuman at Watchet,
that this part of Somersetshire was evangelized from South Wales.'
— Murray, p. 460.

Courtenay his wife, who flourished in the time of Henry V. The figures are richly clothed, the knight, in full armour, wearing his cuirass, bawdrick, belt and sword. His lady has the royal fleur-de-lis on her head-dress, and is clad in mantle, surcoat, and kirtle.

The late Mrs. Halliday, who has treated this monument at great length,* points out the anomalous position of the tomb, the arch running through the soffit of the canopy. The monument appears to have been originally enclosed in the chantry termed in the Patent Roll, 14 Edward IV., 'the chapel of the Blessed Virgin;' and 'the notchings,' says Mrs. Halliday, 'at the base of the eastern impost of the arcade, and on the west side of the second pier from the east, still exist as clear proofs that a screen *once* existed.' The chantry was suppressed in 1547, and the monument wedged into its present position. It will be noticed with regret that both figures are covered with initials and unsightly scratches.

In a recess near the south door is the effigy of a Crusader, Sir Simon FitzRoges, lord of the Manor in the reign of Richard I. He is clad in chain armour, his right hand clasps his sword, his legs are crossed after the manner of the Knights of the Cross, and a long shield lies at his side.

The Rector is to be thanked for having removed the picture tablets to the Phelps family, a very crude collection of paintings, from the walls of the church to

* 'A Description of the Monument and Effigies in Porlock Church, Somerset,' by Maria Halliday. Torquay, 1882.

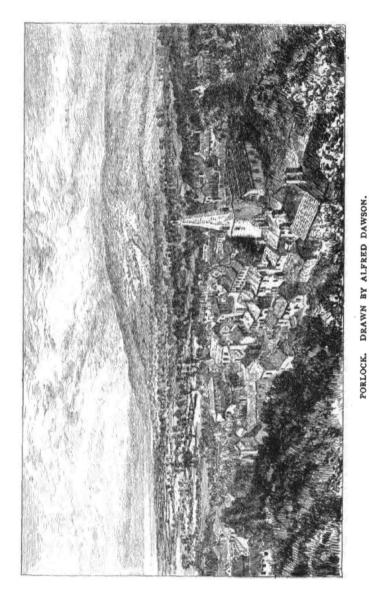

PORLOCK.   DRAWN BY ALFRED DAWSON.

those of the tower. Prominent in each is the tablet commemorating the deceased, over which flutter cherubs and other celestial figures. In the tower, too, is the clock, believed by the Rector to be the oldest in England. In the course of some humorous remarks, on the occasion of the visit of the Somersetshire Archæological Society in 1889, he informed us that it did not go with anything like regularity, and, when it did, it struck at the wrong time, and was neither useful nor ornamental.

Let us pass into the churchyard. Here are the remains of a good churchyard cross of fifteenth century date, which it was once the pride of Porlock to keep in repair. Now the shaft is broken, and the head has vanished altogether—a reproach to the parishioners, Under the wall on the north side of the church is a handsomely carved altar tomb, fast weathering to decay; if practicable, it would be well to remove it inside the church before the elements have done their work. Within half-a-dozen yards is a pathetic epitaph on Thomas and Prudence Rawle, who died within a day of each other—

> ' He first departed ; she for one
> Day tried to live without
> Him, liked it not, and dy'd.'

On the southern side of the churchyard is another quaint inscription, whose dry philosophy is a fine irony on certain monuments we wot of setting forth the grand ancestry and almost superhuman virtues of a departed one, perhaps 'no better than he should be.' It

10

is cut under the name of one Michael Ridler, and runs as follows:

> ' How lov'd, how valued once avails thee not,
> To whom related, or by whom begot ;
> A heap of dust alone remains of thee,
> 'Tis all thou art, and all the world shall be.'

The tombstone bears a date fifty-one years since.

Before leaving Porlock we should pay a visit to the Ship Inn, at the foot of the hill, that hostelry in whose chimney-corner Southey has sat, perchance where he composed the lines which head this chapter. Like him,

> ' By the unwelcome summer rain confined,'

I have sheltered beneath its ancient roof, thankful, after a terrible soaking on Dunkery, to exchange my dripping clothes for the Sunday garments of the good landlady's son, who, luckily was at that time paying a chance visit to the maternal roof.

Although we are now off Exmoor, we have by no means done with it, and although the fine range of sea-ward hills, beginning with Bossington Beacon and ending with Minehead, tempts us to admire, rather than mount, the heathery slopes of Dunkery, it would never do to neglect the monarch of Exmoor, the height of Cloutsham, sacred to the hunter, and the lovely woods of Horner. Leaving the former, then, for a future visit, we turn to the right beyond the church, and follow the lane to the hamlet of Horner, and thence by the wood-land path along the brawling stream to a clam, which will conduct us up a steep hill to Cloutsham Ball. The Horner Water is said to owe its name to the Anglo-

Saxon *hwrner*, a snorer, because of the noisy sound it
makes in its rapid descent from the moorlands. I have
never been able to discover in its tones anything more
sonorous than that possessed by the voice of other
mountain streams, especially those shut in by wooded
hills, and venture, though with diffidence, to suggest
that the Celtic *Aune*, 'water,' is possibly as responsible
for the name as the rather far-fetched Anglo-Saxon
one.

To those who delight in moorland scenery, this valley
of the Horner will present unwonted attractions. Not
only the valley, but the spurs which descend into it are
clad with forest, some to their very summits. But
after awhile the quietude is rather oppressive, the
ceaseless voice of the river monotonous, and it is a relief to find ourselves on the other bank, breasting the
rough path to Cloutsham Ball.

The hill of Cloutsham Ball has a summit of turf free
from trees, if clad in places with bracken, and along this
sward, and in the field adjoining, always musters the
opening meet of the Devon and Somersetshire staghounds. A more beautiful spot whereon to while away
the delay while the 'tufters' are busy working the covers
cannot be conceived. Here in the foreground is woodland; there between the opening in the hills is the sea,
covered with shipping; the rocks of Hurlstone Point
prominent beneath Bossington Beacon. Behind rises
Dunkery, very near now; only a valley, wooded like the
rest, dividing us from his heathery steeps. Far up the
glen to the left is Hawkcombe Head—another favourite
meet of the staghounds—and nearer, hidden, however,

10—2

by the hill, is the lonely village of Stoke Pero,* which
enjoys, with Culbone and Oare, the unenviable distinction of being so remote from mankind that none of
the parsons charged with its spiritual well-being will
live there.   Thus says the local doggrel :

> ' Culbone, Oare and Stoke Pero,
>   Parishes three, no parson 'll go to.'

Also :

> ' Culbone, Oare and Stoke Pero,
>   Three such places you'll seldom hear o'.

A cluster of picturesque cottages forms the hamlet
of Cloutsham.   They are perched on the brow looking
towards Dunkery, and from them a steep lane descends
to the valley.   From the very banks of the stream
running down the bottom, Dunkery begins to ascend,
steep at first, then more gradual.   It is a long, but easy
climb, for nothing more obstructive than heather is to
be encountered.   Indeed, there is but little of this to
him who will follow the track, except near the summit.
About one-third of the way up, and at a distance of less
than half a mile to the left of the path, a rough line like
a plough furrow will be noticed descending the hill.
This marks the course of an extraordinary flood, which
quite recently ripped up the ground for some distance.
At its upper end is a bog, and it is supposed that some
subterranean reservoir beneath suddenly burst, owing
to the severe spring rains.   Whatever was the cause,
the neighbours were amazed one morning to find the
bog burst and an enormous fissure torn in the ground.

* From Sir Gilbert Piro, who held the manor temp. Edward I.

The torrent must have been at least seven feet in depth, for pebbles and other débris were found lodged in the branches of such trees as were able to withstand the rush of the waters. Down into the valley thundered the flood, carrying the crashing trunks of many a tall tree before it, with tons of soil and gravel. The Horner became a raging river, and rose in a moment to an unprecedented height, its banks strewed with the ruins of the woodland. The fissure has since been roughly filled in, but the disturbance is sufficiently marked to be still visible from a considerable distance.

The summit of Dunkery is crowned by the Beacon, a circular pile of stones,* about five feet high, standing upon a large mound. Near it are some ruinous heaps, the remains of the hearths where the beacon-fires were lit in days gone by, and utilised. according to Mr. Blackmore, to light the homeward path of the Doones. Other hearths exist a mile away to the east, at an elevation of about 1,500 feet above sea-level. Westward, along the ridge, are the three cairns called Rowbarrows and Whitebarrow ; beyond again, the pair known as Bendle's Barrows.

Owing to its position, so near the sea, the view from Dunkery Beacon is immensely wide, and, for variety, certainly unsurpassed in the south and west of England ; and though, to quote the words of a traveller, writing of a district far holier in its associations than Exmoor,

* On an ancient map, formerly in the possession of the writer's great-uncle, Dunkery is represented as being crowned by a *tower*. There is, however, no evidence to show that this was ever the case, in spite of the statement in Phelps. *Vide* ' Hist. of Somerset,' sub-title *Dunkery*.

the ' scenery is neither colossal nor overwhelming,' it is ' infinitely beautiful and picturesque.'

It will be well to describe it a little in detail. Well, then, looking north, we have beneath us a sea of foliage, the woods filling the combes of the Horner and its tributaries. In the middle distance is a scrap of the fertile country fringing Porlock Bay, and stretching along the base of the North Hill towards Minehead. Then comes the sea, and even as we look a steamer vanishes behind the rugged promontory of Hurlstone. The whole south coast of Wales is visible ; the humps of the Brecon Beacons, rising, high above the Glamorgan-shire mountains, nearly 3,000 feet into the air. In an easterly direction, Croydon Hill appears quite close, while at no great distance beyond are the Brendons and Quantocks. Further off are the Mendips, and the flattened cone of Brent Knoll. On a clear day the watering-places of Burnham, Weston, and Cleve-don are distinctly visible, and not unfrequently the scattered villas of Portishead. Minehead and Dunster are both beneath their hills. Turning westward we have the whole sweep of Exmoor, from Chapman Barrows to Span Head—both of which are visible—to Ansteys Hill, near Dulverton. And what are those faint specks against the south-western horizon ? they are the Cornish heights of Row Tor, Brown Willy, and Kilmar High Rock, the nearest some sixty miles distant as the crow flies. To their left, and therefore nearly south, rises the grand outline of Dartmoor. Although thirty-five miles of undulating cultivation intervene, we may—beginning from the right—easily identify the following tors: Sourton Tor, Yes Tor (2,030 feet), High Willhays (2,039 feet), Cosdon Beacon, Hameldon, Rippon Tor, and Hey Tor, the twin bosses of the latter being very conspicuous. Such is the view under ordinary circumstances, but after rain the Malvern Hills, in Worcestershire, are visible, and eyes clearer than mine claim to have discerned Inkpen Beacon, in Hampshire, and the high ground about Plymouth. But a panorama embracing an area of 100 miles — for this is about the distance from the Brecon Mountains to Brown Willy—will content most people.

In *Home Chimes* of March 7th, 1885, Miss King tells a pathetic story about a ruined cottage on the side of Dunkery. It was in persecuting days the refuge of two Huguenot ladies, whose extreme poverty caused many remarks in the countryside, nothing but a small quantity of bread being seen to enter their cottage, which was ever jealously guarded from intrusion. After a time they disappeared, and the cottage was visited. Dead and fast locked in each other's arms were the poor refugees. The house was of course searched for comestibles, but nothing was found beyond some pots containing *slugs*, on which, say the people, the exiles had subsisted.

At the very foot of Dunkery lies the village of Luccombe. The situation, as the name would imply— it means the enclosed or shut-in valley—is pleasant ; trees are sufficiently abundant, without excluding too much air and light, and a little brook, rising under Dunkery, runs near, joining the Horner at the hamlet of Bossington. There is a handsome Perpendicular church, dedicated to St. Mary, having a nave, chancel, and south aisle, in which is a good piscina, and another with two holes in the chancel. The pillars have handsomely carved capitals, and in the belfry of the tall tower is a massive altar, or altar tomb, richly carved. In the churchyard are the remains of a fifteenth-century cross, and what is, I think, rather unusual in English churchyards, a row of tall cypresses.

Luccombe once had for rector a celebrated divine, one Dr. Henry Byam, born in 1580. He was educated at Oxford, and in 1612 succeeded his father as rector of Luccombe, and upon the death of his father-in-law obtained Selworthy as well. He was an ardent Royalist, not only espousing the royal cause himself, but placing four of his sons in the royal army. Upon the Parliamentarians obtaining the ascendant, his troubles commenced ; his estate was confiscated, and his wife and daughter, while crossing to Wales, there to seek a more peaceful asylum, were drowned in the waves of the Channel. Byam closely followed the fortunes, or rather misfortunes, of his royal master, and was with Charles II. both in the Scilly Isles and in Jersey. At the Restoration he had his reward—a reward rather inadequate, considering what he had undergone for the Stuart cause. He was made Canon of Exeter and Prebendary of Wells. He died in 1669, in his ninetieth year, and was buried in the chancel of Luccombe Church, where a lengthy Latin inscription records his virtues.

Two miles from Luccombe, and, to a certain extent,

also connected with Dunkery, is another pretty village, Wootton Courtenay. Perhaps it should be claimed rather for Grabhurst than Dunkery, being placed upon one of its spurs; but the latter rises right opposite, and the ascent is very commonly made from this village. The first name is again of Anglo-Saxon origin—*wude*, a wood, and *tun*, a town;* Courtenay, of course, referring to the family of the Earl of Devon. Here is another interesting church, dedicated to All Saints, with a saddle-back tower, more well-carved capitals, and a handsome font. In the porch is a holy-water stoup, supported by a column. Of the churchyard cross, dating from the same century as that at Luccombe, nothing but the carved base remains. The views of Dunkery and the beautiful valleys stretching down towards Dunster are very fine.

Wootton Courtenay, too, has its divine. This was Richard Montague, who in 1628 became Bishop of Chichester, which diocese he exchanged ten years later for that of Norwich.

We shall now descend the southern flank of Dunkery to Exford. It is recommended that the tracks be kept as far as possible. Nothing, except to the initiated, is saved by short cuts. In this country, 'the shortest way round is often the longest way home,' and the wayfarer may be landed on the boggy enclosures (fields they cannot be called) which disfigure this side of the hill.

Exford is a very clean and pleasant village, alive during the autumn with both hunters and fishermen,

* Savage, p. 331.

for here are the kennels of the Devon and Somerset stag-hounds, erected at great expense by Mr. Bisset, in 1875, and bequeathed for the use of the hunt, subject to certain conditions as to management; and here lives that king of huntsmen, Arthur Heal. 'Arthur,' as he is always called, is a thin wiry old man, who cannot be far short of three-score years and ten; and yet age appears to effect little change in his powers, for, though he has been 'at it' thirty-four years, he will still ride away from anyone. And who so punctual as Arthur at the death of a warrantable deer—who so ready in all details relating to the craft which is to him as the breath of life? And then the famous Nimrods he knows! I remember inspecting the kennels with him one August morning, twelve years ago, and was astonished at the familiar, yet respectful, manner in which he referred to the now deceased Major Whyte-Melville. 'Know him? I should think so, sir; and a very proper gentleman too.' To those who only know the author of 'Katerfelto' and 'Market Harborough' by his works, there is a touch of strangeness in hearing of him from the lips of this old huntsman.*

Exford village lies in a valley watered by the Exe: Exford Church is high above, on the top of a very steep hill. It is—the church, not the hill—in the Perpendicular style, and has, it is pleasant to remark, lost nothing by restoration. There is a good porch, and the pillars are handsome. On the south wall is a large tablet, whereon is inscribed, in faded gilt letters, the

* Since the above was written, Arthur Heal has surrendered his horn to the whip, Anthony Huxtable.

'extraordinary virtues' of one Robert Baker. It may amuse the reader to compare it with the philosophical epitaph at Porlock: it runs as follows: ' Close under this wall resteth the body of Robert Baker, whose extraordinary virtues deserve to be had in everlasting remembrance. His life was a pattern of piety towards God, and integrity towards man ; of industry without covetousness ; liberality without pride; charity without ostentation. He was the most upright dealer, the kindest neighbour, the tenderest husband, and the surest friend. He had wisdom to contrive, and courage to execute, the most difficult undertaking for the cause of truth and justice, and in defence of the innocent. He was born of honest parents, and by hard labour increased his substance, which he readily bestowed on all occasions for the honour of God and in support of the needy.' And so on, describing how he married, and died without issue in 1730, leaving much of his substance to the poor. The epitaph, fulsome as it appears, is, if local tradition may be credited, not too exhaustive a description of the character of this worthy miller. Savage has preserved an anecdote which shows him in the light of a modern St. Martin. It relates that while he was at work in a field by the roadside— he was a farmer as well as a miller—one winter day, he was addressed by a starving ill-clad beggar. To him he gave most of his clothes, and the whole of his dinner, and then returned home in very much the same condition as that formerly endured by the man he had so generously relieved.

On Lincombe Farm, about a mile and a half from

the village, and to the east of Court Wood, is a square earthwork, of no great size, known as Road Castle. It is probably Roman. A very good view of it is obtained from the road to Cutcombe, near Exford Church, which commands the hilly field rising from the valley beneath, whereon the camp is situated. It is, as far as I can ascertain, the only antiquity in the immediate neighbourhood, the circular bank on Stone Down being only a fence for the protection of the solitary tree which grows within.

At Exford we may, I think, say farewell to the Moor, for, save the outlying mass of Winsford Hill, the country is pretty well under cultivation. No one however, who delights in the scenery of old-world, rural England should neglect to visit the village from which this fine hill takes its name, for Winsford is the prettiest village anywhere near the moorlands. It lies about five miles east of Exford, part in a leafy combe, part on the hillside beneath the church, a large building with a handsome tower, which is quite a feature in the neighbourhood. There is a wonderfully picturesque inn, the Royal Oak, with mossy thatch and projecting windows, divers quaint cottages, and a curious old paved bridge, covered with ferns, spanning the Exe, one of six—not all over the Exe—for Winsford has nearly as many bridges as London, though most are of Lilliputian proportions. Here more than one pleasant day may be spent in rambling about the deep ferny lanes between the village and the Brendon Hills, and in making excursions about the moorland borders, and down the valley towards Dunster, where the sur-

roundings of the villages of Cutcombe and Timberscombe will well repay a visit. But we ourselves must
return to Porlock, thence to pursue our exploration of
that bold seaward range running from Bossington to
Minehead, which, though now separated from the
Moor by a smiling valley, was doubtless at one time
one of its finest spurs, and as such will be taken in
the division of this work assigned to Exmoor.

CHAPTER IX

FROM PORLOCK TO BOSSINGTON, LYNCH, AND SELWORTHY, AND OVER THE NORTH HILL TO MINEHEAD.

Bossington—A Gigantic Walnut Tree—Lynch Chapel—Holnicote
—Selworthy Green—Selworthy Church—Bury Castle—Bossington Beacon—Bratton Court—Henry de Bracton—Burgundy
Chapel—Greenaleigh—View from Minehead Hill—History of
Minehead.

LEAVING Porlock by the Minehead road, we turn to the left, at the elbow of the hill, and follow a lane to the hamlet of Bossington, lying at the foot of the western end of the North Hill. Bossington is famous for its walnut-trees, the largest an enormous specimen, sixteen feet in girth, and with branches in themselves as large as many a full-grown woodland monarch. The villagers are intensely proud of this their only 'lion,' and it was amusing to note the derision with which an ancient dame heard the suggestion that it must be quite 200, if not 300 years old. 'Lor' bless 'ee!' she exclaimed scornfully; 'he be much more than that; folks do come from all over the country to see 'un.' She evidently thought that 'folks' would not come to visit a mere infant of a couple of centuries or so. Having found argument with these 'oldest inhabitants' quite useless,

I let her have her way, and she retired, with a poor idea of the capacity of the stranger who ventured even to approximate the age of her favourite.

Crossing the Horner, we reach West Lynch, another hamlet, and shall here again pause to examine an old fifteenth-century chapel, until recently used as a barn, but now restored for divine worship by Sir Thomas Acland. At present it is not used for services. The building is well proportioned, and has a good Perpendicular east window, though there is little in its interior to excite interest, the remains of a reredos being the most ancient detail. It is not the only chapel in Selworthy parish; another will be found at Tivington, a third at East Lynch, used as a barn, and the scanty ruins of a fourth on the road to Luccombe. These buildings were used either as district chapels or as private places of worship connected with manor-houses. The architect who accompanied the Somersetshire Archæological Society on their inspection in 1889, supposed them to have been devoted to the former purpose. He also thought that the old oak seats in the adjoining farmhouse—a picturesque building, with a good oak tracery window, massive door and crossbar, and immense ceiling beam—had once belonged to the chapel.

The scenery at this point is very delightful. From the banks of the brook which courses by the roadside the hills commence to rise, clad thickly with woods, from which ever and anon a bold bare brow projects against the sky. The ascent will well repay the exertion, for the distant recesses of Cloutsham and Horner, lying beneath the range of Dunkery, may be explored on the one hand, and the coast for many a mile on the other. But the opportunity for enjoying this magnificent panorama will occur presently; so for the present we continue our route past Allerford, with its two-arched gray bridge, and along the high-road again to Holnicote, the seat of the Aclands, a comfortable country house lying in the open vale between Selworthy, perched high on the hill above, and Exmoor.

Holnicote has suffered much by fire. In 1799 a fine mansion was totally destroyed, and the present house narrowly escaped a like fate in 1851. The war of place-names has waged fiercely here. Savage says the name is traceable to the Saxon *Holeyn*, or *holen*, a species of ilex, a tree very plentiful in the vicinity; while the Rev. F. Hancock, the Rector of Selworthy, who has treated the place-names of his parish very exhaustively, prefers the old English *Hûn*, a personal name.* In the time of Edward I., one William de Holne held the manor, though this fact is of little use in determining the nomenclature, as it was common enough for the lord of the manor to take his surname from the property possessed by him. Certain lands here, it is interesting to note, were in the same reign held of the king in capite by the somewhat peculiar service of 'hanging, on a certain forked piece of wood, the red deer that died of the murrain in the forest of Exmoor' (a very light service, one would imagine, if the denizens of the forest were as healthy then as now; and also, and this was a heavier duty, 'of lodging and entertaining, at his own

* The popular pronunciation is *Hunnicot*.

expense, such poor decrepit persons as came to him, for
the souls of the ancestors of King Edward I."*

Tourists and visitors to this beautiful neighbourhood
owe much to the open-handed liberality of Sir Thomas
Dyke Acland, who has thrown open, to rich and poor
alike, the paths threading the woods which clothe
the spurs of this part of North Hill.   One of the
entrances is opposite the house, and by this we will
find our way to Selworthy Green, a lawn surrounded
by scattered cottages, almost embedded in flowers, the
place of retirement for aged pensioners of the Acland
family, whose lines have certainly fallen in pleasant
places.   Thence it is but a hundred yards to the church,
perched, as we have said, on the hillside, and overlooking Holnicote and all the country Exmoorwards.

It consists of nave, chancel, and north and south
aisles.   The clustering pillars are particularly graceful,
and will at once arrest attention ; but the handsomest
part of the church is undoubtedly the south aisle,
which is lighted by Perpendicular windows of large size
and well-cut tracery.   The tower, sturdy, and of no
great height, is the oldest part, except, perhaps, the
east wall, which, in the opinion of the rector, probably
belonged to an earlier period and smaller church.   The
present building is of fifteenth-century erection.   It
suffered much at the hands of iconoclastic soldiery in
the Great Rebellion, when the screen was destroyed,
the painted windows broken, and even the capitals of
the pillars mutilated.   Cannon-balls have been found
embedded near the building, and it is thought that some

* Savage, p. 198.

engagement must have taken place here. The roofs are all noticeable, particularly that which covers the nave, which is adorned with some very singular picture shields, and it is refreshing to compare the treatment of that over the south aisle with others of the Jacobean period, for the ribs and bosses are not only well carved, but tastefully painted. Above the porch is a priest's chamber, completely overlooking the nave. In the churchyard are the remains of a fourteenth-century cross, and below the church an old tithe barn is worth a visit.

But we must ascend the hill still further, for high above the trees the acclivity is crested by an ancient fortress. This is known as Bury Castle, and it stands upon the western side of the combe, just below a memorial 'wind and weather hut' (to quote the description cut upon it) erected to the memory of the late Sir Thomas Dyke Acland, and whence a magnificent view of Exmoor is obtainable. The shape of this camp is circular, and therefore I presume it to be British.* The wall of stone and earth is about ten feet in height, and was apparently continuous, there being no traces of an original entrance. It is surrounded, except on the side overhanging the combe, by a fosse. The diameter is about 200 feet. A few yards to the west is a crescent-shaped bank, having a height about equal to that of the ramparts of the camp, and protected on the outer side

---

* Phelps says : 'These are, most probably, Danish works thrown up when the Danes made a descent upon this part of the coast at Porlock, in A.D. 908.' This may be, but the position is not such as the Danes would choose ; besides, their camps are generally oval. There was no Danish invasion in 908. He must mean 918.

by a fosse. Whether this was intended for an additional bulwark, or was the commencement of a second camp, the explorer must judge for himself. The walk should be extended a mile westward to Bossington Beacon, a bare brow capped by a cairn, and thence to the rocks of Hurlstone Point. Hundreds of feet below lies the sea dotted with sails, and to the northward, streaked with many a dark cloud, the smoke of the colliers plying to and from the great ports of Swansea, Cardiff, and Newport. The fumes of the furnaces of Landore rise a great white pile behind the seaport first named; the second is concealed by the headland of Penarth, though the shipping in the roads may be discerned in clear weather; the third is also invisible. The two Holms lie on the horizon eastwards, with the heights of Weston and Clevedon to the right. Then the Mendips and flat-topped Brent Knoll catch the eye, followed by the Quantock range and the sweep of coast to Minehead, with its

'Haven under the hill,'

which we shall not see until close upon its outskirts, so abrupt are these hills. Westward are seen Porlock, Porlock Weir, Ashley Combe, and the whole seaward scarp of Exmoor, to the lofty headland of Countisbury Foreland, rising 700 feet sheer out of the sea; while behind stretches the large mass of Dunkery Hill. There are many who prefer this prospect to that obtainable from Dunkery Beacon. In beauty it *may* be equal, but, wide as it is, it must yield the palm to the extraordinary panorama spread at the feet of him who stands on the summit of Exmoor.

For those who are ' sound in wind and limb,' and, it
may be added, sure of foot as well, the ramble (or
scramble, for it partakes of both methods of locomotion)
over these wild hills to the Quay Town of Minehead
cannot be too highly recommended.　But they who are
no longer young, or who, like John Gilpin of famous
memory, ' carry weight,' will prefer the easier descent
through the lanes by Bratton Court, joining the Porlock
road once more just outside the town.　It is a pretty
walk, but nothing very remarkable will occur to render
a halt necessary until the old farmhouse, where, it is
said, Judge Bracton first drew breath, is reached.　It is
pleasantly situated on rising ground, almost at the foot
of the heathery slopes, steep as the roof of a house,
the landward side of North Hill.　The house and
buildings form three sides of a square, the part facing
the lane being pierced by the entrance, a high Perpendicular archway, with an enormous framework of oak.
Tradition has it that the topmost beam has in byegone
times borne the weight of a grisly array of culprits,
though who they were, and for what crime executed is
not said.　Immediately over it a little unglazed window
with carved-oak framework of character decidedly
ecclesiastical, lights ' Bracton's study,' a room about
nine feet square with mouldering gable roof.　There are
one or two more windows with frames of carved oak,
instead of stone, on the opposite side of the quadrangle, but beyond this the farm presents no particular
traces of an antiquity dating back more than a couple
of centuries.

Whether De Bracton really was born at this pleasant

spot, as local antiquaries stoutly assert, it is impossible to say. As with Homer, the honour of giving him birth is claimed by more than one place, though the old house of Bratton, near Minehead, and the Devonshire villages of Bratton Fleming and Bratton Clovelly make but a poor show against the seven cities who disputed for the greatest of ancient poets. However, there is no doubt that the family of Bracton held land in Luccombe, Selworthy and other parishes in this corner of Somerset, the property ultimately passing by marriage to the ancestors of the Earl of Lovelace, in whose possession the court still remains.

Henry de Bracton was born early in the thirteenth century, and after studying at Oxford adopted the law as his profession. In this, as is well known, he rose to great eminence, and was held in such respect by Henry III. that in 1244 he was made a justice itinerant for the northern counties. His well-known work, 'De Legibus et Consuetudinibus Angliæ,' is a wonderful work, considering the times in which it was written, and is even at this day an authority on the common law of England.

It is said that Bracton was also an ecclesiastic. This is not at all improbable, for in the Middle Ages the Law and the Gospel frequently went hand in hand, the Lord Chancellor being almost invariably a Churchman. According to Sir Travers Twiss, the particulars of his different preferments may be found in the archives of the diocesan registry at Exeter, where, prior to 1237, he held a prebendal stall. Mr. W. George, of Bristol, says that he was collated on January 21, 1263-4, to the Archdeaconry of Barnstaple, which he very shortly resigned, becoming, on May 18, 1264, Chancellor of Exeter Cathedral. He was also a Prebend of Wells, and of the collegiate church of Bosham in Sussex. He died in 1268, and was buried in Exeter Cathedral.[*] I have mentioned his priestly offices rather in detail, because the place of his burial is almost as much disputed as the place of his birth, and it is only fair to give the good folk of Minehead, who contend that he sleeps in their church, every chance of proving their argument.

Let us return to Bury Castle. By path and sheep-track we descend to East Myne Farm, and explore the wild gorge of Grixy, one of the many ravines seaming the hills from Minehead to Bossington, from Porlock Weir to Lynmouth. The precipitous steeps descending into the waters of the Channel are as wild and romantic as any part of this grand hill country of West Somerset, clothed from summit to cliff with bracken, whortleberry, gorse, or heather, with here and there an outcrop of rock to enhance the rugged character of the scene. But care must be taken, especially in summer-time, when the turf, burnt a dull yellow, becomes as slippery as glass. At such a time the heedless tourist, disregarding the devious sheep-track, and tempted by a short-cut, may very well slip upon the treacherous grass, and, by spraining an ankle, find that there is some truth in that old proverb, before quoted, which declares that 'the shortest way round is the longest way home.'

As we cross a ravine or gully, about midway between Grixy Glen and Greenaleigh Farm, we shall notice,

---

[*] 'Dictionary of National Biography,' vol. iv., *De Bracton*.

about 200 feet above the beach, the remains of a small oblong building, nearly enshrouded in briars. It lies in the course of a track, plainer than many hereabouts, and in a line with a crag projecting from the declivity eastward. This is Burgundy Chapel; why so named, no one can explain, for it is positively without history. The plain walls now remaining, to the height of but three or four feet, have no window or other tracery to determine the period of their construction, and the only bit of workmanship in the least ornate—a door-jamb—can scarcely be considered as affording assistance. Common report calls the building a hermitage, and its situation—

'Far in a wild, unknown to public view'—

is solitary enough. Except for the faint voice of the sea beating on the boulders beneath, the holy man must, as regards things external, have possessed his soul in a peace of the most perfect kind.

But the next building is of order very different Another mile, or less, along a good path, and we reach Greenaleigh, devoted in summer-time to the high revel of junketing parties, and in winter to sunless silence. For so overshadowed is this farm by the towering hills, that for three long months the sun never touches it. Now it is cheerful enough. About the round tables and rustic benches circulate groups of happy excursionists, discussing that delicious admixture of syllabub and clotted cream for which the West Country is so justly famed. We would fain stop and join them. But no; the western hills are darkening, the sun is just slipping into the ocean, lighting up the Welsh

mountains with a last gleam, and if we would see anything of Minehead this night we must press onward.

. From Greenaleigh to Minehead there is a choice of
routes. We may climb the hill, and pass over its breezy
brow down at the back of the church, having a very
fine bird's-eye view of the town and the country stretching eastward to the Quantocks; we may follow the
road cut in the hillside above the Quay Town, or
leisurely descend, by an older way, to its foot. The
middle course, as is often the case, proves most ad-
vantageous, for we not only save our legs, but have at
the same time a prospect very little inferior to that obtained at a greater altitude, together with a wonderfully
picturesque view of the old street and harbour beneath.

After passing dangerous Culver Cliff, a precipice
sinking from the road to the beach, from which it is
divided but by a crazy wooden railing, we take the
path on the right, and are soon above the roofs of Quay
Street. There it lies right beneath us, perhaps some 200
feet or so. So precipitous is the declivity through which
this alpine roadway cuts, that a pebble could almost be
dropped down the chimney of any one of the cottages.
The decks of the coasters in the harbour are almost as
much at our feet as if we stood in the rigging, and the
ancient mariners, smoking under the lee of the tall,
thatched Custom-house, look like boys. Of the actual
street we can see little but roofs and chimneys, with
here and there a glimpse of sloping garden struggling
up the less abrupt portions of the hillside. In one of
these gardens the author spent a wild stormy night
some thirty years ago. The Channel was one sheet of

foam; the wind roared like a thousand furies; the
shipping in the harbour, though the safest on the
southern coast, broke their moorings, and dashed
against each other, to mutual destruction; and the
sea-wall separating the single line of houses from the
furious waves cracked, wavered and disappeared. And
before daybreak there had been a disaster on the
Welsh coast which has few, if any, parallels in the
history of our merchant navy. Off the rocky shores
of Anglesea the *Royal Charter* had met her doom, and
multitudes of human beings had gone down, to a
watery grave, within touch of the stern rocks. An
awful night indeed!

The road passes onwards, through a fir plantation,
and presently emerges on the eastern side of the hill.
The change is marked. From precipitous slopes,
barren save for some young fir plantations, we have
come upon rich cultivated fields, trending down to that
modern addition to the town known as the Avenue.

To the right lies the church and the hilly, old-
fashioned streets of Upper Town; for Minehead boasts
of three divisions—Upper or Church Town, Middle,*
and Lower or Quay Town. Passing a heavy-looking
castellated house, bran-new and rather out of keeping
with the quiet beauty of the scenery, we reach the
church. And now, before pausing to examine its
interesting interior, let us cast our eyes over the
richly-coloured prospect of level plain and swelling
upland beneath and before us. It differs in many

* Middle Town, however, is now seldom heard of, except among
the aged,

respects from those upon which we have lately looked,
for we have now reached a railway, and, somehow,
where the iron horse intrudes his presence, country—
at any rate, cultivated country—feels the spirit of
change. The town gathers unto itself stark regiments
of brick and mortar called 'streets,' and detached boxes
of like material, called 'villas'; perhaps a tall, unsightly
factory chimney overshadows the landscape, or a brick-
field poisons the air with odours stifling as those of the
bottomless pit. At all events, dark lines of metal rule
the face of the land with unerring precision, bearing
the noisy train and still noisier excursionist to the once
peaceful and still beautiful country. Everyone who
reads these pages can probably call to mind one or
more rural districts 'spoilt' by that civilization whose
ruthless pioneer is a locomotive, and whose sapper and
miner that much-to-be-abused gentleman, the specu-
lative builder. That Minehead still retains most of
its former charm is certainly due neither to the first or
second factor, but rather to the good taste of the
ground-landlord and his agents.

Yet the place has changed. Where is the old overhung 'Watery Lane' that erewhile passed from the
tanyard to the sea? Where the paved pathway that
led from the Quay Town to the church? where the
shady repose of the New Road? Alas! the first lies
buried beneath the Avenue, a wide highway bordered
by modern villas; the second, although still existing in
part, has had its upper end destroyed to make way for
new roads and newer buildings; while the last, though
still 'shady,' can scarcely be called reposeful, when

every summer day a cheap train deposits at the station, on the very verge of the beach, its consignment of pleasure - seekers. But if certain elements of the picturesque and peaceful have been swept away, let us be thankful that most still remains untouched, and be grateful to those who have offered up at the shrine of modern enterprise so few of the older, and perhaps, for that very reason, the more attractive objects of Minehead.

Beyond the shining slate roofs of the Avenue spreads a green and level expanse, once doubtless flooded by the sea, and even now sufficiently marshy. Across it runs the railroad, vanishing to a point somewhere about Dunster Station, thence passing onwards towards Watchet and the soft line of the Quantocks. On the right, and close to the railway, rises the steep wooded cone of Conegar, crowned by a hollow tower; behind slope Grabhurst, Croydon, and other hills running westward towards Dunkery, which, a little higher up the hill, can be seen with advantage. On the left are the sands stretching to the low horn known as Warren Point, the western bound of Cleeve or Blue Anchor Bay. Blue Anchor Cliffs, veined with alabaster and geologically famous, commence the long line of reddish rampart stretching, with but one small break, thence to Kilve, and prominent at the foot of the first headland is a huge square mass of rock, which has fallen from the heights above, leaving a loophole between it and the cliff. Although wanting in the grandeur which has characterized the noble panoramas further west, the prospect is a very fine one.

Of Minehead the history is soon told.   In early days it was, doubtless, a peaceful little port enough, consisting of a few fishermen's cots.   Probably, as was the case with Dunster, ' the glory of this Toun rose by the Moions,' for it was part of the possessions of that family, and still belongs almost entirely to the Luttrells.   At one time it was much harassed by the wild Welsh, and prior to that it is likely enough that the Danes made more than one descent (although the records are silent), for, as we have seen, they attacked both Porlock and Watchet, and the sandy shore of the Warren must have proved a good lying ground for the ' long beaks ' of Scandinavia.   The Cymri are reported by Rishanger to have harried the town and adjacent country to a deplorable extent in 1265, the Sunday before the battle of Evesham.   Their commander was one William of Berkeley, certainly not a Welshman, and what reason he could have had for attacking a settlement such as Minehead does not appear.   The expedition, however, failed in its attempt. Adam de Gurdon, Constable of Dunster, came to the rescue, the invaders were completely routed, and those who escaped the sword driven into the sea.*

If Minehead had a name before Norman William bestowed it upon De Mohun, it has not been preserved. Its present name is but a corruption or contraction of that of its lords, with the old Saxon *heved* added.   It has passed from Munheved, Manheve, and Minheved to its present title.   The connection with the owners of Dunster Castle led to its occupation in 1642 by the Royalist Marquis of Hertford, who, driven from Wells

* Murray, p. 457.

and Sherborne, retired here, and attempted to take
Dunster Castle. In this he was unsuccessful, and
ultimately crossed into Wales. That Minehead was—
as, indeed, might have been expected—intensely Par-
liamentarian is proved by the following extracts from
the church-book referred to by Savage:

1645 Paid the ringers when Bristol was taken and delivered up by Prince Rupert	oo	o3	oo
1648 For ringinge the bells on surrender of Colchester to the Parliament	oo	o4	oo
1649 Paid ringers for ringing for joy of the overthrow against Dublin, by Jones or Marquis of Ormond	oo	o4	oo
June 1st, 1651 Paid for ringinge at the takinge of Scilly by Mr. George Ann, from Sir Wm. Greenvil	oo	o6	oo
1646 Given the ringers when Dunster Castle was yielded up	oo	o4	o8

' And a poor man in distress, having *my Lord Protector's
hand* to his passe, was assisted on his way to Ireland,'
in 1657.

With the exception of a few years in the first two decades of the seventeenth century, when, for some reason,
King James I. seized the franchises, and dissolved the
borough, Minehead returned two members to Parliament from 1st Elizabeth to 1832, when it was disfran-
chised. It is said that when Mr. Luttrell heard the
sad news of the passing of the Reform Act, and that
the town was consequently shorn of its glory, he clasped
his head in his hands, exclaiming, in serio-comic tones,
' Oh, Mine head! Mine head!'

But another and much more substantial ' glory ' has
also departed, and that is the trade of the port, which

150, or even 100 years ago was very considerable. As many as 4,000 barrels of herrings were shipped annually to West Indian, Virginian, and Mediterranean ports, while upwards of forty vessels were employed in the trade to Ireland, whence large quantities of wool, linen cloth, yarn, hides, and other commodities were imported. When this import trade passed to other ports, the decadence of Minehead as a seaport set in, for herrings, even to the amount of 4,000 barrels, will not keep up a trade of any dimensions, and the shipments of oak-bark and grain were inconsiderable. The imports of cattle,* which I can myself remember as occasional events, have also ceased, and the little whitewashed harbour is deserted save for a few small coasters. There can be no doubt that the trade with Ireland was of some antiquity, for Leland, under ' Minheved,' remarks that the ' The toune is exceding ful of Irish menne.' If the Hibernian drover of three centuries ago was as hilarious as his modern brother, *Minheved* must have been a lively place.

* This cattle trade existed as long ago as the reign of Charles II., when for a time the prosperity of the port was threatened by the inforcement of the 'Act against importing cattle from Ireland, and other parts beyond the seas,' passed in the eighteenth year of his reign. The money arising from the sale of cattle seized was to be divided between the person seizing and the poor of the parish. It appears that in 1669 a ship attempted to run the gauntlet, but the cattle were taken, and, with the vessel, sold ; and the moiety of proceeds accruing to the poor was invested in lands, whereof the income became the famous ' Cow Charity.' An account of this curious charity will be found at p. 599 of Savage's ' History of the Hundred of Carbampton.'

CHAPTER X

MORE ABOUT MINEHEAD. DUNSTER

The Church—Curious Sculptures—A Doubtful Tomb—Chained Books—Quay Town—The Hobby-Horse—Novel Marking-ink—Grabhurst—Vale of Avill—Dunster—The Yarn Market—The Luttrell Arms Hotel—Ruins of the Priory—The Priory Church —The Nunnery—The Castle—Its History.

FEW churches in the West of England are placed in a situation more commanding than that of Minehead.* High on the hillside, on the extreme verge of the quaint old cottages of Upper Town, it overlooks the whole place, besides miles of hill and dale beyond. The approach up the steep narrow street immediately beneath is really quite striking. So abrupt is the ascent that the last few yards of road are converted into steps, giving an appearance rather Continental —were it not for the very English-looking thatched cottages—to the thoroughfare. Framed in, as it were, by these ancient dwellings, their walls washed white and yellow and buff, with roofs of dark brown, shot with

* An old tradition says that the level ground near the shore was the site intended, but that the stones being twice removed by supernatural agency during the night, the church was erected upon the spot where they were discovered.

green, rise the battlemented walls of this old church of
St. Michael.   So *overhead* is the entire building, that the
lofty tower stands out against the sky, the background
of hill sinking below the eye altogether.   Indeed,
without throwing the head back, it is impossible to
take in the whole of this striking and unusual picture.

The church is mostly of fourteenth-century work,
but the tower appears to date from about the year
1500.   It has some curious sculptures.   On the south
side is a large seated figure of God the Father, holding
between his knees the crucified form of God the Son.
The pose of the statue is very majestic, though the
elements have nearly destroyed the features.   On
the eastern side, in a shallow square recess, will be
noticed a group of three figures engaged with a pair
of scales.   It represents the dedicatory saint, Michael,
weighing souls.   At one end the Devil is doing his
utmost to bear down the balance, but his efforts are
evidently being frustrated by the Virgin, who presses
the opposite beam.

The interior also presents several features of interest.
To begin with, there is no ' structural ' chancel, the
nave running from end to end without a break.   They
are separated, however, by a very beautiful carved
screen, erected about 1499, and very similar to the
one at Dunster, which is still finer.   I can remember
when school children occupied the rood-loft above, but
the recent restoration has changed all that, very much,
it must be admitted, to the advantage of the building.
The rood-staircase is remarkable for its size, and the
handsome Perpendicular windows which light it.

The table monument, with the recumbent figure in priestly robes, has perhaps caused more discussion than any other object in the church. It is locally asserted to be the effigy of Henry de Bracton, but there are grave reasons for doubting this. In the first place, the monument is probably of fifteenth-century date, whereas the judge flourished two centuries earlier. This, it must be admitted, is not in itself a *very* strong argument against the assertion, as there is no reason why, if the monument were merely cenotaphic, it should not have been erected at a later date as a memorial. But, unfortunately, it was a tomb. I have it on the authority of Savage that it was opened by the late Dr. Ball, of Minehead, and disclosed a remarkable skull, having two rows of upper teeth. So, even if it were possible that the tomb was erected later, and by a sculptor ignorant or heedless of the architecture of the thirteenth century, it is very improbable that so eminent a man as Bracton could have passed away without the fact of the shark-like formation of his upper jaw having been recorded.* Again, the robes are those of a priest, and one hand grasps a broken chalice. Is it likely that Bracton, who was *imprimis* a lawyer, would have been represented as an ecclesiastic, spite of the fact that he held—as has already been shown— more than one sacred office? I think not. Finally, I venture to quote from the particulars handed by Mr.

---

* A well-known Somersetshire antiquary, with whom I visited the monument, thought this malformation an excellent reason for assuming that the skeleton *was* that of the judge, remarking drily that 'Lawyers being *sharks*, the peculiarity was natural enough !'

W. George, of Bristol, an antiquary who has done much for Somersetshire, to the *West Somerset Free Press*, shortly after the visit of the Archæological Society to Bracton's supposed tomb. 'It has recently been established by Sir Travers Twiss,' he writes, 'that De Bracton was buried in the nave of Exeter Cathedral, before an altar dedicated to the Virgin, a little to the south of the entrance to the choir, at which a daily Mass was regularly said for the benefit of his soul for the space of three centuries after his decease; that is, until the reign of Henry VIII.; and it seems to have been always known as De Bracton's chantry. Although doubt exists as to the place of his birth, there can be no question as to the place of his burial.'

Behind the monument, in the north aisle, in a chapel now used as a vestry, is a finely-carved oak chest. The window, which is very beautiful, has near it, on the outer face of the wall, a black-letter inscription, which Mr. Buckle, the architect, renders as follows:

> 'We pray to Jesu and Mary,
> Send our neighbours safety,'

and which, he thinks, rather points to the fact that the chapel belonged to a guild—perhaps of fishermen.

Speaking of black-letter, reminds me of the old books, of which there are five, chained to a desk near the organ. The oldest is a copy of Bishop Jewell's Sermons, 1560; there are also the following: another volume of Sermons, 1562; a Body of Divinity, by Usher, Archbishop of Armagh; the Works of Thomas Adams, 1630; Sermons, by Robert Sanderson, 1657;

and, most interesting of all, a fine black-letter Bible, dated 1639.

As we pass out by the west door we shall not fail to remark the font, which has panels filled with figures of saints; but, as their emblems have been destroyed, it is impossible to identify their personality. In one panel, however, is a monk praying to a weird figure rising from a rectangular vessel or box—perhaps a rude representation of the Resurrection. I give, for what it is worth, Mr. Buckle's hypothesis that the monument in the chancel was that of this priest, who, whoever he may have been, was doubtless, from its position and appearance, a benefactor to the church.

Till quite recently, a statue of Queen Anne, in white alabaster, further adorned the church. It was the gift of Sir Jacob Bancks, a Swede, and an officer in the British navy. His connection with Minehead is explained by his having married the widow of Colonel Francis Luttrell. For sixteen years he was Member of Parliament for the borough. The statue was erected in 1719, I believe upon the pier-head, whence, having suffered from the weather, it was removed to the church. It is now in charge of a builder, waiting removal to the new Town Hall. In the churchyard are the remains of an ancient cross, but no monument of especial interest.

Having descended the hill, and passed through Middle Town, we reach the Avenue. In a court on the left-hand side, just below the Market House, are some almshouses—a low range of buildings, chiefly remarkable for a fine brass Jet into the wall about the centre. Here is engraved a full-rigged ship, and this inscription : ' Robert Quirck, sonne of James Quirck, built this house, Anno 1630, and doth give it to the use of the poore of this parish for ever. And for better maintenance, I do give my two inner cellers at the inner end of the Key; and cursed be that man that shall convert it to any other use than to the use of the poore, 1630.'

Beneath the ship is engraved—

> ' God's Providence
> Is my Inheritance.'—R. Q.

At the top of the court is the shaft of an octagonal cross, which is kept immaculate with *whitewash !* I am told it was, and probably still is, a boundary cross marking the confines of the charity land.

Turning out of the Avenue, below the handsome Tudoresque Town Hall, a road, shaded by lofty elms, and now bordered on one side by villas, leads to the quaint Quay Town, on whose houses we have already looked from the heights above. Nothing but a wall divides the long winding street from the harbour—a massive crescent-shaped horn, erected in 1616, of course by a Luttrell. From the pier-head a good view may be obtained of the irregular line of cottages, overshadowed, indeed, almost overhung, by the precipitous hills. At the back of the quay a narrow strip of shingle-skirted turf stretches to dangerous Culver Cliff, having about midway, close to a shallow pool, some patches of grass said to mark the graves of certain unknown sailors washed ashore from a wreck many years ago. Perhaps they formed part of the complement of the *Lamb*—a transport which left Minehead on February 20, 1736, with troops for Ireland, only to be wrecked a day later on 'Minehead Strand,' when at least fifty-eight persons lost their lives. Whether the cottage at the eastern end of the harbour, known as The Lamb, has any connection with this disaster, I cannot say.

Minehead is the headquarters of a curious custom, known as 'hobby-horsing.' Until recently it was indulged in with much vigour, and is even now, apparently, very far from moribund. On May Day a number of men and boys, accompanied by a drum, perambulated the streets, grotesquely attired, and surrounding the figure of the hobby-horse—a rude imitation of the quadruped, formed by two men concealed beneath trappings, with an imitation of a horse's head attached, and, not unfrequently, a formidable hempen tail as well, wherewith the unwary, as well as those refusing to pay a small fee to the revellers, were lightly beaten. So much for my own recollection. Other items of the performance which were formerly carried out consisted of 'booting' or 'pursing,' *i.e.*, rapping the recalcitrant with a boot. At Dunster Castle the party was treated to refreshments and rewarded for their performances with money. A recent writer on the customs of this part of the world says that the festivities commenced by the inhabitants dancing round the hobby-horse at the cross-roads outside the town in the direction of Bidcombe, and terminated on May 3rd at other cross-roads on the highway to Porlock.

The origin of the hobby-horse has never, perhaps, been quite satisfactorily explained. Of one thing, however, there can, I think, be no doubt, viz., that it is a relic of the old morris-dance :

> 'The hobby-horse doth hither prance,
> Maid Marian and the Morris-dance ;'

and Tollet imagines that it represents 'the King of the May,'* while another fancies that it commemorates 'a religious fracas long ago, in which one party trounced the other.' Savage opines that here it is the relic of some ancient custom of beating the bounds. Whatever it may perpetuate, it was, and is, to adults of the lower classes, an interesting ceremony, though to young children the appalling form of the steed, and the alarming appearance of his satellites, are fraught with some terror. But its popularity is waning now, and many of the quieter folk of Minehead would not be sorry to see written over the custom the epitaph mentioned by Hamlet :

> 'For oh, for oh, the hobby-horse is forgot !'

Those curious in experiments will be pleased to note that (according to Collinson) linen may be marked at Minehead on very easy terms. 'On the rocks at low water,' he says, 'is a species of limpet, which contains a liquor very curious for marking fine linen ; the process is as follows : Lay the limpet with its mouth downward on some solid body, and break it with a smart stroke of a hammer, but not so as to bruise the fish. When the shell is picked off, there will appear a white

* Brand's 'Popular Antiquities' (ed. 1877), p. 150.

vein lying transversely in a little furrow next the head of the fish, which may be taken out by a bodkin or any other pointed instrument.   The letters or figures made with this liquor on linen will presently appear of a light-green colour, and if placed in the sun will change into the following colours : if in winter about noon, if in summer, an hour or two after sun-rising, and so much before setting ; for in the heat of the day in summer it will come on so fast that the succession of each colour will scarcely be distinguished.   Next to the first light green, it will appear of a deep green, and in a few minutes change to a full sea-green; after which, in a few minutes more, it will alter to a blue; then to a purplish-red ; after which, lying an hour or two (if the sun shines), it will be of a deep, purple-red, beyond which the sun does no more.   But this last beautiful colour, after washing in scalding water and soap, will, on being laid out to dry, be a fair, bright crimson, which will abide all future washing.   This species of limpet are, some red, others white, black, yellow, brown, and sand colour ; and some are striped with white and brown parallel lines.'*

And now farewell to Minehead.   Another town of even smaller size lies close at hand, right in our course as we pursue our way past Hopcot Farm, up hilly lanes over mountainous-looking Grabhurst.   For under its northern declivity reposes in a calm, which the adjacent railway has done little to disturb, the beautifully situated and historic town of Dunster.

This hill of Grabhurst, or, locally. Grabbist, rises from

* Collinson, vol. ii., p. 30.

the town with great abruptness to a height of nearly
1,000 feet. From the western side the ascent is easy
enough, but upon the east and north the slopes
are steeper than those of any hill west of Minehead.
Although on one side it is in great part covered almost
to its bare brow with trees, this does not detract in the
least from the boldness of its appearance, for here and
there patches of stones mark the sides, giving it a
striking resemblance to some of the hills of West-
moreland. There is one view in particular, from the
shady lane below Broadwood Farm, on the northern
slope of Croydon Hill, which brought vividly before me
the beautiful brow called Nab Scar, above Rydal
˙Vater. Owing to its abrupt termination at Dunster,

shape changes very frequently; at one point it is 'sow-
back,' at another an undulating though short range ;*
from Dunster Park—the lower one—it rises into a
kind of rounded head ; while from the neighbourhood
of Carhampton it stands boldly up in form a mountain
peak, though in altitude nothing more than a lofty hill.

Situate as it is on the borderland of Exmoor, of which,
indeed, it may be accounted an isolated spur, it commands a surprising view. The beautiful Vale of Avill,
said to derive its name from the Celtic *abell*, an apple
—the Valley of Apples—runs up past Timberscombe
and Wootton Courtenay to Dunkery. At its feet lies
Dunster, nestling about the wooded Tor on which is
perched the castle of the Luttrells, above which, again,
rises the deer-park and the ridge, broken by some rough-

* I have called the whole range Grabhurst ; but the western
extremity is known as Heydon Down.

GRABHURST, DUNSTER. DRAWN BY ALFRED DAWSON.

looking mounds, to which we shall by-and-by devote a
closer inspection. On the other hand is Conegar,
Minehead, and the sea, bordered by flat and fat pas-
ture-land.

Grabhurst appears to be a corruption of *Grobefast*,
for so is the name spelt in ancient deeds. This rather
disposes of Grab hurst, the entrenched wood, while the
story that the name signifies 'pig's back' seems equally
unlikely. There is an absurd legend that the name is
that of a Dutchman who drove the cattle from the surrounding hills to this spot, previous to embarking them
at Minehead. Not far from the eastern end are the
remains of an earthwork. A low bank encloses (except
on the south, where the hillside becomes a precipice)
an area 2,000 feet in circumference.

Let us descend to Dunster. The town is said to owe
its name to two Celtic words, *dun*, a hill, and *tor*, a
tower, which has become corrupted into Dunster. Its
earliest name was Torre, but it soon became Dunes-
torre, and is Latinized into Dunestora, in a grant of the
advowson of the church to the monks of St. Peter's,
Bath, by William de Mohun, dated 1100.*

Dunster is one of the few, the very few, thoroughly
old-fashioned country towns, in this utilitarian nineteenth century, spared to us. Whether we look down
upon it from the crest of Grabhurst, the grounds of the
castle, or from either end of its main street, the same
appearance of almost mediæval aspect is presented, the
same restful air broods over it. Here are no hideous
modern villas, glaring with red brick or gleaming with

* Murray, p. 452.

stucco. In their stead quaint thatched or tiled houses, one or two rich with ancient woodwork under peaked gables, blink in the sunshine at the curious wayfarer. There is a fine view from the corner by the Luttrell Arms Hotel. In the foreground, planted right in the middle of the. widest part of the thoroughfare, is the curious octagonal wooden yarn-market, erected by George Luttrell in 1609. But the kerseymeres of Dunster, once as familiar as the worsteds of the Norfolk town, are no longer known to fame, and ' dunsters ' have ceased to be in request by the good wives of West Somerset. In 1646 the building suffered from the chances of war, and a hole through a beam still shows the passage of one of Blake's cannon-balls. In fact, Dunster possesses little history that is not con-nected with war's alarms. Its political life began and ended in 1360, when it returned members to Parliament for the first and last time.

Although the castle and church claim a previous attention, we may, being at its very door, as well turn our steps first to the old hostelry on the left, once, probably, a residence of the abbots of Cleeve. There is a good fifteenth-century porch, furnished with loopholes cut in such a manner that it was possible to shoot, not only direct, but askance. Upstairs is a well-proportioned room, with a fine oaken gabled roof lighted by windows set in carved oak, the woodwork, indeed, extending downwards and forming a façade. Another upper room has a curious over-mantel in plaster. In the centre of the upper part is a half-figure in the costume of Tudor days, with a rather comical expression of surprise or expostulation in the eyes, though this would appear to be due rather to the indifferent skill of the moulder, than to any intention on his part. Below him, between two female figures in a costume of the same period, is an oval medallion representing a nude form (whether male or female, it is not easy to decipher, the modelling being of the rudest) attacked by hounds. It is amusing to note the guesses levelled at this mysterious work of art. I have heard one suggest that it represents one of Boccaccio's women being torn in pieces for unchastity ; another, Lazarus undergoing the ' licking of his sores ;' while a third, reflecting, perhaps, the general opinion, concluded that the sufferer was Actæon. As, however, that ' peeping Tom ' was turned into a stag before being devoured, we must either relinquish this theory, or arrive at the conclusion that the artist was weak in his mythology. There are other objects of interest in this fine old inn, the principal of which are the highly-coloured arms of the Luttrells, and a ceiling in one of the public rooms.

Perhaps the pleasantest way to the church is to pass up the ascent behind the yarn-market, and approach by the vicarage grounds. Not only are these grounds in themselves attractive, commanding, as they do, an extensive and beautiful view over land and sea ; but they look down upon the few remains of the ancient Priory, with the long line of the church behind, standing out in bold relief against the wooded steeps of the castle. The most prominent objects are the monks' barn and dovecote. The latter contains a pivot, to which is attached a ladder. So that when the monk wished to feed the birds or collect the eggs, he had but to mount the ladder, and travel round the walls, which are honey-combed with nests. A tiled building to the west appears to represent the prior's lodging, perhaps that of the monks as well, for the largest number of inmates at Dunster Priory seems never to have exceeded some half-dozen. Their history is brief. In the time of William the Conqueror,* William de Mohun, grantee of the manor of ' Dunestora,' finding the existing church—it must have been a Saxon one—in ill repair, granted it to the Abbey of Bath, and built for these monks of St. Peter a Benedictine cell hard by. At the dissolution the little Priory, which then had but three monks, fell to the lot of the lords of Dunster Castle.

Behind the scanty remains stands the beautiful church, by far the finest in this part of the country. It is 168 feet long, and 55 feet wide, and in shape cruci-form. It appears on the whole to date from early in the fifteenth century, though there are fragments of an earlier building, notably the west door, which is Norman, as also the piers of a Norman arch on the west side of the tower, and an early thirteenth-century stone altar in the north chapel. The tower, built in 1443, has a height of 90 feet. It rises in three stages. There is a wide but low nave with no clerestory, and north and south aisles, the latter possessing a very handsome flat ceiling, divided into square panels richly carved. The other ceilings are of the waggon kind. Stretching the

* Dugdale's ' Monasticon.' Lyte, however, gives a date between 1090 and 1100—*Vide* ' Dunster and its Lords,' p. 4.

whole breadth of the church is the magnificent rood-screen of fourteen openings. Its situation is nearly in the centre of the building; and 'thereby hangs a tale.' Until 1499 the church was used in common by parishioners and monks. In that year, however, a dispute arose, and waxed so exceeding hot that arbitrators had to be called in, one being the Abbot of Glastonbury. The decision was that the vicar should occupy the nave, and the monks the eastern portion of the church. To mark the bounds between vicar and prior, the rood-screen was accordingly erected a little to the west of the altar, which has since the restoration been removed to the eastern tower arch. Why the cowled brethren should have had so large a portion assigned to them seems incomprehensible; however, as builders of the original Norman church, it cannot be denied that they had a strong *locus standi*, though the vicar might—and probably did — argue that as the original parish church existed before the monks' building, the parishioners had an equal, if not greater, right. But the monks were soon ousted; the Dissolution came, and not long after Leland writes that 'the hole chirch of the late Priory servith now for the paroche chirch,' adding, 'afore tymes the monkes had the est parte closid up to their use.' This 'est parte,' *i.e.*, the Early English chancel, is now used for daily prayers, though it really belongs to the Luttrell family. A volume might easily be written on this fine edifice; and it has, indeed, been pretty minutely described by other and more capable ecclesiologists. Attention will, therefore, be drawn but to a few more points of interest ere we depart for the castle on the hill above. One of these is the ugly arch connecting the south transept with the choir. It was widened some time in the fifteenth century by propping the arch while the jambs below were rebuilt, and two corbels inserted at the springing of the arch, completely altering and as completely spoiling its shape. Others are the chantry, with its altar-stone; the decorated canopy over the body of a lady of the Everard family, against the south wall of the presbytery; and the fine altar-tomb of Sir Hugh Luttrell and his lady, who died respectively in 1428 and 1433. This is also canopied, and bears a certain resemblance to the Harrington monument in the church at Porlock. The octagonal font, too, is handsome; it is sculptured with emblems of the Crucifixion, and of the five wounds of Christ.

Nor must we forget the curious 'Articles of Ringing' painted on a slab now fixed to the wall in the clock-case in the belfry. It will be seen that the treatment reserved by the last verse for the contumacious bellringer was unusually severe. I give them in full, as they are in part nearly obliterated, and are certainly well worth preserving.

I. You that in Ringing take delight,
   Be pleased to draw near;
   These Articles you must observe
   If you mean to Ring here.

II. And first, if any Overturn
    A Bell, as that he may,
    He Forthwith for that only Fault
    In Beer shall Sixpence pay.

III. If anyone shall Curse or Swear
When come Within the door,
He then shall Forfit for that Fault
As mentioned before.

IV. If anyone shall wear his Hat
When he is Ringing here,
He straightway then shall Sixpence pay
In Cyder or in Beer.

V. If anyone these Articles
Refuseth to Obey,
Let him have nine strokes of the Rope,
And so depart away.

Passing through the churchyard, we shall notice the base and stump of a thirteenth-century cross. It may be as well to take this opportunity of mentioning that another is to be seen on the bank by the side of the lane leading to Alcombe, exactly at the top of the steep hill above the town. It is known as the Butter Cross, and is of later date than the one in the churchyard ; according to Mr. Pooley, of the fifteenth century.

At the entrance from Church Street, through which we pursue our way to the castle, is an old timbered priest-house, now occupied by the church caretaker. But another and more striking building a little below—that is, towards the main thoroughfare—will attract greater attention. This is an ancient house known as the Nunnery, a tall structure of about the fifteenth century, with steep tiled roof and gables of decided ecclesiastical appearance. Between the two first stories run tiled pentices, which give the building a look very antique and picturesque. The local tradition is to the effect that it really was a nunnery in connection with the

Priory close by. There is, however, no evidence that such was the case. Mr. Maxwell Lyte states that the name is of modern origin, and that, even within the present century, the building has been known as the High House. It was formerly known as ' The tenement of St. Lawrence,' from the fact that part of the revenue (about £9 per annum) of the chantry of St. Lawrence was derived from it. It is at present divided into cottages.

A very steep road leads to the castle, passing beneath a fine gate-house, probably of the time of Henry V.,* flanked by four towers. The builder is thought to have been Sir Hugh Luttrell. Adjoining the entrance gateway is another, assigned to Reginald de Mohun, and built in the reign of Henry III.; it is the oldest part of the present building. Another Sir Hugh, who flourished later in the same century, rebuilt part of the castle, but the main fabric dates from Elizabeth. The present south front was erected by Henry Fownes Luttrell, rather more than 100 years since. Nothing, as far as I know, is left of the ancient fortress of William de Mohun, or De Moion, to whom the manor, with sixty-seven others, was granted by the Conqueror, who dispossessed the former owner, one Aluric,† who, too,

---

* This may be the ' novum ædificium castri de Dunster' built by Henry Stone in 9th Henry V.; the lower part, however, is in the style of Richard II. (' Dunster and its Lords,' xiii.). At any rate, Leland must be wrong in saying that it was built temp. Henry VII.

† ' William de Mohun holds Torre, and there is his castle. Aluric held it in the time of King Edward, when it was assessed to the geld for half a hide.'—Domesday Survey.

probably had some sort of a fortress on this commanding spot. These Mohuns* were a very powerful family,
enjoying, if Leland is to be believed, even *jura regalia.*
One of them held the castle against Stephen, who, despairing of taking it, merely left Henry de Tracey to stop
his predatory sallies, in which he was successful. It
came into the possession of the Luttrells, who acquired
it by purchase, and have ever since held it, in 1376.
It has been considerably altered and added to of late
years by its present owner.

The interior has a fine hall, with grandly carved
staircase. Over both are rich plaster ceilings, the
latter bearing a date—1681. There is another in the
dining-room. Here, as also in the bedroom occupied
by Charles II., are specimens of the curious plaster
over-mantels so often found in the old mansions of
West Somerset.

In another room are some leather hangings—
commonly, but erroneously spoken of as tapestry—very
highly painted, and varnished, representing the story of
Antony and Cleopatra. The work is Italian. Among
the paintings are specimens of Vandyck (a fine portrait
of Cromwell), Opie, Sir Joshua Reynolds, and others.
A very curious work in the hall by Lucas de Heere
represents the escape of Sir John Luttrell from the
wreck of a ship in which he had been taken prisoner

---

* Old Fuller relates a pretty story of the wife of one of the
Mohuns. 'She hath left a worthy memory behind her, chiefly on
this account—that she obtained from her husband so much good
ground for the common of the town of Dunster as she could in one
day (believe it a summer one for her ease and advantage) compass
about, going on her naked feet.'

during the Scottish war of Henry VIII.   The figure is
nude, and has what appear to be gyves upon the
wrists, though the hands are perfectly free.   A little in
the background a young and very handsome man is
sinking, the face alone being visible.   This has been
thought by some to represent the knight's lady-love,
whom he is saving from drowning.   Unfortunately for
these theorists, Sir John is not only some distance from
the so-called lady, but looking in quite a different
direction.   He is not ' swimming,' but wading waist
deep, and to crown the whole, a moustache deter-
mines at once the sex of the drowning one.   In the
clouds are various female forms, one of which may
or may not mean, ' Victory, ready to crown him with
laurel.'*   In one corner of the canvas is inscribed:

> ' More than the rocks amidst the raging seas,
> The constant heart no danger dreads nor fears.
>   S. H.
> Effigiem renovare tuam, fortissime miles,
> Ingens me meritum facit, amorque tui,
> Nam nisi curasses hæredem scribere fratrem !
> Hei ! tua contigerant prædia nulla mihi.
>   1591, G. L.
>   1550, H. E.'

By which it would appear, that in the former year
(1591) the painting had been restored by a brother of
the hero.   Possibly the English distich superinduced
the belief in the romantic version of the story.

Having regard to its situation, it is needless to add
that the scenery around Dunster Castle is varied
in the extreme.   From all parts of the paths which

* Savage, p. 445.

wind about the wooded slopes of the Tor the most charming vistas present themselves. At one point a wide stretch of sea, backed by the pale heights of Southern Wales; at another the bold bluff of Minehead and the wooded steep of Conegar,* at the opposite end of the bay the alabaster-veined cliffs of Blue Anchor. Eastward rises the wild park, crested with the earthworks of a race older than either Luttrell or Mohun, while southward lies the fair Vale of Avill, with Dunkery blue in the distance. Close at hand, almost overhanging the bowling-green, forming the very summit of the hill, and once the site of De Mohun's keep, towers the sharp line of Grabhurst, with the quaint little town beneath.

As may be imagined, the nature of the ground does not permit of very extensive gardens. The principal attraction is a fine citron-tree, which blossoms and fruits, in due season, against the southern wall, a pretty strong proof of the mildness of the climate. When I saw it, in August last, it was covered with fruit and perfectly open to the air, with nothing but the wooden framework of its occasional covering to speak to its sometime encasement.

The Norman castle of William de Mohun is, as we have said, the first building upon the hill of Torre of which there exists any record. With the exception of the defence against the forces of Stephen, there is little exciting in the history of Dunster Castle until the time

* The tower on the summit was erected circa 1775. Near it is the entrance to an underground passage, said to communicate with the castle, and to have been used by the *Danes !* It is now blocked up.

of the struggle between king and people, when it declared for the Parliament—the Luttrell of the day holding out until, influenced by the royal successes in the West and the arguments of Colonel Francis Windham,* he surrendered it to the king, who appointed Colonel Windham governor. He held it from 1643 to 1646. At one time he had as visitor the young Prince Charles, whose bedchamber, already referred to, is still shown, together with a narrow passage behind the bed terminating in an alcove known as ' King Charles's hiding-place,' though how the prince could possibly need a refuge whilst the guest of a Royalist is not apparent. This Francis Windham was a man of renowned valour. It is said that on hearing that the Parliamentarians had pillaged his kinsman's house of Sandhill and ill-treated the women, he left the castle with only thirty followers, and, falling upon them at Nettlecombe, routed no less than 250 men, returning in triumph to Dunster. Again, in 1646, when Blake lay siege to the fortress, he is reported to have sent the following answer to the Parliamentarians, who threatened that if he did not give up the castle, his mother, a prisoner among them, should be placed in front to receive the first fury of his cannon. 'If you doe what you threaten,' said this intrepid warrior, 'you doe the most barbarous and villanous act was ever done. My mother I honour, but the cause I fight for and the masters I serve, God and the king, I honour more. Mother, doe you forgive me, and give me your blessing, and let the rebels answer for spilling that blood of yours, which I would save with the losse of

* Clarendon, vol. iv., p. 110.

mine owne, if I had enough for both my master and yourselfe.' The mother, brave as her son, replied: 'Sonne, I forgive thee, and pray God to blesse thee for this brave resolution. If I live I shall love thee better for it; God's will be done.' It is said that the siege was raised by Lord Wentworth and the mother saved.* This siege by the redoubtable Blake—the man who

> ' Made Spain and Holland shake,
> Made France to tremble, and the Turks to quake—'

lasted nearly six months, and is celebrated for the brave defence of the garrison. Only once do they appear to have been relieved. This was by Lord Hopton, who, on February 5, 1646, drove Blake from his position, and brought food to the starving Royalists. But Blake, strengthened by the troops of Fairfax, soon returned, and, on April 19, Windham surrendered.

Not long after—in 1648—a somewhat notable man was sent as prisoner to Dunster Castle; William Prynne spent seven months in durance vile within its walls, having offended Cromwell and his party by asserting that the king ' had satisfactorily answered the propositions for peace.' A schedule of Luttrell muniments, which he spent his enforced leisure in arranging, is still extant. One of them contains information show-

* Timbs' ' Abbeys, Castles, etc., of England,' p. 155. It seems, however, that this story is wholly mythical. ' The siege was not raised, the castle was not relieved at this time, and the supposed chief actors in the affair were then in Cornwall, or on the western borders of Devon.'—Lyte, p. 90. The only relief was by Lord Hopton, on February 5, 1646.

ing that Dunster in early days possessed a harbour.*
It is a 'broken plea, supposed to belong to the 12th
of Elizabeth, of the attorney-general's concerning
Dunster Haven within the Manor of Dunster, that
it always belonged to Thomas Luttrell and his ancestors, who took the profits thereof.'   The only place
for a ' haven' would have been the mouth of the stream
watering the Vale of Avill, which, under the name of
Hone or Horne (query, the Celtic *aune water*), here
meets the sea.   All traces of a harbour have long disappeared.   Even the tide has been confined within
proper limits, and the flat meadows between the town
and sea, formerly overflowed by the salt waters, are not
only embanked, but divided by the unromantic railway.
Tempora mutantur!

* *In vol. i., part 8, of 'Somerset and Dorset Notes and
Queries,' Mr. W. George notices that in 1380 a Catalan merchant
ship, bound from Genoa to Sluys, was driven by a storm into
Dunster, and taken as a prize by Joan Mohun, Lady of Dunster.
King Richard II., however, ordered the merchandise to be delivered to the owners.   Rymer's 'Fœdera, Tonson's edn., vii., p. 233.
Vide also 'Dunster and its Lords,' p. 17.   The Genoese captain
must have been blown very far out of his reckoning, indeed, to get
into the Bristol instead of the English Channel.

CHAPTER XI

FROM DUNSTER, OVER CROYDON, AND THE BRENDON HILLS

Water Lane—Cæsar's Camp—British Camp—Croydon Hill—
Another British Camp—Stone Enclosure at Dumbledeer—Withy-
combe Fire Beacon—Red Girts—Chargot Lodge—Monkham
Circle—Slowly—Langridge Kistvaen—Treborough—Leigh Wood
Cascade—Brendon Mines—The Dunstone and Naked Boy—
Raleigh's Cross—Discovery of Roman Coins—Elworthy Barrows.

THE breezy slopes of the park are, in themselves, sufficient temptation for the walk, but he who is archæo-
logically disposed will need no impetus for the climb,
when he hears that two fine camps are up above yon
wood. The artist will be fain to stop at the old bridge
at the foot of the hill, and at the end of Water Lane,
for here is as picturesque a bit of colouring as will be
met with in the vicinity. In the clear stream, spreading
over the shady lane, the gray arches lie reflected, a
faithful double, while beyond, the perfect cone of Grabhurst, here seen end-on, towers, clad in green bracken
and purple heather, above the foliage creeping over his
feet.

But the path ascends upwards beneath the trees
for about half a mile. Soon after passing into the open,

it becomes a green ride, and from this, about 300 yards from the wood, we shall diverge to mount through the bracken to the summit of the ridge. While yet distant, the fallow deer stare at us curiously, but upon a nearer approach are off like the wind, to pause again on the slope beneath, and wonder at the impertinence of the biped who dares intrude upon their domain. Suddenly some mounds come in sight against the sky-line, and in another moment we find ourselves standing upon the vallum of a large enclosure—the so-called Cæsar's Camp.

The camp is said to be octagonal, but, after a careful survey, I came to the conclusion that it is very nearly square, the corners being rounded off. The length from north to south is 130 paces, or about 390 feet; the breadth from east to west about 115 paces. It is encircled by a double vallum of stones and a fosse, the latter having a depth of about nine feet, in places more. But on the southern side, where a very abrupt declivity rendered such a precaution unnecessary, the vallum is single and the fosse disappears. So steep, indeed, is this hillside, that a pebble may with no great exertion be thrown clear into the valley beneath. There are entrances on the east and west only; that on the east is defended by parallel banks running at right angles to the vallum for about forty paces. A short distance—I did not measure it, but apparently some 200 yards—still further eastward is a zigzag rampart or outwork, about six feet high.

That this is not a pure Roman camp the reader need scarcely be told. It is not rectangular, and has but two places of ingress. However, it is much more Roman than British, and the fact that Roman coins—I believe of Maximian and Constantine*—have been discovered in the neighbourhood goes some, if but a little way towards fixing the nationality of its sometime occupants. The Rev. Prebendary Scarth appears to be of opinion that it protected the road by which the miners of Brendon would bring their ore to Minehead for export. It remains but to be added that the inner vallum is much broken in places, and of very irregular height, at one point not more than seven feet, at another exceeding twelve.

The view from the ramparts is beautiful. Looking north, we have in the foreground beneath the wooded Tor and castle, and the tower-crowned height of Conegar. Beyond the level meadows gleams the sea. Eastward, over the fertile lands about Carhampton, Old Cleeve and Washford, stretches the bold line of the Quantocks, and faint in the distance isolated Brent Knoll and the Mendips. Turning, the eye rests upon heathery Black Hill, and dark Croydon, from which we are divided by the well-wooded valley running up towards Broadwood. Westward, or rather south-westward, is Dunkery, the beacon very plain against the sky, and, crossing the vales beneath, the glance sweeps over the bold range of the North Hill to Mine-head, resting finally upon Grabhurst, and the little town between it and the castle.

On the hill to the north-west, and at a lower eleva-

* I have since learnt, from Mr. Luttrell, that coins of these reigns were discovered in the park near the old Carhampton road, con-cealed under some stones in a little gully.

tion, is another camp.   This is circular, and has a diameter of seventy paces.   It is surrounded by a fosse and
stone vallum about ten feet high.   There is an entrance
on the south only.   This hill-fortress overlooks the
Vale of Avill, and, although not perched on the edge of
such a glacis as its neighbour, does, nevertheless,
occupy a position sufficiently commanding.   It is
known as the British Camp.

Descending the hill southwards, and passing an old
and dangerous quarry which, unprotected by a railing,
yawns abruptly at the traveller's feet, we descend a
winding path into the valley, and, climbing a shady lane,
rich in ferns, come out upon the open moorland at the
foot of Croydon Hill.   As the base is skirted, the
country towards the Brendon Hills opens out.   Yonder
is Lype Hill, barrow-crested, and almost islanded by
cultivation; then comes Goosemoor, with its minestack
and deserted engine-house, both part of the long line of
Brendon, which bounds the horizon.

For the sake of the view—and, as Croydon is the
loftiest hill hereabouts, it is very wide—we will ascend
to the summit.   In our search for antiquities, however,
we shall, I think, be disappointed.   Murray states that
there are 'several hut-circles or remains of ancient
British habitations' on this dark height.   That there
may be 'remains' of 'habitations' I am not prepared
to deny, but it would puzzle the most enthusiastic
archæologist to make a hut-circle out of the scattered
stones which lie here and there on the slopes.   There
are some queer piles of stone on the southern declivity,
locally known as 'stone heaps,' which *may* be burial

cairns, but anything approaching a stone circle is not to be found. I have cross - examined numberless whortleberry-gatherers on this and the neighbouring hills, but not one could remember ever having encountered anything circular except these piles. On the crest a ruined cairn has been converted into a kind of chair, which forms a capital shelter, as I myself can testify, from the storms sweeping across from the uplands of Dunkery. There are several ruinous heaps of a like character hard by.

There is, however, one item archæological, on the south-eastern slope, which the traveller will do well to visit, though its discovery will certainly entail a long and perhaps unsuccessful search. This is another British camp similar to that upon the hill in Dunster Park, but having a less diameter. It measures forty-seven paces, and is so covered with oak coppice and ling as to be quite obliterated, save for a few feet on the south, where, as usual, there is an entrance. It is marked plainly enough upon Savage's map, but is inaccurate in point of size, being, as I have said, considerably smaller than the Dunster Park specimen, instead of (as he makes it) larger. Nor is it as far down the slope, the stream, which in his map touches its eastern rampart, being quite a quarter of a mile distant. To those who would visit it I can only say that it lies exactly opposite some scattered stones, which are very conspicuous on Black Hill, across the valley eastward, and on the edge of a pathway descending to Broadwood Farm. At the upper end a solitary fir will also assist the explorer in identifying its position.

Considering how near these two camps are to each other, one is disposed to wonder that there is no settlement for whose protection they were designed. But although it is true that there are no traces of a village in the *immediate* vicinity, we have not to proceed far before coming upon traces of one. If we strike over the shoulder of Black Hill, and descend to Higher Dumbledeer, a small hill-farm, we shall find, close to the gate opening upon Withycombe Common (which is the easterly continuation of the ridge in Dunster Park), the indistinct remains of a large stone circle. Forty or fifty years ago there were traces of several hut-circles within the walls; but these have now entirely vanished. The tenant at the adjoining farm told me that great quantities of stone had been carted away for draining and like purposes, and that, having cut the fern which grows thickly all over the enclosure, for thirty-six years, he was quite sure there was no sign of a basement remaining. Nor, after several visits, and much trampling down of vegetation, can I do otherwise than corroborate his statement. An imperfect rampart, about 3 feet high and 130 feet in diameter, within which the ground appears to have been partly excavated, is all that remains of this old village. The summit of the hill above is called the Fire Beacon, but there are no remains of hearths; the cone is evidently quite a natural formation.

As to the position of the village with regard to the camps, it seems to me not very far-fetched to imagine that the earthwork overlooking the Vale of Avill would protect the approach up the valley towards Broadwood;

that that upon the slope of Croydon would overlook the pass between it and Black Hill; while the Fire Beacon on Withycombe Hill would warn the inhabitants both of the settlement and the camps of any approach from the south or east.

Under the Fire Beacon lies the picturesque old village of Withycombe. The Perpendicular church has a remarkably low massive tower, probably the oldest part of the church, and the font is, I think, Norman. It is a small building, nave and chancel being on one level, but separated by a good carved screen in excellent preservation. There are two name-less monuments : one in the recess of a window on the north, apparently a nun ; the other in a recess in the south wall, representing the rudely-carved figure of a lady in the costume of, I think, the fifteenth century. Both are recumbent, and both, as far as can be ascer-tained, without history. Beneath the altar, placed there by the present vicar for preservation, is a seven-teenth-century slab, on which appear the names of Basset of Bewpir (Beaupré), and Morgan (now of Tredegar), two well-known Glamorganshire families.

In this parish is Sandhill, anciently Sandell—a former home of the Wyndhams, now a farm. The vane on the gable bears the initials F. W., those of Colonel Francis Wyndham (or Windham), who, as we have already seen, held Dunster Castle for the king. The letter which induced Mr. Luttrell to surrender was written from this house, and is still in existence. It is a fine old house, and retains some old wood-framed windows and oaken-wainscot bearing the date 1588, the year of the Armada. An upper room is said to be haunted by the ghost of Madame Carne, a reputed witch, and worse—she is said to have made away with one or all of her three husbands. A brass preserved in the vestry of Withycombe Church announces that she married, first, John Newton of Sandell; next, Charles Wyndham; and, lastly, Thomas Carne of Ewenny, Glamorgan. She died in 1612, and was duly buried in the parish church. But she could not rest. When the party returned from the funeral there she was —frying eggs and bacon!

From Withycombe we shall proceed to Carhampton, which gives its name to the hundred. Here is a good, but rather plain, Perpendicular church. It has, however, one ornament, a magnificent screen of eleven openings, stretching the whole breadth of the church. It has been recently painted, and it is a question whether the effect is wholly satisfactory. The tower is new, and supplants a plainer one, which was adorned, like many others, with stucco.

Behind the village, on the hillside, is the old thatched farm of Aller. There is nothing striking about it now; but it was once the seat of the Everards, who, says Savage, held it of the Mohuns by the tenure of castle-guard. The only remains of former greatness will be found in a large room on the ground-floor, where the ceiling is divided by plainly-carved (and whitewashed) oak beams. From Dunster Park, close at hand, is another very striking view of the castle and Grabhurst Hill.

To return to Dumbledeer. It is a pleasant walk over

the dip dividing Black from Rodhuish Hill. The pathway skirts the side of a deep but narrow valley or gully,
watered in dim and invisible recesses by a rocky
stream, and clothed with mountain-ash and the most
magnificent bracken I have ever seen. In many places
it is quite seven feet high, and so thick that once I had
to turn back, being unable to force my way through this
miniature forest. The wayfarer who would descend
into this ravine should exercise caution, as the banks
are rather precipices than slopes, and should he come
to grief, human aid may be a long time in reaching him.
The spot is called Red Girts, a name presumably
traceable to former mining operations. Within recent
years, indeed, iron-ore has been sought in this glen, but
with, I understand, results the reverse of satisfactory.

We are now well on our way for the Brendon range,
which has been of late frequently visible, and which, as
we reach the top of the ridge above Red Girts, stands
forth plainly across the Roadwater Valley. Midway,
in the bottom, is Luxborough, seated among charming
combes, and close to the beautiful grounds of Chargot
Lodge, a mansion which, though of no great size, can
boast of delightful surroundings. It lies on the slope
of a narrow valley, bounded by wooded hills, which close
in at the upper end, an amphitheatre of foliage. Down
through the verdant meadows rattles a merry stream,
feeding a chain of ponds, where the trout swarm in
great numbers, and where an occasional swan may be
seen reflecting its white image in the clear water.
Little, if any, of all this can be seen from the summit
of Black Hill, but a descent to Luxborough and a visit

to these picturesque grounds will well repay those who have the time.   But our steps take a different direction.

A little eastward of Black Hill, and really part of it, is a spur known as Monkham Hill.   About half a mile below the brow, on the southern slope—that is, between our present position and Slowly Wood—Savage's map shows a circle, to which he thus refers : ' On Monkham Hill, on the north side of the parish (Luxborough), there is an extensive circle of large stones, and two barrows close to it.'   The barrows are still *in situ ;* not so the stones.   They appear to have been on the top of the hill, for Camden says that the circle commands a view of the Channel.*   No one nowadays even remembers them, nor have I been able to discover the slightest trace. Were it not that another antiquity, lying further down the valley, calls for an examination, it would be as well to descend to Luxborough and climb to the Brendon Hills, or, as the range is almost invariably denominated in West Somerset, Brendon *Hill.*   As it is, we will follow the summit and slope of our hill towards Slowly Farm.   All along the top, at intervals of a few hundred yards, are large barrows more or less ruined : one, on that part of the down called Rodhuish Hill, which is a prominent object to all the country round, I measured, and found 180 feet in circumference, and still 10 feet high.   On the slope towards Slowly Wood are more

* 'On the summit of Monkham Hill, further west, are several barrows, and a circular enclosure of loose stones piled up forty feet in diameter, which seems to have a Druidical origin, though perhaps used as a signal station, as it completely commands the whole line of coast from Porlock Bay to Quantock's Head Point.'— Camden, Gough's edition, 1806.

'stone heaps,' one of immense area, though of no remarkable elevation.

In the gullies about these uplands the honeysuckle attains to remarkable profusion. I remember one in particular, at no great distance from the cairn alluded to, which was literally one mass of bloom, so much so, indeed, that the leaves were barely visible, and the air for many yards around was laden with the perfume. It stands on the very edge of a sudden rift made by bog drainage, and is really quite a floral curiosity.

Nearer Slowly Farm, in fact not more than a hundred yards behind the tall sycamores on the common above, is a very small and ruinous hut-circle, the only one I have discovered in the neighbourhood. There are traces of some tracklines near it, which show, perhaps, that in a former day this bare hillside was under cultivation. Here the staghounds occasionally meet—to the neighbours the liveliest day in the year—perhaps the *only* lively one, for Slowly is remóte from the 'busy hum of men.'

East of Slowly is Drucombe Wood, of course assigned to Druidism. West of that, again, is Langridge Wood. It lies on the further side of the road to Washford, on what, as its name implies, is a *long ridge*. On the highest part of this ridge, and close to the left of a grassy walk will be observed a large clump of heather and low shrubs. This marks the débris of a cairn destroyed in 1820 to make a rough road for hauling timber. To their astonishment the workmen came upon a large stone, which covered a kistvaen about seven feet in length, two and a half in breadth, and a yard deep,

14

formed of five slabs.* This contained the skeleton
of a human being, 'perhaps,' says Savage, who, like all
writers of his period, was bitten with Druidical mania,
'from its proximity to Drucombe, that of some Druid.'
Whether Druid or warrior, the poor fellow was not
allowed to remain in his ancient resting-place. The
skeleton was re-interred in the parish churchyard at
Treborough (!), where, it is to be hoped, the contiguity
of Christian bodies does not make the pagan uncomfortable.

By a pretty rough scramble through this and an
adjoining wood we get into the steep road leading to
Treborough, passing some large slate-quarries, quite
recently abandoned, much to the sorrow of the neighbourhood, as they afforded employment to a large
number of men. The village has nothing of interest
to detain us, and the plain stuccoed church, with its low
tower, will not attract the ecclesiastical antiquary. The
country, however, is very pleasant : here a wild combe
carved in the face of the hills, here a softer fold ' dank
with heavy foliage.' In one of these, and a tremendously deep one it is, below the road leading across the
hills, reached by a path opposite a cottage called
Sminhays, an additional attraction presents itself in the
shape of a cascade.† A tiny stream, little more than a
runnel, after a course of less than a mile, slides over a
cliff of black slate. In summer the fall is insignificant,
though the accompaniments of nodding fern and over-

---

* Phelps' measurements are, 7 feet 6 inches by 2 feet 6 inches.
† A Celtic friend suggests that Treborough may owe its name to
this cascade—*tre berw*, the place of the waterfall.

CASCADE IN LEIGH WOODS. DRAWN BY A. DAWSON FROM A SKETCH
BY J. LL. W. PAGE.

hanging hazel render it at all times beautiful; but in winter it is truly imposing, standing out white as milk against the dark rock. In height it cannot exceed thirty-five or forty feet, though I fancy the 'bye-dwellers' imagine it much higher—an ancient inhabitant giving it as his opinion that it was 'main high.'

From this glen—Leigh Wood or Lincombe* is its name—to the deserted iron-mines is but a mile. The gaunt chimneys, the ugly pumping-houses, do not improve a landscape already rendered sufficiently dreary by the rows of ruinous cottages bordering the roadside. There is in particular a chapel, inscribed 'Beulah' whose blistering walls, boarded windows, and overthrown railings are a sad commentary on its title. A parish doctor told me he could remember the time when over one hundred families of miners occupied the village; now, with the exception of half a dozen cottages, let at next to nothing, the place is worse than Goldsmith's deserted village. Somehow, it is believed owing to the influx of iron-ore from Spain and the heavy expenses attending the carriage of the raw material to Watchet, and its transhipment to Wales, the undertaking did not pay. The Ebbw Vale Company ceased their operations, and labour sought fresh fields. The railway made from Gupworthy, four miles away to the westward, along the almost level tableland, down the Roadwater Valley to the sea, is almost deserted—only two trains per diem run now, and these only come as far as Combe Row, at the foot of the hills, carrying, of course, passengers alone—and silence reigns where, a dozen years since,

* The cascade is known as Lincombe Shutts, *i.e.* shoots.

the air resounded with the cheerful, if not always melodious, voice of commerce.

But how, someone may ask, did the trains of trucks get to the top of the hill, 1,000 feet or so above the sea. Let us approach that pile of slate débris on the edge of the slope, and we shall see. We look down a long incline cut through the woods—in places through the rock too—which, at a gradient of one foot in four, comes straight up to our heap from the station below, looking, at this elevation, no bigger than a box. Passengers for the hills are transferred from the train to a truck (which, by the way, might be more comfortably fitted), and drawn by a fixed engine to the summit. The sensation is rather curious than agreeable. One must lean well forward on the plank bench, or run the risk of toppling back into the dusty bottom of the impromptu vehicle. But the steep journey is made at last, and our truck runs over the top of the heap and emerges on the breezy hill.

No one will call the crown of the Brendon range interesting. From its commencement at Lype Hill, to Elworthy Barrows, some twelve miles, the elevation does not alter more than about 200 feet, and, with the exception of a narrow strip of heather running along some parts of the summit, and occasionally spreading over the slopes of a combe, Cultivation has claimed them for her own. Nor are there any very notable antiquities. There are occasional barrows; one of those on Lype Hill is seventy-four paces round, and nine high, with a shallow trench encircling it. Some have names, others not. There is Leather Barrow, for instance, not far from the iron-works, which, like Lether

Tor on Dartmoor, may owe its name to its steepness;
and there is Wiveliscombe Barrow—a long way from
the town, though; and again, Elworthy Barrows, which
are not barrows at all. By the side of a cart-road,
leading through the fields to Middleton Farm, is an
immense mass of pointed rock, eight feet high, known as
the Dunstone (probably the *Hill* Stone). It has been
questioned whether this was not a menhir, but it is like
no 'longstone' I have ever seen, and could certainly
never have been placed there by human agency. It is
simply a shapeless lump of natural rock, perhaps
exposed by denudation. The 'Naked Boy,' a somewhat similar, but much smaller, stone, a little further
west, by the side of a by-road, said to be part of the
ancient trackway leading from Combwich over the
Quantocks and Brendons to Devonshire, is evidently
of the same nature. It marks the boundary of two of
the hill parishes and of the Trevelyan estates.

Of course the prospect is delightful, though, unless
you attain a rising somewhat above the ordinary level, it
is scarcely possible to see that on both sides from the
same spot. And as we are more or less shut in
westward by the hills about Dunster, little beyond the
pretty bay of Blue Anchor, and the fertile vale
stretching away to the Quantocks, now quite close at
hand, is to be seen. The valley, through which the
unseen railway threads its way to Washford, is marked
by almost continuous lines of wooded hills. Haddon
Hill, near Dulverton, rises a few miles to the south,
and Dartmoor again rears its rugged walls in the misty
distance.

The minerals of these hills appear to have been

worked from very early times. Many ancient piles of
refuse have been found, particularly at Syndercombe
(which, in spite of spelling, is supposed to derive its
name from the scoriæ there found), while Roman coins
and mining implements have been discovered at Treborough and Luxborough.   .

From the incline we follow the road for another mile
to the Raleigh's Cross Inn, a large, but now rather
desolate, hostelry. In former days, before the
Barnstaple Railway was thought of, it was a favourite
house of call for drovers going to Taunton Market;
but the iron horse has changed all that. On the
edge of a triangular piece of grass, nearly in front of
the house, stand the remains of the monument from
which it takes its name—Raleigh's Cross. A rough
but massive base supports about two feet of an
octagonal shaft.

At the visit of the Somersetshire Archæological
Society in 1883, Mr. Beamer stated that he had heard
from Mr. Babbage, the aged steward of the Trevelyan
estates, to whom the story had been handed down from
his father and grandfather, ' that the cross was erected
when Nettlecombe was owned by the Raleighs, the
hill being then an open common, and traversed only by
pack-horses from Bampton to Watchet,' and that it 'was
fixed by the side of a dangerous bog, called the Snipe
Bog, in a field below, and to the north-west of where it
now stands, as a mark of danger and warning to
travellers to keep to the south side of it.' The bog is
still visible, but now partially drained. When the hill
was enclosed, about forty or fifty years ago, and a road

cut from Sticklepath Gate, the cross was standing in its original place, but, by order of Sir Walter Trevelyan, Mr. Babbage then removed it, and put it where it now is, as a boundary-stone parting the Trevelyan and Carew properties.*

This statement elicited a reply from Sir Charles E. Trevelyan, who stated the family tradition to be that the cross was erected by an ancestor, one Simon Raleigh, of Agincourt memory, and the last Raleigh living at Nettlecombe, in memory of his first wife, Joan, who was brought from Devonshire to Nettle-combe for burial. Its former position was at the cross-roads, and the body might very likely have rested there prior to interment. He recollected the cross being removed about fifty yards, and then restored to its original position at the cross-roads, and adds that 'when the enclosures were made on both sides, the lines of the old roads were so far departed from that the cross was left under a hedge on the north side of the new road from Bampton to Watchet.'†

In cutting through another hedge, or earth-bank, in this neighbourhood, the boundary between the parishes of Upton and Withiel, in November, 1847, a small earthen vessel was brought to light, containing eight coins—seven of brass and one of silver. The bank, a very ancient one, had been erected right across this deposit, which was two feet under ground. Two of the coins are in the collection of Mr. Spencer G. Percival, and are (1) a large but dilapidated brass of Hadrian, the

* Som. Arch. Soc., xxix., pp. 47, 48.
† *Ibid.*, xxxi., p. 74.

inscription nearly obliterated: obverse, laureated head of Trajan; reverse, figure of Fortuna. (2) A denarius of the same reign, in good preservation as to the inscription, but with one half missing. The obverse has IMP. CAES. NERVA TRAIAN, and a portion of a laureated head; the reverse, P. M. TR. P only, with part of a winged figure of Victory holding a garland.*

The Sticklepath above referred to is a very steep and rough hill, doubtless owing its name to the Anglo-Saxon *sticele*, steep. The name is common throughout the West of England, and is invariably associated with an abrupt ascent. In Devonshire the name is borne by a picturesque village right, under Cosdon Beacon on Dartmoor, from which a toilsome track winds up the hill. And every trout-fisher knows that a *stickle—i.e.*, a rapid in a stream caused by a fall in its bed—is a likely place for sport.

Did we descend this hill, we should, on reaching the valley, pass the great house and park of Nettlecombe, once the home of the Raleighs, who have given their name to the Raleigh aisle in the parish church, where lie several of their monuments. An opportunity, however, of visiting this pleasant combe will occur by-and-by.

We are now standing by the mutilated cross, and must, for the present, continue our exploration of the hills. There is, however, not a great deal more to see of this Brendon range. Another two miles between tall beech hedges, with rough fields or open moorland

* *Somerset County Gazette*, Sept. 9, 1882.

on either hand, and we mount a gentle hill (crossing at its foot the head waters of the Tone, or one of its tributaries) to Elworthy Barrows, the highest spot, *point* would be quite a misnomer, 1,283 feet above the sea. As we ascend, and pause to look back, we have a good view of Dunkery and other Exmoor heights, with a glimpse of Croydon, Grabhurst, and the coast ridge beyond Minehead. To see the Channel, however, it will be necessary to get the other side of the enclosure, whence a very fine view may be obtained. The 'soft-looking, wooded Quantocks' are now a pronounced feature in the landscape, sloping down from the lofty Fire Beacon Hill to the richly-wooded park of St. Audries, washed by the, alas! now somewhat dingy waters of the 'Severn Sea.'

Elworthy Barrows, or Burrows. as the country people pronounce the word, lie on the right of the road. That they are not tumuli at all, in the ordinary sense of the word, has been before stated, though even such an authority as Professor Boyd Dawkins said that 'he saw what *appeared* to be the remains of an old rampart, though it might be anything else.' How it can possibly be 'anything else' but a camp, I for one, fail to understand. The mounds are certainly, in several places, quite detached from the main line of rampart, but they all fit into the circle, and enclose an area of at least fifteen acres, with a diameter of about 825 feet. The rampart is very irregular, but in some places rises to ten feet or more. There can be little doubt that it is a Belgic-British camp, which was for some reason—perhaps because the fall of the hill was for some little distance practically nil—never completed.* On the south and west the fosse shows plainly. A stone celt, now in the Taunton Museum, was discovered here ; while, in a field adjoining, a solitary barrow, destroyed about 1833, disclosed a ring of stones encircling a quantity of ashes, among which was a stone or flint spear head—unfortunately not preserved.†

At this point, the termination of its most westerly spur, we say farewell to Exmoor. Strictly speaking, it may well be doubted whether it should be included in an account of the great moorland of West Somerset at all ; for at least two miles intervene between Lype Hill and the enclosures upon the slopes of Dunkery ; but perhaps it has as much right to be considered a part of Exmoor as have Croydon, Grabhurst, and the North Hill. At any rate, we are fortified in our classification by the important opinion of a great, though now no longer living, geologist, and, under the ægis of such an authority, feel that we cannot have greatly erred.

* An ingenious theory appears in Phelps' 'Hist. of Somerset.' He considers that the camp may have been hastily commenced to resist the onward march of Ostorius, and as hastily discontinued and abandoned on his retreat, or, rather, return to quell the insurgent Silures and Brigantes (*vide ante*, chap. iv.).

† *Somerset County Gazette*, Sept. 7, 1882.

CHAPTER XII

BETWEEN THE BRENDONS AND THE SEA

Hartrow—Willet Tor—British Urns—Combe Sydenham—The
Drake Cannon-ball—Stogumber—Monksilver—Nettlecombe—
Knap Dane—Castle Hill—Huish Barton—Roadwater Valley—
Cleeve Abbey—Chapel Cleeve.

FROM Elworthy Barrows the hills descend in long
slopes into the undulating country stretching down into
the valley of the West Somerset Railway and towards
the town of Taunton.   In this neighbourhood is much
pleasant scenery, and more than one interesting church,
manor-house, and cottage.   There is the quaint little
church of Elworthy, with its chancel set askew—typify-
ing, it is said, the position of the Saviour's head when
on the cross—two miles below, on the left, but still on
high ground—and Clatworthy, near which, overlooking
the Tone, is another large camp, called Castle Hill*—

* Castle (the British *Castell*) Hill is a very common name for
camps in West Somerset. Two miles south of this camp is another
earthwork, also called Castle Hill.   And there are at least three
others : one in the parish of Bathealton, another near Wiveliscombe, and a third—described later—in the parish of Nettlecombe.
The one near Clatworthy is supposed to have been occupied by the
Romans, as a protection for the miners at Syndercombe close by.

and Brompton Ralph, both pretty hamlets, far beneath on the right.   There is Hartrow Manor, a large modern antique mansion, erected about 150 years since on the site of an older sixteenth-century house, which has a noble hall, lighted by windows containing some fine heraldic glass, Flemish, Swiss and Bavarian, and interesting old armour; and the Jacobean house of Gauldon, in Tolland parish, which, though now a commonplace-looking farm, owns a large room with a richly ornamented ceiling and frescoes.   But all these lie somewhat beyond our beat.

There is, however, an outlying eminence, which should be ascended for the sake of the view which it commands.   This is the wooded knoll known as Willet Tor, crowned by an ornamental tower or ' folly.'   From it the whole of the Quantocks are visible from St. Audries to Kingston.   Looking towards the sea, the most distant church tower is that of Bicknoller; then in the valley, midway, is Stogumber; opposite is Crow-combe, close to the great pile of Crowcombe Court. Towards Taunton are the towers of Kingston, Bishops Lydeard, and Combe Florey.   The latter parish had for its pastor that most amusing of divines, Sidney Smith, and many a laughable story of his sayings and doings may still be picked up in the neigh-bourhood.   Behind is seen, close at hand, the tall bare tower of Brompton Ralph, and farther away the smoke of Wiveliscombe.   Beyond that, again, closing

Roman coins have been ploughed up within its area, which is now cultivated.   The shape is irregular, and it was probably originally Celtic.

the southern horizon, is the almost level range of Black-down, marked above Wellington by the tall obelisk erected to the memory of the Iron Duke.

In 1834 an interesting discovery was made near Willet. Within a circle of upright stones, six feet in diameter, the stones being about three feet in height, was found a large urn, full of fragments of burnt bones and ashes, and the remains of another. They are both British. The first, which I have myself seen, is in the possession of Mr. Blommart, of Willet House; the pieces of the other are in the collection of Mr. Spencer G. Percival, of Henbury Clifton.*

To reach the Quantocks is now an easy matter, the valley being but four miles across, and a road—cover-ing, however, a considerably greater distance, for these Somerset lanes wind like a labyrinth—will conduct us to their feet. But the time has not yet come. There is a good deal of an interesting nature down among these northern spurs of the Brendons, beyond Elworthy there, which we should be mistaken in passing by, and we will, therefore, descend to the thatched cottages of Rooksnest, and take the road westward.

This road, descending from the high ground near Elworthy, runs through the wooded bottom and on to Minehead, opening to view en route some of the most delightful combes this side of Exmoor. The first after leaving Elworthy is Combe Sydenham, a very deep and narrow vale, luxuriantly clothed with fine trees, and damp, even in summer, beneath the heavy foliage. It is watered by a bright trout stream, which, after feeding

* *Somerset County Gazette*, Sept. 7, 1882.

some pretty ponds, flows merrily past Combe Sydenham House, an ancient Elizabethan mansion close to
the road, and quite unmistakable, with its gabled tower,
about which the pigeons wheel in myriads, rising from
the centre of the house. The date, 1580, is carved
above the porch, which is further adorned with the
Sydenham and Stourton arms, much weatherstained,
and an inscription in old English letters as follows:

> 'Porta tuis semper Georgii generose patebo,
> Ingratis animis janua clausa patens.'

There is some remarkably fine tapestry in the drawing-
room, a large and lofty apartment, and other curiosities.
Combe Sydenham is haunted. The ghost is that of
Sir George Sydenham, a Royalist officer, who died in
1596. Every night he rides down the combe, somewhere between midnight and cockcrow. At one time,
too, he 'walked' the hall, but I understand that he has
not been seen of late years. Tradition does not give
him a very reputable character.

His daughter and heiress, Elizabeth, married Sir
Francis Drake. There is no record of the fact in the
parish registers, but the marriage settlement, dated
August 25, 1595, places the matter beyond doubt.
Some time prior to the marriage she adopted another
lover, assuming that Drake, who had been long absent,
was dead. But as she was about to confer her hand
on the new love, a 'cannon-ball' fell between her and
the gallant, effectually preventing the ceremony. It is
said to have been fired by the great circumnavigator
from the Antipodes, and, under the name of the 'Drake
cannon-ball,' is still preserved at Combe Sydenham.

It is a large polished ball of iron, a foot in diameter, and weighing 120 pounds. As Mr. F. T. Elworthy, from whom I first heard the story, remarks, it is no doubt a meteorite. That it is a heavenly rather than an earthly body is further shown in some information furnished by Mr. W. H. Greene to the eighth volume of the 'Western Antiquary.' Under the title 'A Curious Legend of Sir Francis Drake,' the author tells how Sir Francis and Mistress Sydenham plighted troth, and how Drake, saying that he might be away at sea for years, conjured her to be faithful, threatening that, if she wavered in her fidelity, he would send a token to assure her that the vengeance of Heaven would overtake perjury; how the other lover presented himself, and how, despairing of Drake's return, she consented to marry the substitute. In graphic language we are then told of the wedding-day, of the bridal party hesitating to leave the mansion in consequence of an impending thunderstorm, and of the impetuous bridegroom-elect, hurrying the lady forth to the horses. Then comes an awful peal of thunder, a ball glowing hot falls on the stones of the pavement, which split asunder, and rolls between the horrified pair. 'It is the token from Drake,' Elizabeth Sydenham cried. 'He lives! and has sent this fearful thing to reprove me for my inconstancy: I will not go to the church.' And she kept her word, and married Drake after all. Whether her second husband, William Courtenay, of Powderham Castle, was the rejected suitor, 'history,' says Mr. Greene, 'does not declare.' At the spot in Combe Sydenham Hall where the mysterious ball stopped, there it still remains, and there, according to vulgar tradition, will it ever be, utterly refusing all efforts to roll it elsewhere.

Two miles away, over the hill eastward, lies the village of Stogumber.   Combe Sydenham is in this parish, and its handsome church would have been the scene of the nuptials of Elizabeth and Drake's rival, had not the 'token' interfered. It is a large building in two styles of Perpendicular, though the tower appears of earlier date.   The arcade separating the nave and chancel from the north aisle is fine, and consists of five large and two smaller arches. All the pillars have beautifully carved capitals; on one are shields bearing symbols of the Crucifixion.   The columns of both the smaller arches are pierced with elegant arched openings forming a double hagioscope.   This only occurs in two other churches in England, if not the United Kingdom.   The arcade of the south aisle is much less ornate, two octagonal pillars, indeed, being of very rude design.   The chancel is rather gorgeous in colouring, but the reredos, representing a fine sculpture of the Ascension, is chaste and pleasing.   Under a canopy close by, between the Notley aisle—a portion of the south aisle—and the chancel, is the recumbent figure of the aforesaid Sir George Sydenham, and his two wives.   At the foot, in bas-relief, is a female figure engaged in prayer, facing what look like three mummies, but which probably represent infants.

The north, or Halsway, aisle was built by Cardinal Beaufort, whose seat, Halsway Manor, we shall pass by-and-by.   At the eastern end both of this and the south aisle were chapels.   Under a window is a fine brass to Margery Wyndham ; and this is the only monument of note. Every bench-end throughout the church is carved, some very handsomely.

The exterior of the building, owing to the sculptured battlements and gargoyles, has a peculiarly rich appearance. There is nothing interesting in the churchyard except a restored cross, decorated but heavy-looking.

Just beyond Combe Sydenham is Monksilver, pleasantly situated beneath a wooded hill, where the fallow deer may be seen grazing. It gets its name from a gift of the Manor of Silver (probably originally *silva*, a wood) to the Priory of Goldcliff in Monmouthshire, the donor being the then Lord of Stowey, Robert de Candos, who flourished about the time of the Conquest. A neat little Perpendicular church, with plain tower, but well-carved battlements and pinnacles adorning the nave and chancel, stands half-way up the hill. We shall notice among the gargoyles on the southern side an extraordinary representation of a mediæval dentist at work. The bench-ends are again a feature, and there is a good screen. The churchyard cross is remarkably handsome. It marks the grave of the late rector, the Rev. W. F. Chilcott, and to his memory it was restored twenty-five years since. At each angle of the socket stand statuettes representing the symbols of the Evangelists.

The road now follows a fairly level *strath* to Nettle-combe. The combe is on the left, and consists for the most part of the beautiful park of the Trevelyans, through which a road winds towards the hills, which

15

form an effective background. The fine manor-house of Nettlecombe Court—Tudor as usual—almost touches the church, an interesting building, mostly Perpendicular, with nave, chancel, north and south aisles. The nave is partly lighted by an Early English clerestory, and is divided from the aisles by good pillars with carved capitals. In the wall of the south, or Raleigh, aisle are two deep-arched Early English recesses, containing the recumbent figures of a Crusader, and of a knight and his lady. There are no inscriptions, but they are said to be the effigies of members of the family from which the aisle takes its name—once the owners of Nettlecombe Court. In the same aisle is the font, a very handsome piece of sculpture, each of the eight panels being filled with Scriptural scenes. The principal objects in the north aisle are the two windows of old stained glass, containing figures of saints. The pulpit is approached by two narrow arches, and a stair in the wall—doubtless the rood-stair. The nave possesses a few carved bench-ends.

A coffin-shaped slab of sandstone, part of an old tomb, is inserted in the outer wall of the north aisle. A raised cross is the only ornament; there is no inscription. The churchyard cross is of a kind very uncommon in West Somerset: it is a large Latin cross, and stands upon a massive calvary; the cross is covered with ivy, the base with hart's-tongue fern, and the eye is at once attracted by this picturesque object. Indeed, the whole grouping of mansion, church and gardens, with the park in the foreground and the wooded hills behind, is undoubtedly pleasing.

This neighbourhood is not without historical legend. As we ascend the hill to Fair Cross, we shall notice, just beyond some allotment gardens, a high round field; this is known as *Knap Dane*, and either here or hard by was made the discovery of human remains to which I have already referred.* It was while examining the surface of this and the adjoining field (which present nothing remarkable, save what may perhaps have been lines of earthwork, now nearly levelled by the plough) that an incident occurred, showing in a remarkable manner the extraordinary confusion which prevails in the uneducated mind with regard to names having a similar sound, though very far indeed from being synonymous. An old man was pointing out a field on the hillside across the valley to the south, on which some kind of inequality was plainly visible. 'It is a place where the Romans were,' he said, 'and they do say there was fighting; it be called Castle Hill, and the *Roman Catholics* had a castle there.' Perhaps I should have gently pointed out that Romans and Romanists were scarcely identical; but he was very old, and why disturb his cherished fictions? It would have been cruel.

Whether Castle Hill was a camp, Roman or other-wise, is extremely doubtful. Local legend speaks of fighting having taken place there, and one person thought that weapons had been dug up, but at what time and of what period no one knew. The field in which it is situated is on the slope above Huish Barton Farm, and the appearance in its centre of a raised

---

* *Ante*, Chapter IV.

mound, roughly square, is peculiar. The plough has played sad havoc with this eminence, but it still rises some four feet above the surface of the natural ground. There are no signs of entrances, and the enclosure within, if it can be called such, is level with the ramparts —levelled, probably, by artificial means. The area I should estimate at about an acre.

An interesting house is Huish Barton. The drawing-room, though low, has a wonderfully handsome ceiling, divided into deep rectangular panels, each decorated with ornaments of fruit or flower. The uninhabited portion was evidently at one time of some magnificence; there is a stately upper chamber—now, alas! decayed, and used as a wool store—with ornamented plaster ceiling and marble hearthstone. Over the wide fireplace is more plaster, with the date, 1698, in figures of fanciful shape. Of course there is a ghost, and I was shown a door in the corridor leading to this room, which, prior to the arrival of the present tenant, had not been opened for many years. He, however, rose superior to the dread of the 'lady in silk,' and nothing has happened to him yet.

Not far from Knap Dane the road drops to the hamlet of Tarr, otherwise *Torr*. On the way we shall get a glimpse of the long valley of Roadwater, running up to the Brendon Hills, and threaded by the grass-grown railway, down which a melancholy-looking train crawls dolefully to and from the little port of Watchet.

This narrow Roadwater Valley is finely wooded. High on either side of the railway rise the tree-clad hills, while the meadows are divided by a swift brook

—the same that makes the cascade in Leigh Wood—
until at the long village, which gives to the vale its
name, the stream from Chargot swells its flood, and
the blended waters follow the line to the sea. Between
Roadwater and Washford the hills become lower, and
presently the valley opens out into bright green
meadows, varied here and there by ancient orchards—
the 'Vallis Florida' of monkish records. In the midst
of these meadows, and close to the railway, rise the
crumbling walls of Cleeve.

Cleeve Abbey was founded just 700 years ago
by William de Romare, or Romara, youngest son
or nephew of William de Romare, Earl of Lincoln.
'This William, youngest son of the foreseid William
de Romare, and of the seid Luce hys wyff, found the
Abbey and Monastery of our seid blissed Lady of the
Cliff, in the foreseid countie of Somerset, in the nyneth
yere of the reigne of King Richard the First, late King
of England; and that by the hondes and oversight of
oone Hugh, then Abbat of the foreseyd Monastery, and
Abbey of Rewesby, the which stalled and made then
first Abbot of the foresyd Monastery of Cliff aforeseid
oone Raff, as hit apperith by old wretyngs in the seide
Abbey of Cliff.'*

The abbey had many benefactors besides the founder.
Richard, Earl of Cornwall, granted to the monks lands
in that county; Hubert de Burgh, land in Rugeham;
Reginald de Mohun and William de Mohun, lands at
Slaworth and Stortmanforde respectively; and King
Henry III., 'our manor of Branton in the County of

* MS. Cott., Tib. E. 8, f. 208.

Devon.' But the fraternity was never a very large one. According to the Rev. F. Warre (quoting Tanner), there were, shortly before the Reformation, seventeen monks, with an endowment of £155 10s. 5¼d. per annum, which, though a small sum in modern eyes, was in those days far more considerable. At the Dissolution William Dovell, the last abbot, had a pension of £26 13s. 4d.* Among the celebrated men who have been monks of Cleeve may be mentioned Hooper, Bishop of Gloucester, burnt with Cranmer and Latimer by ' Bloody ' Mary.

The grounds are approached by an old bridge across the Roadwater Brook, or, as it is here called, the Washford Brook, within which, at a distance of a few yards, stands the thirteenth-century gatehouse. The lofty entrance archway is flanked by buttresses, one of them, a hideous modern addition, evidently erected to prop the decaying walls. Immediately over the arch is a Latin inscription, ' Porta patens esto nulli claudaris honesto,' which may be rendered, ' Gate, stand open; nor be shut to any honest man.' Above this is a square-headed Perpendicular window, unglazed; and over this, again, in the gable, are two niches, the lower empty, and the upper containing the figure of the Virgin and Child.

Passing through a passage, forty-six feet long by thirteen feet wide (and which was once arched through its entire length, and has over it a large guest-chamber, and at its side two arched recesses, supposed to have been the entrances to stables) we reach the inner side of the gatehouse, which has above the crown of the arch a

* Dugdale's ' Monasticon.'

rectangular medallion, with the name of Dovell, the last abbot, another square-headed window, and in the gable three niches, the central one canopied and containing a crucifix. This front appears to be of later date than the general fabric, and is thought to have been constructed by Abbot Dovell.[*]

A wall runs from the gatehouse to the moat, which extends nearly to the brook, and which, with another line of wall, protected the abbey, its mill, two fish-ponds and farm 'against any sudden attack of robbers, a precaution which the state of society at the end of the twelfth century must have rendered very useful to a body of foreign ecclesiastics.'

The enclosure, through which runs the old millstream, has some fine sycamore and walnut trees, almost concealing the modern farmhouse erected within the precincts. Crossing it, we enter the remains of the fifteenth-century cloisters, now only existing on the western side of the quadrangle, around which are grouped the refectory, the dormitory and the south wall of the church. The refectory, said to be the work of Dovell, is a magnificent upper chamber, fifty-one feet long and twenty-two feet broad, lighted by nine beautiful Perpendicular windows, five on the north and four on the south, and reached from below by a stone staircase. On the eastern wall is an old fresco of the Crucifixion,

[*] This is Mr. Warre's opinion. Mr. Buckle, the architect, who accompanied the Somersetshire Archæological Society in 1889, thought that the whole of the upper story of the building was Dovell's work, and that the figure of the Virgin and Child, of earlier date than the sixteenth century, had been utilized by him.

and on the southern, up a few steps, the recess where, while his brethren dined,

> 'The preacher droned from the pulpit,
> Like the murmur of many bees,
> The legend of good St. Gutblac,
> And St. Basil's homilies.'

The roof is of Spanish walnut, exquisitely carved, and resting on corbels of angels. Its wonderful state of preservation is accounted for by the fact that this wood is never attacked by worm.

It will doubtless be remarked that the position of this refectory is, for a Cistercian abbey, somewhat unusual, the ordinary position being at right angles to the cloisters, as at Beaulieu and Rievaulx. The flooring of the earlier refectory, to the south of the present building, has lately been unearthed. It is laid in encaustic tiles, representing the arms of certain benefactors.

Descending into the quadrangle, and entering an Early English door, we mount another staircase and enter the dormitory, over 137 feet in length, and twenty-four in breadth, now divided by a rough modern wall. The windows here are lancet-shaped and small, a good thing for the monks, as in the days before glazing the shutters proved a very inefficient protection. A door and staircase communicated with the church. Under the north end lies the sacristy. The circular opening in the eastern wall, formerly supposed to be for the transit of a monk's body into the burial-ground, was probably a window, as there are traces of an altar beneath it.

Further on, beyond a small chamber, is the entrance into the vaulted chapter-house, having on either hand a beautiful Early English window with shafts of blue lias. Further south, beyond the slype, is the monks' common room, also lighted by Early English windows.

Outside the north wall of the quadrangle was the church, a fine large building, now, with the exception of the foundations, no longer existent. It is said to have been ' 161 feet in length, of the purest Cistercian type, consisting of a nave of five bays with cylindrical pillars, fragments of which remain, a low central tower, short transepts, each with two square chapels, and a shallow, aisleless presbytery.' The style appears to have been Transitional and Early English. Many of the encaustic tiles which formed the floor still remain, and are, except when under examination, carefully covered with loose earth. The arms of Richard, Earl of Cornwall (commonly called King of the Romans), Clare, Mohun, and others, are as plain as when the tiles were first fired.

And here our account of Cleeve Abbey must end. Those who desire more minute details will find their curiosity more than satisfied by a perusal of the late Professor Walcott's little brochure, or the interesting paper of the Rev. F. Warre.* From both I have derived considerable assistance.

At the Dissolution the abbey met with the usual fate of such religious houses :

> 'Bluff Harry broke into the spence,
> And turned the cowls adrift.'

---

* 'Old Cleeve Abbey,' a paper published in vol. vi. of the 'Proceedings of the Somersetshire Archæological Society.' I believe a very exhaustive account is to be contributed to the volume for the present year. The author is Mr. Buckle.

It was granted to Robert Earl of Sussex. The present owner, Mr. G. F. Luttrell, of Dunster Castle, deserves, and has, the thanks of the community for the care he manifests in the preservation of the beautiful old place. No longer, as was the case within the writer's memory, are the cloisters used as cattle-sheds and other buildings devoted to the storing of farm produce; but swept, if not garnished, the archæologist can examine traceried window or Early English doorway without clambering over sheaves of straw or tumbling backwards on to a pile of apples.

An ancient pitched path led, indeed in several places still leads, from the gatehouse nearly to Chapel Cleeve, and in all probability formerly extended to the more ancient chapel of St. Mary le Cliff, which once stood on the cliff to the east of Blue Anchor, but of which no vestige now remains. It was destroyed by a landslip in the reign of Edward IV., the only relic uninjured being an image of the Virgin. From an interesting pamphlet entitled 'Past Times in Old Cleeve,' by Mr. Clement Kille, we learn that ' in recognition of what was then thought to be the miraculous providence of God in thus preserving the image intact, King Edward IV. granted a charter establishing a market and fair, the profits of which were to go to the support of the new chapel, which David Juyner, then Abbot of Old Cleeve, at once commenced to erect further inland at what we know as Chapel Cleeve.' Chapel Cleeve is a modern mansion, in which are incorporated the remains of this later building, which contain one or two good Perpendicular windows and an ancient fireplace. At the angle of the house adjoining this chapel is a large ivy-mantled archway, in which the sockets of hinges still remain. To what this archway led I have never heard suggested; perhaps another building, which may have served as a hospitium, flanked it, and the gate opened into a yard or quadrangle, around which lesser buildings were placed. This is, however, pure surmise, and there are not wanting those who think that the existing fragment was itself a hospitium, and question whether a chapel, in the ordinary sense of the word, ever existed at all. These doubters cannot, however, have seen a copy of the charter above mentioned,* which, after reciting that divers miracles had been worked in the former chapel, and that it—'by reason of an in-cessant abundance of rain and mighty down-flood of waters horribly fell, and in falling had entirely pros-trated, cast down and shaken to the ground the same chapel'—and the miraculous preservation of the image, refers to the erection of another chapel (*aliam Capellam*) 'in a certain other place within the precincts of their aforesaid manor, that the memory of the said blessed and glorious Virgin may in the same place, by the de-voted and faithful servants of Christ, be honourably held in praise and veneration, as it used to be of old.'

* Published in the 'Proc. Som. Arch. Soc.,' vol. vi., p. 43, where also a copy of the original Latin document may be seen

CHAPTER XIII

ALONG THE COAST TO WATCHET

The Monks' Path—Old Cleeve—A Curious Epitaph—Blue Anchor —Marshwood Farm—Watchet—Dawes Castle—St. Decuman— Monuments and Epitaphs — A Resurrection — Williton — An Imitated Monument—Doniford.

AT Washford the railway is reached, and we may take train to Williton for the Quantocks. No one, however, will regret the longer route by Blue Anchor Cliff to Watchet, half a dozen miles full of interest. Let us, then, abandon the railway, and pass over the hill to the village of Old Cleeve, by a road which practically follows the Monks' Path.

Up some steps, 'Cobbler's Steps,' I think they are called, and into a steep field we climb, at once coming upon a fragment of the ancient way. Presently, when we reach the lane, it becomes more defined, while over the brow, known as Cliddons,* there is a long and remarkably well-preserved portion, serving, indeed, as a causeway. On the very top is the base and stump of a ruined cross, in former days directing the wayfarer to the church of Old Cleeve, just beneath. The view,

* A corruption of Cleeve Down.

descending, is very beautiful. Through the branches
stretching from the tall hedges appears the square
massive tower of the church, rising above the lowly
thatched cottages at the foot of the abrupt descent.
As a background spreads the dark amphitheatre of hills,
Conegar in the foreground, Grabhurst behind, Dunkery
far away on the left, Minehead near at hand, on the
right thrusting out an arm that embraces the sweep of
Blue Anchor Bay.

The church is well worthy of examination. It is
built on the side of the hill, and I can well remember
the day when the nave, following the fall of the ground,
sloped boldly from the west door to the chancel. But
the 'restoration' has changed all that, though there still
appears a slight, a very slight, rise. The tower is en-
riched by a broad band, or string course, of plain shields,
which is again repeated over the west door. Its
breadth, for a Perpendicular tower, is remarkable. The
interior consists of nave, chancel—handsomely decorated
—and south aisle. The cradle roof of the nave has
oaken ribs, supported by angel corbels. Each angel
grasps a shield, painted with the cross of St. George.
As St. Andrew is the patron saint, it will occur to most
that *his* symbol would have been more appropriate.
There is handsome carving, too, in the sloping roof of
the aisle. A hagioscope or squint may be seen in the
chancel wall on the right side of the arch, and in the
northern wall of the nave an arched recess, containing
the recumbent figure of an unknown layman of the
fifteenth century. The east and west windows are
filled with stained glass, the gift of the Halliday

family, whose mansion of Chapel Cleeve is not far distant.

In the churchyard is the tall shaft of a cross. Some sculptured portion of the head still remains. It stands on a lofty calvary, and is, as usual, octagonal. The epitaph-hunter will find, almost beneath its shadow, as quaint an inscription as that afforded by any God's acre in the country. It is cut on the tombstone of one George Jones, who died in 1808, at the age of sixty-seven. As may be inferred from the words, the deceased was by trade a blacksmith. The verse runs thus :

> ' My Sledge and Hammer lie reclin'd,
> My Billows, too, have lost their wind.
> My Fire's extinct, my Forge decay'd,
> And in the Dust my Body's laid.
> My Coal is burnt, my Iron's gone,
> My Nails are drove, my Work is done.'

It will be noted how the local pronunciation of ' bellows' appears upon the stone.

Below the church we again take up the Monks' Path, which crosses a field to the highway, where it is finally lost. The road passes the old sixteenth-century farm-house of Binham and the picturesque lodge of Chapel Cleeve, and, ascending the hill, skirts the woods at the back of the house, and drops again to Blue Anchor—a mere handful of houses on the edge of the sea, here bounded by a great bank of pebbles bristling with heavy piles. The rising ground behind is the spot whence Turner painted his somewhat exaggerated picture of Dunster Castle. The prospect of mountain, strand, and sea was, and is, one would have thought, grand enough to enable the artist for once to dispense with artistic license.

Between Blue Anchor and Carhampton is Marshwood, formerly a manor-house of the Luttrells, now a farm. In the porch are two extraordinary plaster bas-reliefs: the one, a representation of Abraham—*in the dress of a knight of the sixteenth century*—preparing to sacrifice Isaac; the other showing a man in like costume bound to a post, and pelted by a crowd. In one upper room is a plaster overmantel, with the Luttrell arms flanked by two men; in another, a nude figure holding a couple of hounds, and with stags on either side.

The road to Watchet ascends the hill, and runs along the top of the ridge, having the sea on one hand and the wide vale on the other. There are many pretty peeps down through the broken cliffs to the water, or through gates in the hedges towards the Brendon and Rodhuish Hills. The Quantocks rise straight ahead, their highest point, Willsneck, away to the south-east, looking anything but the height it really is; while the fine Fire Beacon Hill, rising above the deep glen of Weacombe, looks far more lofty, instead of being, as is the case, nearly 250 feet lower. Presently we turn a corner, and the outskirts of Watchet come into view, the fine church of St. Decuman, across the valley, looking down upon the ugly buildings of the paper-mills, and the rows of cottages that stretch up the hill eastward.

The whole of this little seaport may be viewed from the top of the hill by the limekiln, whose dilapidated walls, perched on the summit of the cliff, look at a distance like a ruined fortress. With the exception of the harbour, consisting of an eastern pier of stone and a western breakwater of wood, there is nothing very picturesque about it. The entrance is marked by a small lighthouse. Part of the harbour was constructed by Sir W. Wyndham, Queen Anne's Secretary of State for War, whose descendants, the Earls of Egremont, had their seat at Orchard Wyndham, a picturesque old manor-house near Williton. The title recently became extinct, but the property and much land in this locality still remain in the family.

The present is a favourable opportunity for relating how this Sir W. Wyndham, in the succeeding reign, managed to elude the officers who, on account of his Stuart proclivities, were sent to arrest him. It was in 1715, in the dawn of an autumn morning, that the *posse* arrived with the warrant for the apprehension of this suspected adherent of the Pretender. Sir William, throwing on his dressing-gown, descended to meet them, and was at once claimed as prisoner. However, on his stating that his coach would be ready at seven to convey the party, they allowed him to return to his room to dress, and, it is almost needless to add, saw him no more. The crafty knight slipped out at the rear of the premises, and, adopting the disguise of a divine, maintained his liberty for some time. Ultimately, however, he surrendered, and was sent as prisoner to the Tower, whence, after a few months' confinement, he returned on bail to his home.*

The trade in iron ore has ceased since the closing

* Murray, p. 448.

of the iron-mines on Brendon Hill, but there is still enough in flour, timber, and paper from the mills up the valley to draw a few small coasters to the port.

Mention has already been made of the ancient history of Watchet.* This limekiln may, perhaps, mark the spot of a fight consequent upon one or other of the Danish descents referred to in the Anglo-Saxon Chronicle. When excavating for the kilns, a quantity of human bones was discovered, and quite recently others were laid bare by the breaking away of a portion of the cliff. These remains were reinterred higher up the field by the lime-burner, who declined handing any of them over to an antiquary unless he guaranteed their burial in the parish churchyard. Like the workmen who discovered the skeleton in the kistvaen in Langridge Wood, he appears to have thought that they demanded, not exactly Christian, but some kind of burial. At all events, he considered, with a respect for the dead which does him credit, that these bones, whether of Briton, Saxon, or heathen Viking, deserved more decent treatment than they would have, perhaps, met with at the hands of the curious. No weapons, however, have been found.

The spot is known as Dawes Castle. The sea has doubtless swallowed up the greater part of any earth-

* Its ancient name is said to have been Veched. What this name means I do not know, but it is probable that it took it from the now nameless brook—the same as that which flows down the Roadwater Valley. Washford (on this same brook) is called in ancient documents *Wachetforde*. Watchet also appears as *Weced*, *Weced-poort*, *Wecheport*, *Wesedport* and *Weseffort*. *Vide* Camden's 'Britannia,' Gough's ed., 1806.

16

work there may have been, but I think I could trace considerable remains of a rampart on the southern or landward side, just above the road, and in this the late owner of the field agreed with me. It is merely a segment of a circle, and is now full of the stumps of thorn-bushes. Were it not for its shape, I should have hesitated to regard it as more than an old hedge; indeed, there are indications, where the line breaks near the cliff on the western side, which make a positive opinion somewhat doubtful. Along the cliffs towards Blue Anchor, which are here very irregular and clothed with coppice, is a cover now called 'Warrens.' A local legend says that this is a corruption of the ancient name *War End*, and at this spot the fight, presumably Celtic,* which commenced at Battlegore, near Williton, came to an *end*. I give the story without comment.

Some have thought Dawes (or Daw's) a contraction of Danes. But the ancient beacons were called *Dawns*, and it is more probable that Dawes Castle, as well, perhaps, as more likely-sounding Danesborough, owe their names to the signal-fires that once blazed upon their summits.

Of modern warfare Watchet has known little; still, it was, to a limited extent, mixed up with the war between King and Parliament, as the following extract from the life of Blake† will show : 'The King's party

---

* *Vide ante*, Chapter IV.

† 'The History and Life of Robert Blake, Esq., of Bridgwater, etc., written by a gentleman bred in his family.' *Vide* articles by Somersetiensis, pp. 145, 227, vol. i., ' Notes and Queries for Somerset and Dorset.'

in Wales had sent a Ship from thence to Watchet;
what its Loading was is not mentioned, but the Tide
being at Ebb, and the passage for Horse made thereby
commodious, Captain Popham's Troop, then on the
Coast, rode into the Sea, and attacked the men aboard
with a brisk Fire from their Carbines, which soon did
such Execution among the Welch Gentry, that they
did their utmost to weigh and be gone, but Popham's
Troopers plyed them so thick with their Carbine Shot,
that, to save their Lives, they Surrendered the Ship and
themselves. The greatest Rarity of all which is, that a
Ship in the Sea was taken by Troop of Horse; for
the Troopers rode into the Water, their Horses Breast-
deep, to come near enough to fire effectually at the
Enemy.'

We now wend our way to St. Decuman's Church.
The position is unusua.ly commanding, and this church
'set on a hill' is a conspicuous object from both land
and sea. Like St. Dubritius, St. Decuman was a
Welshman, or, at any rate, crossed from Wales into
Somerset. His method of transit was, to say the least
of it, peculiar. He crossed upon a faggot (some say a
hurdle, others a *cloak !*). His only companion appears
to have been a cow, who 'of her own accord accompanied him in all his wanderings and fed him with her
milk.' On this hill St. Decuman lived a hermit until he
met with martyrdom. He was beheaded—when, lo !
a miracle. The saint took up his head, and bore it to
a spring, where he washed away the blood. Whether
he then interred his trunk, together with the decapitated
member, we are not told. There seems some reason,

16—2

however, for believing that he lived some time headless, for a variation of, or addition to, the legend asserts that he swam the Channel with his head under his arm !—it is presumed on his return journey to Wales.

In architecture the church is mainly Perpendicular, though there exists Early English work in the chancel. The oaken ribs of the waggon roof of the nave are supported by angel corbels standing on brackets, and holding shields, some with armorial bearings. The arms of Clare are, as at Cleeve Abbey, conspicuous, and the patch of encaustic tile in the chancel floor will also remind us of those at the Abbey of ' Vallis Florida.' There are the remains of a screen, plainer in character than those of most churches hereabouts, and made hideous near the centre by an intruding blunt arch, I believe formerly part of the Egremont pew. Some of the pillars have niches. 'Iconoclastic rage' has emptied most of them; but one still has an ecclesiastical dignitary in each of the four flutings, while behind the pulpit a pillar is adorned with the effigies of St. George slaying the dragon, and a bishop.

But the most interesting detail is the brasses. The first commemorates in lengthy verse the virtues of Sir John Windam and Lady Elizabeth, his wife, who died in 1571. The inscriptions, surmounted by full-length figures of the deceased, are let into the top of a table monument standing beneath a canopy on the north side of the chancel. Behind this, under the east window of the north aisle, are more brasses to the same family— the spelling of whose name is very various. In a dark slab in the wall are the brazen effigies of Sir John and

Lady Florence Windham, who died in 1572 and 1596 respectively. Both figures are represented in full dress, and are about half life-size. Armorial bearings further adorn the stone. Beneath the brass recording the names of the deceased is another brass, bearing a curious triplet, in which the speakers are the husband, the wife, and Fate. It runs as follows:

MARITUS	When changeless Fate to death did change my life
	I prayd it to bee gentle to my wife
VXOR	But shee who hart and hand to thee did wedd
	Desired nothing more then this thie bedd
FATVM	I brought y⁰ soules that lınckt were each in either
	To rest above y⁰ Bodıes here togeıther

Side by side with this are other brasses. These are embossed and gilded, and are half-length portraits of John Windham and Joan his wife, who died in 1645 and 1633 respectively. They are also accompanied by armorial brasses, and there is a long Latin inscription.

The last is in the chancel floor, in front of the altar rails; it represents the full-length figure of Edmund Windham, who died in 1616.

I know no country church so well supplied with these memorials of the dead as that of St. Decuman. And there is an unusual amount of finish in the work, which those familiar with ancient brasses will at once recognise. The details of the dresses of the period are cut with great nicety, and form an imperishable record of the costumes worn by our forefathers of the sixteenth and seventeenth centuries. The poetical effusions, too, are a feature, though this is not confined to monuments in brass. The more humble stone is favoured in a similar manner; one, a flag in the chancel, close to the brass last mentioned, is specially noticeable, expressing in somewhat forcible terms the disappointment of a loyal Wyndham left, like too many others, unrewarded by King Charles II. It commemorates the sufferings of Sir Hugh, who died in 1671, son of the Governor of Bridgwater, and one of the six hostages exacted by Fairfax at the surrender of that town, and announces that

> ' Heere lies beneath this ragged stone
> One more his Princes then his owne
> And in his martered Fathers warrs
> Lost Fortune Blood gained nought but scarrs
> And for his sufferings as rewarde
> Had neather countinance or regard
> And Earth affording noe releafe
> Is gone to Heaven to ease his greefe.'

The use of 'then' for 'than' will be noticed both in this epitaph and in that beneath the brasses of Sir John and Lady Florence.

The principal stone monuments are to be found in the north aisle. There is a large one inserted in the wall, where are represented, life-size, the kneeling forms of the brothers Henry and George Windham, who died in 1613 and 1624, and another to William Wyndham, who died in 1683. Standing beneath the first is a handsome table monument to the late Earl of Egremont, covered with a rich slab of blue marble.

As we depart we shall notice, close to the south door, the font, which is supported by a carved column, the basin being upheld by angels. In the churchyard is a tall cross lately restored. It is octagonal, with a small ornate head, and stands on a rough calvary. The grave-stones present us with several curious epitaphs. The first is on an exciseman, and is often quoted ; though I must confess that, except in its good sense, a quality not always conspicuous in monumental in‧ scriptions, I see nothing very remarkable about it :

> ‘ Praises on tombs are trifles vainly spent ;
> A man's good name is his own monument.’

Another, recording the death of Betty, wife of Richard Hales, who died in 1819, is far more curious, and reads at first very much like a conundrum :

> ‘ You now that weep and at my grave attend
> Within these walls was made your dearest friend
> At eighteen months a child no more a wife
> For that dear babe I did resign my life.’

The nautical element is well represented. No less than three graves have the whole or part of the following :

> ‘ Tho Borus blast and Neptune's waves
>   Have toss'd me to and fro
> In spite of both by God's decree
>   I harbour here below
> Where I do now at anchor lay
>   With many of our fleet
> Yet once again I must set sail
>   Our Saviour Christ to meet.’

This is from the tomb of Thomas Sully, who died in 1824. Another close by has the same, except that the plural is substituted for the singular, while the third adopts the first verse only, and this with a slight variation.

A very quaint epitaph was, until the late restoration (when it was found to be too much broken to be pieced together) in the church. It is a good instance of the forced rhyming and playing upon words of two centuries ago.

HEERE UNDERNEATH THIS STONE
INTERR'D DOTH LYE
THE CORPSE OF THOMAS NORRIS
ESQ BY
FIVE OF HIS CHILDREN FOUR
SONNS DAUGH^R ONE
TWO THOMS TWO JOHNS
ELIZABETH ALONE
SOME DY'D BEFORE AFTER
HIM SOME ALL MUST
HE DYD ABOUT Y^E TENTH
DAY OF AUGUST
1650 AGED 44
DEATH IS A CHANGE HOW SMAL A CHANGE IS HIS
BEFORE HE WAS NORRIS & NOW NOT IS
HE NOR IS NOR IS NOT SINCE GOD & FAME
HE DEAD ETERNIZE BOTH HIS SOUL AND NAME

Beneath the church, on the margin of the stream, is the old manor-house of Kentisford. It is now a farm, but the lofty rooms, porch, and Tudor windows plainly show that it was once a mansion. In this house resided one of the Wyndhams, and from it the body of his wife was borne to its last resting-place (as was supposed) at St. Decuman's. But in the middle of the night the lady returned clad in cerements, doubtless very much to the consternation of the household. A wicked sexton had entered the vault, bent upon annexing to his own use the jewellery of the dead. Finding a valuable ring immovable by ordinary means, he resorted to extra-

ordinary ones, and, drawing forth his knife, proceeded
to sever the finger from the hand.   This awoke the lady
from her trance, and, rising suddenly, she passed the
horrified sinner, left the vault, and returned to Kentisford.*   Her image, and those of two children, one of
them born almost immediately after this miraculous
escape from living burial, may be seen carved upon one
of the bench-ends in the pretty little cruciform church
of Sampford Brett, two miles distant beyond Williton.

Nothing is to be gained by descending the landward
side of the hill to Williton, a large straggling village
lying in a shallow valley, with a background of cultivated hill and dale.   Its chantry chapel, built by
Robert, brother of Reginald Fitz-Urse, one of Becket's
murderers, retains few marks of the period of its
erection, and the heavy shaft of the mutilated cross
hard by its doors, and of another by the Egremont
Hotel, are not worth turning from our route to inspect.
By the way, the assassins who delivered their master
from ' this pestilent priest ' appear to have been well
represented in this part of Somerset ; the vestry of the
church of Sampford Brett contains the recumbent
effigy of another—Richard le Bret, or le Brito, which in
a former day stood under a canopy—now removed—
in the north transept.

It is now pretty generally known that the stone in

* There is some doubt as to the attempted cutting of the lady's
finger, though none as to the felonious intention ; for another
version states that the sexton *found* her alive, and liberated her.
Perhaps the cut finger addition—if an addition—is to be found in
a somewhat similar story related of a London church, where the
sexton actually did draw blood.

the wood at Blackdown, behind Orchard Wyndham, with its inscription to Julia Martima, is a forgery, and a forgery without even the merit of accuracy. The original stone is at Ellenborough in Cumberland. The fraud, if such it can be called, was exposed by Mr. W. George, of Bristol, one of our most untiring antiquaries. The people about Williton call it '*Mother Shipton's Tomb*'!

We have diverged. Let us now descend the hill from St. Decuman's to Watchet, and follow the road by the coast to the hamlet of Doniford—*the ford of the hill*—at the foot of the Quantock slopes. Here, over a well, is the base of another cross, though so dilapidated that the casual wayfarer would scarcely notice it. We cross the stream, a large brook referred to by Leland, and at once begin to climb towards the ferny downs which 'renne in crestes from Quantok-Hedde toward Tauntoun.'

CHAPTER XIV

THE QUANTOCKS—THE LANDWARD SIDE

'Away to the Quantocks come wander with me,
As fleet as the wild deer, as blithe as the bee.
The heather is blooming on Cothelstone's crest ;
The bracken is waving o'er Bagborough's breast.

STEPHENSON.

'CITIZEN SAMUEL, this is the very place to talk treason
in.' 'Nay, Citizen John, it is a place to make one
forget the necessity of treason.' There are few lovers
of nature who will not agree that Coleridge was right
in this reply to Republican Thelwall, who thought a
wild spot on the Quantocks a suitable place for
seditious utterances. The cheerful beauty of the
Quantocks, as one who is now no more* describes the

---

* The Rev. W. L. Nicholls, of Woodlands, near Holford, whose
little book, 'The Quantocks, and their Associations,' though very
brief, contains much interesting information about the earlier days
of the 'Lake Poets.' He died in the summer of last year.

spirit of this lovely range, should not induce thoughts of discontent and rebellion. Rather let the man who thinks he has reason for girding at the powers that be, retire to some less happy spot—the central morasses of Dartmoor, for instance—where he may brood undisturbed over the supposed unsatisfactory state of the country, encouraged in his humours by the ungenial waste around. But the Quantocks, with their waving bracken and glowing heather, their far-reaching combes and wooded glens, are no refuge for unappreciated patriots. Nature is too strong.

The end at which we have now arrived—the seaward end—is to my mind immeasurably the finest. Here the hills rise steep and sudden from the fertile vale ; here heather, rather than tree, is king ; here, in short, is wildness and freedom that will be sought in vain where the heights about Cothelstone sink down towards Kingston and Broomfield into cultivated or wooded undulations. Here, too, we find the nearest approach to peaks, for although no hill of the Quantocks assumes the form of a true cone, not a few crests between St. Audries and Willsneck are in their abrupt fall westward more or less mountains in miniature. Leaving, therefore, any further remarks anent the poets who have done not a little to make them famous, until we approach their former dwelling-places, let us set our faces against the long, rather than steep, hill which is nowadays the natural approach to their solitudes.

Except the view in our rear, which every moment grows in extent and beauty, there is nothing in particular to arrest our attention until we reach St. Audries.

There is, indeed, a small archæological item in a field on the left, between the lane and the high-road coming up from Williton, and on a farm known as Rydon; but this need hardly detain us. It is a large circular tumulus, bearing the extraordinary name of Bloody Pate. It has never been opened.

Crossing the high-road, then, we ascend a rough lane through the hamlet of Staple, and are, in a few moments, on the moorlands once more. And now stop and look back, or rather look down.

Immediately beneath is the beautiful park of St. Audries, undulating down to the sea. Here and there the gleam of some tree-environed lakelet catches the eye, while life is added to the scene by the troops of fallow deer resting under the tall elms, or browsing peacefully on the verdant slopes. The mansion, a large handsome pile, is modern, but it contains a rare collection of antiquarian objects, collected by the owner, an enthusiastic archæologist. To us, who are, perhaps, chiefly interested in local relics of bygone days, the collection of British antiquities will prove most interesting. These consist of portions of swords and sheaths, daggers and knives, leaf-shaped and barbed spearheads—the latter, I believe, unique; the British Museum, at any rate, cannot match them— more than a score of celts, of sections square or oval; palstaves, gouges, and a disc of molten metal. All these were discovered in Wick Park, on the Fairfield Estate, to the east of the Quantocks.

Above the house, just under the trees, there stands the perfect Gothic Church of St. Etheldreda—commonly

known as St. Audries, the parish church of West
Quantoxhead—with its polished stone pillars and carved
capitals, erected within the last few decades on the site
of a more ancient building, whereof no traces remain.
In the churchyard the base and stump of a weathered
cross will alone attract the antiquary.

The eye follows the coast-line to Minehead, whose
white cottages are seen clustering at the base of the
great North Hill, ten miles away. In the middle distance the upper houses of Watchet are also visible,
dominated by the dark tower of St. Decuman's. In
countless undulations of grass, corn, and timber, the
fertile land stretches to the towered knoll of Conegar,
and the fine forms of Grabhurst and Croydon, over
which, a paler blue, looms Dunkery. More to the
south lie the Brendon Hills, separated from us by the
deep wide valley we have before so often seen, out of
which rise more than one church-tower. Where it
opens into country less confined, the smoke of
Williton will be observed half concealing the long
line of cottages.

And now upwards again towards the pole marking
the summit of Fire Beacon Hill. We pass the dark
woods that climb the western slope of Staple Plains, as
the level piece of moor hereabouts is named, and presently emerge on the brow of a deep glen—Weacombe.
Late summer is the time to see Weacombe. Not only
is this brow, but the steep wall of the combe, rich as a
Turkey carpet with the golden furze, the purple heather,
the fading bracken. In the hundreds of miles of moorland tramped, I do not know that I have ever seen any

ST. AUDRIES CHURCH. DRAWN BY ALFRED DAWSON.

of Nature's colouring so vivid as that upon this hillside.
Of Weacombe must a well-known local writer on rural
scenery* have been thinking when he wrote thus:
'Then the low whortleberry-bushes, with but gleaning
left of their damson-coloured fruit, are rich in their
scarlet-splashed foliage. Then the ripe green of the
seas of bracken is diversified with chrome and ochre,
with here and there an oasis in their midst, a vivid
emerald lawn of mountain turf, with, it may be, the
green eye of a tiny lakelet reflecting the still heaven
above; or down the hillside, the bright, narrow line of
mossy green, which traces the course of a streamlet
oozing out of the rock. And what can be said of the
heather in its glory? The splendour of its purple and
rose, with masses of the golden gorse interspersed—a
carpet is a poor thing to which to compare it; but it
does overspread the hillside and the tableland with rich-
ness of deep velvet-pile glowing from the loom of the
summer.

> ' " These are words,
> Their beauty is their beauty." '

Standing now by the ruined cairn on the hilltop, we
have a repetition of the view from below, only wider.
For now is again seen the long extent of Channel,
the distant Mendips, the terraces of Burnham, overlooking the mud-flats at the mouth of the winding Parret.
We look down upon a great part of the country lying
between our hills and the inland port of Bridgwater,

---

* The author of the 'Harvest of a Quiet Eye.' ' The lakelet' and
' the bright line of mossy green ' are very distinguishing features of
Weacombe.

a tract dotted with villages, and we see the hilltops stretching away towards dark Willsneck, loftiest of them all. There is camp-crowned Danesborough, here the bald brow above Bicknoller, here barrow-crested Thorncombe, just concealing the top of more shapely Hurley Beacon, sloping down towards the unseen woods of Crowcombe.

Here and there, a little below the summits, stand a few dark pines—here singly, there in groups of three or four. In them is the louder music of the Quantocks, passing from the mournful cadence caused by the summer breeze to the deep diapason of winter, when the wind roars through their groaning branches in furious blast, when snow shrouds distant Exmoor, and when the Welsh coast is dim in storm-wreaths, and the yellow tide—a thousand feet below—lashes the pebbly beach in futile anger.

But that coast is near now, nearer, indeed, than has been the case during any part of our pilgrimage, and the elevated church of Penarth—Coleridge's 'kirk,' perhaps, or, rather, its successor—the lighthouse of the Flat holm—undoubtedly his 'lighthouse-top'—are plainly to be seen.*

The nearest village visible towards the sea is East

---

* 'The ship was cheered, the harbour cleared ;
   Merrily did we drop
  Below the kirk, below the hill,
   Below the lighthouse-top.'
              ' *The Ancient Mariner.*'

As is well known, this poem was composed during a walk along this, the southern, coast of the Channel, with the coast of South Wales full in view.

Quantoxhead, standing, as its name would imply, at the very head or end of the hills from which it takes its title. 'I saw,' says Leland, 'a fair Park and Manor Place of the Lutterelles caullid Quantok-Hedde bycause it standeth at the Hedde of Quantok-Hilles towards the Se.'

It is noted, for an Elizabethan manor-house, a fine but rather grim - looking building, owned by the Luttrells, who have, indeed, in direct line held the manor since the Conquest, when it was granted to Ralph Paganel. It stands at no great distance from the cliffs. So near as to conceal the greater portion of its walls, is the church, an edifice of no particular architectural pretensions, but with some good bench-ends, and on the north side of the chancel a fine altar-tomb under a canopy, bearing this inscription, 'Here luyt hugh luttrell knyght wyhe departed 1522 the fyrst day of february, here lyt andro luttrell knyght his son wyhe departed the yere of our lord god mccccccxxxviii the iiii day of may on whoys souly ' ihu have mcy.' The spelling, even for the early years of the sixteenth century, is very barbarous. In the churchyard are the remains of a fourteenth-century cross.

Perhaps the best way of seeing the more interesting features of these hills will be to follow along the slopes. However delightful the walk across the summits may be, however fine the panorama on either hand outspread, villages are entitled to some notice, and there are many spots sheltering under the ferny or wooded declivities attractive both to artist and antiquary. Descending, therefore, from the Beacon to the level of the sur-

17

rounding moor, we skirt the head of Weacombe and
pass down another gate in the hills, Bicknoller Combe,
where grows that rare fern, *lastrea oreopteris*.   Bicknoller, close to its mouth, and under a tremendously
steep hill, is a picturesque hill village, with a pretty
Perpendicular church.   The tower has unusually pronounced angle buttresses, and is ornamented near the
battlements with immense, though sadly dilapidated,
winged gargoyles.   The porch, a very lofty feature,
at first appears to have an unnecessarily tall gable.
This is, however, caused by a parvise with an old oak
waggon roof.   There is a good deal of rich carving in
the battlements of the nave; in fact, the church, for its
size, possesses more sculptured work than many in this
district.   The pillars dividing the nave from the aisle
are particularly good, with handsome capitals, and the
bench-ends are, as is the case with nearly every church
of the Quantocks, handsomely carved.   But the glory
of the church is the screen, a beautiful specimen, with
five openings, finished at the north side, above the
pulpit, in fresco work.   The rood staircase is still open.
In the chancel is the fragment of what was probably a
columnar piscina, placed for safety in a recess near the
altar.   The pulpit and cradle roofs are, with the exception of the bosses, modern.

In the churchyard is the headless shaft of a fourteenth-
century cross, and beneath the 'east window a
curiously-worded tombstone, to divers members of the
family of Bartholomew Safford, the Presbyterian
minister, who, from 1646 to 1662, supplanted the Rev.
J. O. Baynham.   At the restoration, a few years since,

it was found lying neglected on the grass, and set up in its present position. The inscription is wholly in verse, and runs, as far as I can read it, as follows :

> ' Three Saffords out of view
> Mabel, Mary, Bartholomew
> Bartholomew Saffords flesh and bone
> His wife, his sister and his son
> Mabel became for worms a bait
> December 9th in forty eight
> Mary was fitted for the bier
> On March the 4th that same year
> Death on Bartholomew did fixe
> On March the 2nd forty six
> Wife sister brother father dear
> Christs minister and pastor here.'

*   *   *   *   *   *

The two concluding lines are illegible. The omission of the *century* is very unusual.

On the slope of the hill behind the village, a little to the east, we notice a large earthwork, which, though in reality a rude oval, from the valley beneath appears almost square. It is known as Trendle's Ring—presumably from the Anglo-Saxon *trendle*, a circle. On the east the ground falls suddenly to a combe of no great length, appropriately named Short Combe. The camp—if camp it were—is surrounded by a rampart of stone and earth, from eight to ten feet high, except at the lower end, where it measures nearly fifteen. It is further secured by a fosse. There is but one entrance, at the upper end. The length and breadth are equal, 98 paces, or close upon 300 feet.

In the country beneath, and about a mile distant, bisected by the railway, is another earthwork, of which very few traces remain, called Turk's Castle. It occupied a rocky knoll, but what with the railway cutting, an orchard and other cultivation, little can be made of it. Local legend says that fighting once occurred between it and Trendle's Ring, but is silent altogether as to the period. The camp was, without doubt, circular.

Just across the brook that runs down the little valley, to the south of Turk's Castle, is an abrupt rising, more or less covered with trees. Here, almost concealed by the wood, is yet another camp, which we will call, as it has no other name, after the farm on which it is situate, Curdon Camp. No doubt the farm owes its name to the camp, rather than the camp to the farm, for *caer dun* means the fortified or enclosed hill. The vallum is irregular, and the fosse ceases altogether on the side facing the stream, which is very abrupt. As far as can be ascertained, it is of much the same shape as was Turk's Castle, and probably about equal in size. It is, I think, not unlikely that a line of these earthworks once stretched right across the valley to Elworthy Barrows on Brendon, thus completely barring a hostile approach up the depression between the two ranges.

Some people, inspired, perhaps, by the fact that Roman coins have been found at Bicknoller, have dubbed Trendle's Ring a Roman camp. This—*ab initio*—I am pretty confident it was not, its shape alone, notwithstanding its apparent inclination to a square, precluding such an idea being entertained. That the earthwork was British seems reasonably

CROWCOMBE. DRAWN BY A. DAWSON FROM A SKETCH BY J. LL. W. PAGE.

certain; that it was one of the *castra æstiva* is matter of pure conjecture.

Passing Thorncombe—the hills are becoming more wooded now—we reach the fine manor-house of Halsway, said to have been built for a hunting seat by the great Cardinal Beaufort. It was also occupied at one time by the Cade family, one of whose scions, the notorious 'Jack,' was the hero of an insurrection in 1450, when, at the head of the Kentish men, he advanced upon, and even entered, London. But here, in spite of his precautions, his followers committed an act of depredation, and were, in consequence, repulsed by the citizens, Cade soon after being killed by a Suffolk gentleman named Iden. The house, that is, the old part, for it has been added to of late, is long and low, the front divided by three pinnacled towers. There are some fine bay-windows and curious gargoyles, the most remarkable representing the devil seizing a lawyer. The situation is high on the slope of the hills, with a pleasant view over the valley towards Willet Tor and the Brendons. In another mile we reach Crowcombe.

Seated beneath the thick woods that climb from behind the church almost to the hilltop, with Willsneck's bold slope bounding the view to the east, and Hurley Beacon, with the largest barrow on the Quantocks for its summit,* rising bravely westward, the white cottages and picturesque church of this pretty village have an

---

* It is 225 feet round at the base, and still, though half ruined, seven feet high. Thorncombe Barrow has a circumference of 195 feet.

effect truly charming. Yet no one would imagine that it was once a borough and market town. Of the borough, except the bricks and mortar, or rather the cob and thatch, nothing remains; while the only relic of the market is a remarkably slender octagonal cross, about fifteen feet high, standing on a rough calvary by the roadside, at the turning to the stables of Crowcombe Court. The head appears to be a kind of ornamented Maltese. Some years since it was broken, owing to the strain of a line of flags stretched from it to a neighbouring tree. The fracture was carelessly repaired, with the result that the head is a trifle askew.

The great red-brick pile of Crowcombe Court, standing in beautiful grounds under the hill, has some valuable paintings. There are several Vandycks, a Holbein, two Knellers, two Jansens, two Rubens, two Poussins, a Da Vinci, two Rembrandts, a Carlo Dolce, and others, besides many curiosities.

Close at hand, above the highway, is the church, a striking building, with deep porch and richly sculptured battlements. The tower was once surmounted by a spire, but this was destroyed by lightning in 1735.[*] The interior has good arches, though the screen, compared with others in these parts, is poor. The place of the north aisle is occupied by a large chamber belonging to the Carews; it is raised four steps above the rest of the church. There is a handsome modern reredos in white stone, with effigies of the four evangelists flanked by angels. The bench-ends are fine; some, indeed, curious. The best are in the south aisle,

* Murray, p. 470.

where is one in particular, representing a naked man fighting with a double-headed dragon. On the octagonal font of yellow sandstone (which has been partially restored) are figures of kings and bishops. It is supported by a good carved pedestal. The cradle roof is modern, but in keeping with the rest of the edifice; that of the porch is groined and handsome.

Just outside the porch a rather fine fourteenth-century cross will be remarked. It stands as usual on a calvary, and is octagonal in shape. The height is about nine feet. The head, small and mutilated, is evidently a modern addition. Its interest consists in three figures in relief. That on the north is John the Baptist; on the west is an unknown bishop. On the east a female form is represented. From her dress, that of a religious order, she is thought to have been a prioress of the Convent of Studeley, a Benedictine house founded by Bernard de St. Wallery about the year 1184, to which convent Godfrey de Crowcombe, grandson of the Earl of Mortaigne (the Conqueror's grantee) conveyed the manor.* The Saxon owner appears to have been Gytha, wife of Earl Godwin, who gave it to the See of Winchester, from whose possession it was soon torn by the rapacious Norman.

Facing the church gates is an ancient building, now deserted. An outer stair leads to an upper story, once a charity school, founded, I believe, by a lady of the Carew family; the lower part was divided into dwellings. The villagers appear to know nothing of its history, and an old lady whom I encountered, collecting

* Pooley's ' Crosses of Somerset.'

sticks from the interior, was much more anxious to draw attention to a county magnate riding by than to afford the minimum of inaccurate information whereof she could boast.

Instead of approaching Willsneck by road, which will entail a very fatiguing climb, it will be well to betake ourselves to a rough lane, and gradually ascend the hills to Triscombe Stone, as it is called, a point on the ridge, marked by a rough block, where the staghounds meet once or twice in the early part of September. Below, dividing us from Willsneck, is the deep valley of Triscombe; at its foot a farm, an inn, and one or two houses. The name *Tre-is-cwm* is said to mean the dwelling at the foot of the valley, and certainly describes the situation to a fault. Right up this valley, deep in shadow most of the day, comes the road to Stowey and the country east of the Quantocks, and few rides are more beautiful than that winding down the side of Cockercombe, one of the largest and loveliest glens of these hills. Tall trees overshadow the way for almost the whole of the descent, the spaces here and there filled up with rhododendrons, but not so as to deprive the traveller of frequent glimpses of the opposite steep, and of the sullen back of Willsneck, from whose slopes a brisk streamlet rattles down the glen. Many have turned away down this tempting path rather than incur the ascent of Willsneck, although from Triscombe Stone the battle is half fought, as the mountain wall—it is nothing less—across the valley has been circumvented.

Except on its western slope, where the fir-woods of

Bagborough climb nearly to its brow, Willsneck is covered with heather. Its summit is not at all interesting, being simply a long flat tableland, a sort of 'hog's-back.' But the view is of course a wide one.

We are getting towards Taunton now, and the fertile valley of Taunton Deane lies outspread away to the left, bounded by the Blackdown Hills. Many combes run up into the eastern buttresses of Willsneck, not bare, as further north and west, but well wooded and watered by numerous tinkling streams. On the side of one the gray church of Asholt stands forth boldly against a background of heavy foliage.

Willsneck has three tumuli. The one forming what summit the hill possesses, 1,261 feet above the sea, is crowned by a pile of stones, and is surrounded by a little path. All have been opened.

Beneath the next hill, Bagborough, where, in some cairns called Rowboroughs, Roman coins have been found, is the village of the same name. Bagborough is not an interesting village; what attractions it possesses centre about the church, which is almost surrounded by the gardens of Bagborough House, whose walls come close to the east end. There is nothing very remarkable about the church, but it is a good Perpendicular building, and has been well restored. Here are more carved bench-ends carefully affixed to moden pews. But they are not so handsome as those of Crowcombe. An old sundial, with the date 1648, is over the porch. The tower, square and substantial, has no battlements.

Bagborough House was the seat of the late W. Fenwick Bisset, and perhaps the most interesting object within it—at any rate, to the hunter—is a magnificent painting by Mr. Samuel Carter, presented to the 'Master' at a dinner at Dunster in 1871. It represents an autumn evening on Badgworthy Water. The stag is at bay in the stream, and Mr. Bisset, on his powerful gray horse, cap in hand, is watching the despairing creature with a touch of sadness in his eyes. 'Arthur' is approaching from behind for the *coup de grâce*, while the excited hounds splash about the water in their eagerness to pull down the lordly monarch of the forest. Prior to presentation the picture was hung in the Royal Academy, where it attracted numerous visitors. The grave of this unselfish and hard-working master of staghounds is in the church-yard hard by. It would perhaps little become one who knew him not personally to say much in his honour, but the concluding words of a chapter in the Hon. John Fortescue's work on stag-hunting may, perhaps, not inappropriately be here quoted. 'Mention his name,' he writes, ' to any of the yeomen or farmers who knew him in the stag-hunting district, and they will say, " Mr. Bisset ! Ah ! he was a good gentleman." *A good gentleman.* Take the words as they are spoken, in their fullest sense, and you can add nothing to give higher praise. Such Mr. Bisset was, and as such he is and will be remembered by high and low in North Devon and West Somerset.'

After traversing the long street of Bagborough, a pleasant walk by field and lane takes us to Cothelstone

Lodge, a large Grecian mansion, finely placed in an extensive sloping park stretching far up the hill. Below is a tree-environed lake, and beyond rises the little church and the restored manor-house, once the residence of the Stawels. Of the earlier mansion, as will be seen presently, little or nothing remains.

The lands of Cothelstone came into the posession of the Stawels at the Norman Conquest. In this, their native county, many were famous, notably Sir John, an ardent Royalist. In 1646 he raised three regiments of horse, and one of foot, for King Charles, and bid fair to become one of the most powerful foes of the Parliament in West Somerset. But no one could stand against Blake. Marching from Taunton, he encountered Stawel's levies near Bishops Lydeard, and after a sharp skirmish routed them. So the gallant knight retired to his fortified mansion of Cothelstone, and there defied the Roundhead soldiery. But the house was unfit for protracted defence: Blake's cannon soon made breaches in the walls, and the garrison was forced to surrender. Being 'too dangerous a man to trust at large, Sir John was lodged in Newgate, where, under a fine of £25,000, he remained thirteen years. Meanwhile his lands were sold or appropriated, his timber cut down, and his house nearly demolished. At last the Restoration came, and Sir John emerged from his confinement to welcome his master's son at Charing Cross. The Restoration of the king meant also the restoration of the Stawel lands —at least, of a considerable portion. But the burden of debt incurred in consequence of the Civil War weighed heavily upon the good knight, and in order to discharge his liabilities much was sold. Cothelstone, however, he contrived to retain. He did not long survive his imprisonment, dying at his seat of Netherham, near Somerton, in 1661. His heir became a peer, under the title of Lord Stawel—a title now extinct.

As for the ruined house, it appears to have lain waste for about twenty-five years, when it was converted into a farm. It is only within the last four decades that it has been restored to its former appearance ; of it we shall now proceed to give some account.

Cothelstone Manor, as it is now called, is a peculiar type of Jacobean—a type which the late Mr. Esdaile, grandfather of the present owner of the Cothelstone estates, was at great pains to follow. The result of his labours is in every way satisfactory, and there can be no doubt that the present building, restored—almost rebuilt, in 1855—represents very accurately the mansion bombarded by Blake. The twisted pillars dividing the windows, and flanking the entrance, constitute the most curious feature ; several of the original still remain. In the hall is a relic of former days. The fireplace bears the date 1681—a date which probably refers to the building of the farm, which, as we have seen, arose on the ruins of the old mansion. By the way, it is a farm still, though presenting rather the appearance of a country seat.

The house is approached from the road by an outer gateway and an inner gatehouse, whose architecture corresponds with that of the main building. This, I believe, was little injured by Blake's cannon, and is one of the few really good specimens of a gatehouse of the Jacobean period. The outer gateway formerly spanned the road, but has been recently taken down and rebuilt in its present position. On the arch, that judicial butcher, Judge Jeffreys, hung Colonel Bovet and Mr. Blackmore, two of Monmouth's adherents, whose blood, according to local tradition, ran down to the Gore at Bishops Lydeard. This sanguinary name is not, however, due to the execution of these two unfortunate gentlemen, but to that of another rebel named Gore, who there paid the penalty of his rashness. Colonel Bovet was a Taunton gentleman, and Jeffreys caused him to be hung here out of spite to Lord Stawel, who, although, like his forbears, a Royalist, too plainly showed his disgust at the inhumanities of the ' Bloody Assize.'*

Of the Norman home of the Stawels no vestige now remains, unless, indeed, in the shape of some under- ground chambers marked on a plan of the ruins made in 1855 ' dungeons,'† and where, indeed, fetters were

* Locke's ' Western Rebellion,' p. 9, note f.
† For an inspection of this plan and sketches of the house, both after the bombardment and as a farm, I am indebted to Mr. C. E. J. Esdaile, of Cothelstone House. I would also thank him for his ready permission to peruse his grandfather's diary, which contains a long and most interesting account of the Stawels and their mansion. Speaking of these very dungeons, the writer quaintly says : ' It was nothing but natural that a place for the safe deten- tion of prisoners was had. At the time we are speaking of, there were no Petty Sessions, with the attendant attornies. No—no ! My Lord was the Petty Session, and a grim Domestic his attorney —did man or woman disobey orders, summary conviction followed, and the Dungeon received its victim.'

found. But of a Perpendicular mansion, there are considerable traces. To the west of the house is a building measuring eighty feet by twenty—'chiefly,' writes Mr. Esdaile, 'apportioned for the great hall, in which the retainers dined and slept; it had not any apartments over, but an open roof of carved oak, after the fashion of the Middle Ages.' It was unconnected with the main building. In conclusion, I may say that no prettier group lies beneath the wooded slopes of Quantock than that made by the manor, a still-house above, now divided into cottages, the church, and a picturesque thatched cottage, with black beams dividing its whitewashed walls, high on the slope above.

The church is a mixture of Transition, Norman and Decorated. The Norman work appears in the two arches dividing the nave from what was aparently a chapel, evidently at one time reserved to the ancient lords of the soil. Here there are two fine table monuments—I presume to Stawels—but the pews come so very close to their sides that any inscription there may be is completely hidden. The older monument represents a knight in armour and his lady, and appears to date from the fourteenth century. The other supports similar figures, in the costume of the seventeenth. There are well-preserved tablets to the Stawels in the little chancel, that on the right commemorating in Latin the loyalty and misfortunes of the Royalist Sir John. Other details will be found in the well-carved bench-ends, pulpit and reading-desk. There is also a hagioscope and a good font. For so small a church, the building possesses not a few features of interest.   The battlements and pinnacles of the tower are a late addition.

In a sloping field (every field here slopes), between the church and vicarage, is a curious little building, known as St. Agnes' Well.   I could not ascertain its history, but do not think it of earlier date than the old manor-house, which it supplied with water, and with which it was connected by a leaden pipe.*   It is a very rough dome, entered by a diminutive round-headed arch, and contains anything but the most palatable water.   The outer wall is nearly shrouded in ivy, thorn, and dog-rose.   Close at hand is an aged walnut, about eighty feet high and eighteen in girth.

Another ruin will be noticed well up on the slope westward, behind Cothelstone House.   This is a shattered square tower, called by the neighbours a hunting-tower, but in reality nothing more nor less than a ' folly,' built, probably, in the last century.   A strange object appears higher up on the right.   A little prospect seat is surmounted by a top-heavy and inexpressibly hideous and inartistic nude figure, presumably a man, and with less doubt a hunter, as a dog couches at his heels.   The Roman nose (broken), wig-like locks, and generally barbarous appearance, would fix as the date of its erection the debased period of a hundred years ago.

Below—in fact, immediately at the rear of the mansion—stands a group of cottages, which bear traces of better days.   One, now occupied by the butler, owns a

---

* Mr. Esdaile's MS. There is a wild, and, so far as I can gather, wholly unauthenticated tradition, that the well is a survival of a religious house.

good ornamented plaster ceiling and overmantel, while
in an upper room is another, ruder but more curious,
representing Samson slaying the Philistines with the
jaw-bone of an ass.   There is no date, but, from comparison with those at Dunster and elsewhere, I do not
think that these decorations have seen the light of more
than two centuries.

We have had almost enough of churches lately, but
another, though some little distance from the hills,
should be visited, ere we mount once more into the
upper air.   In the opening vale below rises the lofty
and magnificent tower of Bishops Lydeard, considered
by many the finest in the West of England, though it can
scarcely bear the palm while the slender and still loftier
tower of St. Mary Magdalen pierces the smoke of
distant Taunton.   Still, it is a wonderfully beautiful
piece of work, and we shall do well to follow the road
downward before pursuing an upward course, and note
in detail not only its proportions, but those of the church
beneath its shadow.

The tower is in four stages, each lighted by windows
of delicate tracery.   The battlements are beautifully
fretted, but the effect of the slender pinnacles is rather
spoilt by the network of rods ensuring their safety.
The body of the church consists of nave, north and
south aisles, and chancel, the latter nearly new, and
very handsomely stencilled.   A lofty arcade of pillars
separates the south aisle from the nave ; that marking
the north aisle is much lower, and has a curious and
not altogether pleasing effect.   A magnificent screen
crosses the church from the wall of the south aisle to

the northern pillar of the chancel arch. It is admirably decorated in red, blue and gold, as also is the more modern pulpit and cradle roof. A low screen of much later date crosses the north aisle. Out of fifteen windows, no less than eleven are filled with stained glass.

Much time may be spent in examining the bench-ends—also decorated—which are as fine as they are curious. One has rabbits, another a stag. There is a windmill, with miller and packhorse and birds between the sails. There is an ancient ship against a blue ground, and a gilded shield with azure fleur-de-lis and lion supporters under a crown. Another gilded shield bears sacred emblems—the pierced hands, feet and heart of the Crucified, surrounded by the crown of thorns, the cross, ladder, mallet, spear, scourge, pincers, and lictors' staves.

The most interesting monument is a small brass, which will be found under the east window of the south aisle. It is to Nicholas Grobham (founder of the alms-houses in the village) and Eleanore his wife, who died respectively in 1585 and 1594. There is a picture representing them kneeling at an altar, with their three sons and two daughters, flanked by an angel and the nude figure of a boy blowing bubbles. The epitaph is better poetry than that usually composed, and for this and the odd spelling is worth copying:

> ' Behold the end of mortall fleshe
> for earth to earth must needes returne
> behold the pampred corpes of mane
> A praie unto the sillie worme

18

by merites of our Saviour Christ
eternallie our soules doe reste
With angels brighte and saintes of god
as to his mercie seemed beste
Deathe in the grave a lingringe sleepe
our bodies must a whiles detaine
Till Christ his trumpet sound retreit
to call them home with him to raine
As you therfore with earthlie eies
doe now behold our fatall tombe
So let your hevenly eies foresee
the end that unto you must come.'

The churchyard cross is the finest in the district. It is, as usual, octagonal, and dates from the fourteenth century. On the eastern face is a canopied relief containing figures of John the Baptist and two others. Each of the eight sides of the base is filled with figures of the Apostles, except those facing the east and west, which contain representations of Christ in glory and the Resurrection. The head is new, and was, I believe, supplied by the late rector, Mr. Warre, a well-known local antiquary. There is also a fragment of what must have been a still handsomer village cross, fixed on the top of a very ugly calvary of red sandstone. Canopied figures of the Virgin and Child, and four others, much weathered, can be made out. With the exception of one figure on the right, all are crowned.

But it is time to return to our hills. The high-road winds up through a fine beech-wood, past a lodge, and then round the northern side of Cothelstone Hill towards Bridgwater. There is, however, a short-cut up the glen at the back of the vicarage, which will take us right over the summit, and this we shall now follow. It is a pretty spot, watered by a swift runnel breaking from the hillside, and is remarkable for containing thistles so enormous as to be quite curiosities. There are many as high as a man, and a dozen or more running up to seven, eight, and even nine feet. This combe was within living memory the abode of a modern cave-dweller, known as Blackietops or Blackatops, who lived a solitary life in a hole beneath a rock in the hillside, and was famous throughout the country-side for his eccentricities. The cave is now filled with earth.

Almost the whole of this south-western side of Cothelstone Hill is wooded, and the traveller emerges upon the grassy and ferny summit rather suddenly. The highest part is crowned by a prospect tower. Its history is altogether unknown, but it was probably built at the same date as the manor-house, now some hundreds of feet below. The shape is circular; there are one or two empty windows and a round-headed doorway. There are no means of ascent, and its most appreciative visitors appear to be sheep, of which there are always a couple or more sheltering from the heat of summer or the cold of winter; for Cothelstone is an exposed spot.

On every side there is a charming panorama. We are now standing on the last lofty eminence of the range, for Buncombe Hill is of no great account, and the eye embraces all the country from near Williton to the Blackdowns, the town and vale of Taunton, the plain of Bridgwater, and about half of Somersetshire. More of the eastern spurs and combes of the Quantocks are visible hence than from any other point, and, of course, there is a lengthy stretch of sea.

Referring to the extensive view to be obtained from Cothelstone, Mr. Jeboult tells an amusing anecdote. It appears that a gentleman, with the aid of a telescope, made out the time upon the market clock at Taunton, seven miles distant. A rustic asked to be allowed a peep through the wonderful instrument, and having discovered that the hand was upon the hour of twelve, the gentleman asked him if he would like to hear the hammer strike. The amazed rustic assented, and again placed the glass to his eye. A repeater was then held at the end and struck, when the yokel exclaimed, ' Zure the ould Nick hisself must be in the 'fernal pipe; I nevver heard sich a thing afore.'

And now we turn our steps to the more gradual and undulating slopes which characterize the eastern side of the range, for there is still much to see, ere, having worked back almost to the point whence our survey of the Quantocks was commenced, we bid farewell to the hill-country of West Somerset.

CHAPTER XV

THE SEAWARD SIDE

Holwell Cavern — Broomfield — Ruborough Camp — Quantock Lodge—Igneous Rocks—Nether Stowey — Coleridge and his Friends—The Court House—Castle Mount—Robert de Candos —The Audleys—The Trackway—Danesborough—Dodington Court—Sir Francis Dodington—Holford—Alfoxton.

AT the back of Cothelstone Hill, a little beyond an inn called the Traveller's Rest, and below the Bridg-water road, is a geological curiosity. We have been *over* the Quantocks; we now go *under* them, though for no great distance, to inspect Holwell Cavern, a fissure in the grauwacke slate, discovered many years since during quarrying operations. As the entrance is barred by an iron gate, it will be necessary to visit the farmhouse of Great Holwell and secure the services of the janitor. The cavern is—according to our guide— sixty yards in length ; the breadth from four to twenty feet; while the height is from five to thirty. In several places, however, impending crags oblige the visitor to bend nearly double, and to escape a broken head requires some care. The beauty of the spot is due to crystals of white and pale pink arragonite (now

somewhat sullied by smoke of lamp and candle),
minute spars of which thickly encrust the roof, while
masses of stalagmite have formed whimsical objects
similar to those in the larger caves at Cheddar. Here
are seen the 'loaf,' the 'elephant's ear,' and other of
the creations so eagerly sought in the grand caverns of
the Mendips. Another small aperture branches off
about midway on the right. This is only accessible
on the hands and knees, an uncomfortable mode of pro-
gression, and by no means to be recommended, as the
floor is anything but clean. Traces of Reynard may
be detected in the softer spots, and bats flutter in
numbers within an inch of the visitor's head, or hang
from the roof. The cave is fairly dry, except at the
extreme end, where there is a small spring, and in
winter possesses an atmosphere far warmer than the
outer air. I remember exploring it when a thin
coating of snow lay on the hills above, and the keen
northern blast cut like a knife, and was surprised at
the contrast in temperature. The guide said that the
cavern was as good as a weather-glass, as it invariably
became wet before rain. At the time of my visit it
was dry, and I remarked that no rain, beyond a few
drops, fell for several days.*

* In the second volume of 'The Proceedings of the Somersetshire Archæological Society,' an interesting paper on Holwell
Cavern is contributed by Mr. Andrew Crosse, a well-known
scientist, who, as the sometime resident of Fyne Court House,
Broomfield, had many opportunities of making experiments. He
says that the water has peculiar properties, very quickly forming
stalagmite, and that stones thrown into the little pool at the end
become covered with crystallized carbonate of lime in the form of
dog-tooth spar.

At no great distance is the village of Broomfield. It may be reached by returning to the cross-roads to Taunton and North Petherton, and then following the latter over the ferny and wooded slope of Buncombe Hill. It is a tiny hamlet, there being nothing beyond the church and vicarage, pleasantly situated Fyne Court House, and half a dozen cottages. The church has a pretty tower, surmounted by a short slated spire. The style is the usual Perpendicular, and the pillars again have handsome carved capitals. There is some good ancient stained glass in a window in the nave, and the richly carved bench-ends are notorious. The church-yard cross dates from the thirteenth century, and differs from all in the neighbourhood. In the first place, it has no calvary, but in lieu thereof a very deep socket; in the second, it is square instead of octagonal; and, in the third, has sculptured angles. The head is missing, but there still remains the carved corona from which it sprung. The shaft is remarkably elegant, and, with the base, rises to a height of about fourteen feet. Close to it is a table-monument to the Cross family, elaborately decorated in the somewhat inartistic style of the seventeenth century. Part of the churchyard is shadowed by aged yews.

Passing down the hill, and through an iron gate below the vicarage, we cross a common and descend into a combe, a picturesque spot, watered by a stream descending from the hills above. Almost all the land hereabouts is cultivated; the Quantocks have practically ended, dying away into rolling plain towards Bridgwater. As the hill towards Lydeard Farm is climbed, there is a pleasant peep at Broomfield Church, among the trees, on the top of the opposite steep. Soon we emerge into another road running to the Traveller's Rest, parallel with the one over Buncombe Hill. This we follow to some poor-looking cottages by the roadside, where it will be necessary to requisition a guide, for on the hill above, part of Withybees Farm, lies an antiquity which has excited no little speculation.

This is Ruborough Camp, a large oblong* enclosure, now planted with young firs. It is 330 paces in length, and 275 in breadth, and is surrounded by a deep fosse and lofty vallum, the latter having an average height of, perhaps, fifteen feet. There are entrances at the upper and lower ends, *i.e.*, at the east and west.

The surface of this camp, owing to its position on a spur, bounded on the north and south by deep combes, is very irregular, and much higher in the centre than at the sides. The vallum is overgrown with trees and brambles, which, with the fir plantation occupying the enclosure, will in a few years render the discovery of the camp a work of difficulty. At a short distance from the upper end is a fragment of another vallum, extending for about 100 paces, defended by a fosse almost shrouded in briars. What this was intended for, I know not; perhaps, as it stands on that side of the camp most exposed, as a further protection. Between it and the camp is a field, known to the neighbourhood as 'Money Field.' Here Roman coins have been discovered, and either in the field or camp other

* Mr. W. B. Broadmead calls it 'triangular.' I cannot agree with him.

remains, including some querns. Of course, as has been before suggested, this is no conclusive reason for laying down an absolute theory that Ruborough Camp is Roman. Nevertheless, its shape is a very strong argument in favour of its being such, and it is certain that no other Roman camp exists on the Quantocks. Its position is sufficiently commanding, overlooking the approaches to the hills from the Parret, but it does not guard the British trackway from Combwich as narrowly as might have been expected. A subterranean passage, 100 yards long, now filled in, gave the occupants of the camp access to a spring of water on the side of the hill.

I was told by my guide that an old woman had picked up some 'cannon-balls' ten or twelve years since, and at once went in search of her; but she was not to be found, and an explanation of this curious, and, of course, quite unexpected, artillery is among the things that await another excursion into this charming but remote neighbourhood.

From the Traveller's Rest we descend, by winding and occasionally terribly rough and steep lanes, to Asholt, most delightfully situated of all villages that cling to the skirts of the Quantocks. It lies on the side of a spur, at the back of Willsneck, and is as tiny as Broomfield. The church, a quaint little building, mainly Perpendicular, though the piscina is Early English, has a nave, with some hideous modern windows, and a very short south aisle. The chancel— its walls tastefully ornamented with encaustic tiles— has a pretty, if Liliputian, reredos, with symbols of the

Four Evangelists. There are good outer and inner
arches to the porch, which still contains the stoup for
holy-water. The ground behind rises so abruptly that
the top of the little churchyard, only some forty feet
from the east window, is on a level with the belfry of
the plain gray tower. The view from this spot is very
fine. In the foreground are some tall pines—half as
high again as the tower—which serve but to accentuate
the soft beauties of the long winding valley stealing up
towards dark Willsneck. On the further side is a
picturesque-gabled farm. Down the bottom comes the
usual stream, flowing onward, between wooded hills,
to Spaxton and the Parret.

Spaxton Church, with its curious bench-ends, beautiful fourteenth-century canopied cross, and old court-
house, we do not visit. It is not a village of the
Quantocks, but lies in the lowlands beyond their
furthest spur.

From Asholt there is a pleasant walk to Over Stowey.
On the way we pass Quantock Lodge, a modern
mansion, formerly the residence of Lord Taunton, but
now of Mr. Stanley, the member for the Bridgwater
Division. In a quarry on this estate is found an
igneous rock, hard in texture and grayish-green in
colour, which carves well and takes a high polish.
Specimens may be seen in the house and in the church
of Buckland St. Mary, near Taunton. Sir Roderick
Murchison pronounces it a volcanic ash, and, upon
visiting the spot, not only felt confident that he stood
before a volcanic rock, but was of opinion that the
very cone of elevation was before his eyes. While

referring to this outcrop, it may not be out of place to mention the syenitic dyke, near Hestercombe, discovered by Mr. Horner, and of which there are only two or three similar patches between the Quantock and Malvern Hills.

The church of Over Stowey is throughout Perpendicular. There are several memorials to Lord Taunton, the most interesting being two stained windows at either end of the north aisle, designed by Mr. Burne Jones, R.A. The reredos has for centrepiece a beautiful white marble figure of the Good Shepherd, erected to the memory of Edward Stanley, who lived but one day. There are some good bench-ends, and a very fine eighteenth-century brass candelabra, made at Bridgwater. Another, apparently an exact counterpart, is in Burnham Church. The tower, more ancient than the church, has some quaint gargoyles. In the cemetery, an uncommon appendage to so small a village, is a cross to Lord Taunton, similar to the old market-cross at Crowcombe.

And now we approach Nether Stowey, a small town at the foot of the hills, chiefly memorable as the sometime residence of the poet Coleridge, who appears to have entertained for it feelings of deep affection :

> 'And now, beloved Stowey, I behold
> Thy church tower, and, methinks, the four huge elms
> Clustering, which mark the mansion of my friend ;
> And close beside them, hidden from my view,
> Is my own lonely cottage, where my babe
> And my babe's mother dwell in peace.'

The poet's 'friend' was 'Tom' Poole. 'Tom' Poole's

memory is still green at Stowey. A more benevolent man than this worthy miller never existed; and his personal integrity was so highly esteemed, that he was, says De Quincey, 'the general arbiter of the disputes of his fellow-countrymen; the guide, the counsellor of their difficulties; besides being appointed executor and guardian to his children by every third man who died in or about the town of Nether Stowey.' It was, indeed, as he himself tells us, 'in order to enjoy the society of his dear and honoured friend, T. Poole, and to have leisure for the study of ethics and psychology, and the foundations of religion and morals,' that Coleridge came to Stowey.

'Tom' Poole's mansion is now a shop, and the 'elms,' like himself, have been 'cut down,' while the 'lonely cottage,' inhabited by the poet in 1796, has become the Coleridge Cottage Inn, the last house on the left-hand side of the town going towards Williton. In the following year his friends Wordsworth and his sister took Alfoxton House, near Holford, where they were frequently joined by Southey. With such a galaxy of poetic talent, it is not wonderful that the hills and dales of the Quantocks are full of memories of the three 'Lake Poets,' or that the beautiful scenery about their homes coloured, in no small degree, their writings.

But Coleridge's political opinions did not meet with favour from the Government, and they were placed under espionage. A Government spy, with a *long nose*, who was sent down to watch them, thought that they were talking of him as *Spinoza*.* ' C. was believed to

* Murray, p. 467.

have little harm in him, for he was a crack-brained, talking fellow; but that Wordsworth, they said, is either a smuggler or a traitor, and means mischief. He never speaks to any one, haunts lonely places, walks by moon-light, and is always *booing* about by himself.' Poor Wordsworth! Had the long-nosed one heard Southey's exclamation, when apprised of the death of Robespierre at 'Tom' Poole's dinner-table, he might, judging a man by his company, have had more reason for suspicion. 'I bring you great news,' said the miller's nephew, bursting into the room; 'Robespierre is dead!' 'Good God!' exclaimed Southey, '*I would rather have heard of the death of my own father!*'

Whether Wordsworth really did give the Government good cause for suspicion, I do not know. The fact remains that they were not permitted to remain at Alfoxton. The lease was refused, and in the autumn of 1798 the 'smuggler or traitor' left for Germany.

Yet, notwithstanding these annoyances, the life at Stowey and Alfoxton was a peaceful and happy one, and often regarded by the trio in later years as one of the most enjoyable of their existence. Says Words-worth:

> 'Upon smooth Quantock's airy ridge we roved,
> Unchecked we loitered mid her sylvan courts.'*

They rode, they walked, they loitered over the breezy downs, or along the wooded vale of Seven Wells, Butterfly Combe, or Holford Glen. At the latter spot occurred that disastrous picnic which has so often

---

* 'The Prelude.'

raised a laugh against them. Owing to carelessness, a beggar made off with the cheese, and the brandy-bottle was broken by Coleridge, leaving the not very satisfying meal of bread and lettuce for the holiday-makers.

Stowey Church, a plain Perpendicular building, larger than most in this locality, presents little to interest either tourist or antiquary. Perhaps the most attractive thing about it is a tablet commemorating the virtues of Tom Poole.

In the churchyard wall is an odd-looking monument to the Blake family, descendants of the warrior admiral born at Bridgwater, and dreaded by all Royalists from Taunton to Dunster.

Adjoining is the fine Elizabethan manor-house called the Court House. I call it Elizabethan, for such it now is, but the foundations date from the days of the Queen's grandfather, Henry VII. It was commenced about the eleventh year of his reign b that Lord Audley who, in 1497, headed the Cornish insurrection, incited by Flamank and Joseph, against the collection of a subsidy, and which was dispersed very speedily at the battle—if such it can be called—of Blackheath, after which all three were executed on Tower Hill. Upon Lord Audley's attainder, the half-finished building fell to ruins ; but the king, having restored to his son such lands as he had not already conferred upon others, the Manor of Stowey again came into the possession of the family, and in the latter part of the reign of Elizabeth the great-grandson of the rebel built, or restored, the house as it now stands.

There is a story that a Norman cell of the monastery of Bec formerly occupied the site of the buildings; but I can find no authority for the statement, and the present lord of the manor tells me that he has never heard of the existence of such an edifice.

On the knoll at the top of Castle Street is a very prominent circular mound, about 25 feet in height, and at the top perhaps 120 feet in diameter. Until about thirty years since it was simply a bare grassy hill, known—as it still is—as Castle Mount. Its mention in certain manuscripts led to its being opened by Sir Peregrine Acland, the then lord of the manor, with the result that the foundations of a small rectangular building, 60 feet by 45 feet, were laid bare. Five chambers can still be traced; the deepest is locally dubbed the Dungeon.

The mound is surrounded by a deep dry ditch, called, and doubtless rightly, the Moat. Its average depth is twelve feet. On the side nearest the lane the fortalice was apparently further protected by a vallum, or perhaps wall, with an outer ditch—presumably the barbican. The surface of the ground is so broken and confused that it is quite possible that other buildings existed here, and that the ruins on the Mount are those of the keep. But the history of Stowey Castle is so very meagre, that it is impossible to arrive at any very definite conclusion respecting it.

In the days of the Conqueror the Lord of Stawel was one Robert de Candos, and in him and his descendants it remained until the reign of Edward III. In the seventeenth year of this reign Philip de Candos, last of

the line, died.   He had no issue, but having made his
wife Alianora, sister and co-heiress of William Martin,
Lord of the Manor of Combe Martin and Barnstaple,
joint tenant of his Stowey lands, the property devolved,
on her decease, to her nephew James, Lord Audley, a
notable warrior who fought under the Black Prince.   In
the following reign Sir John Touchet had the lands,
and he assumed the title of Baron Audley.   And in
these Audleys (subject to the afterwards-reversed attainder above mentioned) it remained for centuries.
In the time of Henry VIII., John, Lord Audley parted
with the estate, presumably to one Edward Walker ;
for we find that ' the castle and part of the demesnes,
called the Red Deer Park, were, 20th Henry VIII., the
possession of Edward Walker . . . . probably the
purchaser from Lord Audley.'*

But the castle, at any rate, seems to have again come
into the possession of the Audleys, for Mervin Touchet,
son of the Lord Audley who restored the manor-house,
sold the Stowey estates to Angel Grey, of Kingston
Maureward, Dorchester, who, having espoused the
royal cause, placed a garrison there, thereby incurring
the vengeance of the Parliament, whose soldiers not
only took it, but burned it to the ground.†

And this is all we really know about it.   Although

---

* These particulars were gathered from a MS. of the last
century by Mr. Thomas Palmer, of Fairfield, in the possession of
Sir Alexander Acland Hood, Bart.   They are copied, almost verbatim, by Collinson, who was, Sir Alexander tells me, indebted to
this MS. for most of his information about this neighbourhood.

† *Vide* a paper entitled ' Sketches in North-West Somerset,' in
the *Somerset County Gazette*—date unknown.

history does not tell us by whom it was built, it is no unreasonable assumption to attribute its erection to the first lord of Stowey, the aforesaid Robert de Candos: he is certainly as likely to have been the builder as Cromwell to have been the destroyer, for this is the story in Stowey. Cromwell is said to have advanced from Bridgwater; but was he ever there? The general who took that town was Fairfax, and it fell, as is well known, on the twentieth of July, 1645. Fairfax, therefore—or perhaps Blake—is more probably the person responsible for the destruction of Stowey Castle, which has thus been a ruin for nearly two centuries.

The Palmer MS., in one of its references to the castle, adds, 'Near it was a church, dedicated to St. Michael; but both are now ruined, so that no footsteps remain of either but the castle ditch.' This building, which has even less history than the castle, in that it has none, has indeed 'left not a wrack behind.'

One more antiquity ere we depart from Stowey. In a field on the right of the road to Over Stowey, just after leaving the town, is a portion of the trackway to which reference has more than once been made as running from Combwich on the Parret, over the Quantocks and Brendons, into Devonshire. It can only be traced the length of the field the hedge of which it follows. It is lower than the field, and presents the appearance of a hollow way. The wonder is that ploughing and agricultural 'improvement' has not caused it to disappear altogether. The width is, I think—I did not measure it—about eight feet. An attempt to trace this old British road up the valley and across the hills would be interesting, but this I have not had time to do; and it would, under any circumstances, be a work of extreme difficulty, for it must be now in a very broken and fragmentary condition.

Almost from Stowey begins to rise the fine height of Danesborough, on this side wooded up to the earth-works that crest its summit. I have never ascended from Stowey direct, but can speak to the climb from the Castle of Comfort Inn,* two miles further on the road westward, and of the bare slopes towards Holford. Whether from the inn, or from the old coach road near it on the Stowey side, we must pass through thick woods and oak coppice, thus losing the backward view, which is the finest on this side the Quantocks, for of these eastern hills Danesborough is king, being but six feet short of 1,100 feet.

As to the origin of the name there are many theories. One authority suggests Dinas-borough, the fortified-place; another, Dawesborough, by which name it is known in ancient deeds, and which he thinks is derived from the *dawns* or beacons, also called dauntrees, lighted to warn the countryside of an enemy's approach. Mr. Nicolls, who says that the hill is locally known as

---

* 'This, some years ago, was the scene of a great annual merry-making, known as "Dodington Rit." On the Sunday before Mid-summer, shoals of visitors arrived from Bridgwater and other places, and, after striving as to who should find the first whortle-berry, held high jinks in the pretty arbours which the landlord had constructed. Stalls were set up on the roadside, and the gathering partook of the nature of a fair, which lasted two days.'—*Somerset County Gazette.*

Dousborough, thinks the name a corruption of How's-borough, the hill fort.* From whatever source this hill is named, no one supposes that the Danes have anything to do with its nomenclature. Collinson, indeed, says that the earthwork is Roman, and that its shape—an irregular oval—is no objection, all Roman camps in Britain being fashioned according to the ground ; and that the station was probably at Putsham, in the parish of Kilve, where, as before stated, a large number of coins have been found. There is no doubt in my own mind that the camp is Celtic, though it is likely enough, as in numerous other instances, that the Romans subsequently used it as an æstiva, or summer quarters.

The vallum, which is 740 paces in circumference, or about 2,200 feet, is very abrupt, and from fifteen to twenty feet high. The area within is given by Mr. Nicolls as more than ten acres. A deep fosse surrounds it. It is said that there is an outer and lower vallum, but I do not think this is anything more than the natural fall of the ground. Of the three entrances two appear doubtful. The only original one is either that by the flagstaff—where some rough piles of stone probably mark the site of fire-hearths—or the opening near the mound at the northern end. This mound, which has a diameter of thirty feet, is perfectly flat on the top, and is more likely to be the site of a prætorium than the grave of a Belgic chief, which, except in its circular form, it does not at all resemble. It has not been opened; so the riddle, for the present, remains unsolved. On the western declivity Mr. Nicolls points out a

* 'The Quantocks and their Associations,' p. 13.

raised road leading to the British trackway coming up from Stowey.

From Danesborough Camp we have our last glimpse of Exmoor. It is only a glimpse, because the intervening hills which stretch away westward cut off all but the tops of the higher ground. Dunkery looks very far away now, cold and bare in contrast with the warm colouring around us. But he looks grand too, grander than any of these hills of the many openings,* none of which approach him in altitude, the loftiest falling short some 450 feet. On the other hand, we look down upon the rolling plain that spreads to the Severn Sea, upon the towers of Stoke Courcy—now corrupted into Stogursey, as Stoke Gomer has become Stogumber—where the De Courcys dwelt, and where the scanty remnant of their castle may still be seen, though hardly from here; on Fiddington and Stowey and others more distant; on the red spire of Stringston and Quantoxhead, within sound of the sea. Immediately beneath, hidden by the trees, is Dodington, with its fine old manor-house, Dodington Court, now a farm, but still retaining many traces of its former importance. This we shall presently examine more closely.

Descending Danesborough, in the direction of Holford, other signs of its Celtic defenders will be noticed. The first, lying on the slope to the right of the green path, is a large cairn surrounded by a shallow trench, somewhat similar to that dug in the present day round a soldier's tent. Just over the brow beyond is a

* *Gwantog*, full of openings—the original name, according to Mr. Jones.

pit, thirty-five feet in diameter, and marked 'outpost' on the new Ordnance map, and as such regarded by Mr. Nicolls, whose late house is just beneath. He thinks that it was connected with the camp on the hill-top above, and was 'probably roofed over in a beehive shape, to form a shelter for the guard.' On the Stowey side, in a field close to the highway, near the drinking fountain above the Castle of Comfort, is a barrow, or, at any rate, a mound of some sort. It has never been opened.

Dodington Court is a good example of an Elizabethan Manor. From a date over a window it appears to have been built in 1581. The exterior, fronting the road, presents a long façade, with gables and projecting porch. In the great hall is a fine Renaissance chimneypiece (its place would formerly have been occupied by the daïs), but the principal feature is an oaken screen and minstrels' gallery, discovered through the instrumentality of the late Sir Peregrine Acland. The work for the period is singularly rough. The drawing-room has a handsome cornice, ornamented with escutcheons. Bishop Clifford, as reported in a local paper, states that the property is mentioned in 'Domesday Book,' as coming into the possession of the Dodington family in the reign of Edward I., and remaining in it till 1740, when the representative at that time, in consequence of political troubles, retired to France, obtaining there a precarious livelihood by the sale of buckles and knives. Collinson, however, quoting from the Palmer MS., states that the exile was Sir Francis Dodington, who, for his zeal in the Royal cause, was expressly excepted in all treaties between the Parliament and the King. He afterwards returned to Dodington Court. The Royalist proclivities of this cavalier appear occasionally to have taken a wrong direction. Of him it is related, that meeting a minister on the highway, he demanded fiercely whom he was for; and on the minister replying 'For God and His Gospel,' he ran him through on the spot.

There is nothing very noteworthy about Dodington Church, with the exception of a handsome piscina, supported by a column in a corner of the porch, and a fifteenth-century cross in the churchyard. But an entry in the register (which commences in 1538) is curious, if rather horrible. 'February 25th, 1770, was buried James Protherow (a Welshman), as he was travelling from Carnarvon to Westminster in London, his parish, being eaten up by lice, through the inhumanity of the parish officer through whom he came. All possible kindness being shown him in this parish, but he lived in it but a few days, and died a most miserable spectacle as was ever seen, aged sixty-seven.'

We approach the end of our pilgrimage. North of Danesborough is Holford, with its saddleback church tower, its combes and its glens. Holford Glen, a 'cleeve' in the hills, is watered by a stream running between banks of turf, with oak-covered steeps as a background, while that of Alfoxton is a wooded ravine in the grounds of Alfoxton, down which a sparkling stream, cradled in the combe above, races to the not very distant sea beyond Kilve. How often Wordsworth and his brother-poets wandered in these woodlands, and beside these hurrying waters! How must they have traced the windings of the combe, and marvelled at the great fields of digitalis making purple the lower slopes! And many a time must the villagers of Holford—quaint hamlet, looking as if it were dropped from the skies—have watched their meditative forms, one of them perhaps even then composing the poem with which Holford is associated—'The Last of the Flock.'

It is worth our while to climb the hillside once more, and look down upon Alfoxton, the quiet sedate house where our poets read and wrote and talked, and where they probably plotted, too, more than one pitfall for wary 'Spinoza.'

The park climbs far up the hills, a rolling expanse of vivid green broken with clumps of trees. But it ends at this line of beech, and the free hills assert themselves, rising in rounded outline far against the sky. Down in the combes there is oak and hazel, and larch and briar; here is nothing but heather, bracken or gorse, and perhaps one or two wind-tossed pines :

> ' The hills are heathy, save that swelling slope,
> Which hath a gay and gorgeous covering on,
> All golden with the never bloomless furze.'

And here let us say farewell. What fitter spot whence to look our last ' on seaward Quantock's heathy hills ' and their lovely surroundings ? They who would again view the whole of our hill-country must mount to the western summits beyond: there is the flagstaff on Beacon Hill plainly standing against the gray sky, but two miles distant, commanding the vast sweep of hill and dale from Dunkery Beacon to Mendip. But here

> ' The many-steepled tract magnificent
> Of hilly fields and meadows, and the sea,
> With some fair bark, perhaps, whose sails light up
> The slip of smooth, clear blue betwixt two isles
> Of purple shadow,'

is quite enough to fill our souls with beauty, enough to stamp upon our senses the loveliness of this western land, enough to last us for many a day to come, when, in city counting-house or stifling street, we shall look back with a sense of pleasure, not untinged perhaps with regret, upon our journeyings through the hill-country of West Somerset.

APPENDIX A

PERAMBULATIO forestæ de EXMORE, in comitatu Somerset, per visum Malcolmi de Harleigh et Johannis de Crokesleghe ad dictum visum faciendum per dominum regem assignatorum, et per visum Baldrici de Nonyton et Hugonis de Popham militum, de comitatu prædicto per eosdem Malcolmum et Johannem electorum et eisdem associatorum ad dictum visum testificandum, convocatis et præsentibus Petro de Hamme tenente locum Sabinæ Pecche, custodis dictæ forestæ, et Gilberto de la Putte admeans, viridariis ejusdem forestæ, facta ibidem vicesimo secundo die Martii, anno regni regis Edwardi vicesimo sexto, per sacramentum Willelmi de Staunton, Willelmi Trivete, et Walteri de Loveny militum, Johannis de Reyny, Johannis de Pouleshull, Philippi de Woleford, Henrici de Gernvile, Johannis de Radyngton, Ricardi de Avele, Rogeri de Mandehulle, Roberti de Mandehulle, Roberti de Escote, Thomæ Terel, et Roberti de Chubbworthe, qui dicunt, quod bundæ forestæ prædictæ, juxta tenorum cartæ domini Henrici quondam regis Angliæ, patris domini Edwardi regis nunc, de foresta, incipiunt ad quendam locum qui vocatur Cornesyete, et abinde procedendo per quandam viam, inter dominicum domini regis et feodum Willelmi de Kytenore, usque illas petras quæ vocantur *Fistones*: et abinde descendendo per quendam ductum qui vocatur *Lillescumbe*, usque aquam que vocatur *Ore*: et abinde descendendo ultra brueram usque illum montem qui vocatur *Blakebergh*: et abinde procedendo usque brueram atque illum montem *Osmundebergh*: et abinde procedendo ultra brueram usque illum locum qui vocatur *Spracombesheved*: et abinde descendendo per quendam ductum usque aquam quæ vocatur *Exe*: et abinde

ascendendo per quoddam vetus fossatum usque illam petram quæ
vocatur *Radston:* et abinde procedendo inter feodum Johannis
Moun et feodum abbatis de Neth usque illud vadum quod vocatur
Reddeford: et abinde ascendendo ultra brueram directè usque illum
locum *Schepecumbeheved*, usque illam petram quæ vocatur *Deresmarke:* et abinde procedendo ultra brueram, inter dominicum
domini regis et feodum abbatis de Neth usque locum qui vocatur
Stonchiste: et abinde descendendo usque locum illum, in aqua
Berghel, usque aquam de *Schureburn*, descendit in aqua de
Berghel, qui locus vocatur *Schureburnessete:* et abinde descendendo ultra brueram directè usque illam petram quæ vocatur
Hockleston: et abinde descendendo, usque quoddam vadum quod
vocatur *Wylleneford*, in aqua quæ vocatur *Dunmokesbroke*, in con-
finio dictorum comitatum, usque Cornesyete, ad locum ubi prius
dictæ bundæ inceperunt. Et dicunt quod totum à dextris intra
bundas prædictas in toto circuitu est foresta domini regis. Et quod
omnes terræ et bosci subscripti à sinistris extra bundas prædictas
fuerunt afforestati, ad dampnum tenentium, post coronationem
domini Henrici quondam regis Angliæ, filii Matildis imperatricis, et
debent deafforestari juxta tenorem cartæ prædictæ, videlicet, omnes
terræ et tenementa et bosci, cum bruens, inter prædictas bundas et
mar . . . . quæ Johannes Kelly tenet. Villa de *Kytenore*, cum
boscis, brueris et aliis pertinentiis suis, quam Willelmus de Kytenore tenet. Villa de *Yervar*, cum boscis, brueris et aliis pertinentiis, quam Johannes de Meler tenet. Villa de *Porloke*, cum
boscis, brueris, et aliis pertinentiis suis, quam Simon Roges de
Porloke tenet. Villa de *Bosynton*, cum boscis, brueris, et aliis
pertinentiis, quam Henrici de Glasten tenet. Villa de *Westloctun*,
cum boscis, brueris et aliis pertinentiis: Villa de *Wyveresmeresham*,
cum boscis brueris, et aliis pertinentiis, quas Galfridus de Loctun
tenet. Villæ D'Overey et de *Estloctun*, cum boscis, brueris et pertinentiis quas Baldricus de Nonyngton tenet. Villa de *Broggelesnole*
et *Lovecote*, cum boscis, brueris, et aliis pertinentiis suis, quas prior
de Taunton tenet. Boscus qui vocatur *Worthe*, cum bruerâ et aliis
pertinentiis suis, quas Johannes de Kellynton tenet. Villa de *Stoke*
cum bosco et aliis pertinentiis, quam Gilbertus Piro tenet. Villa de
Chittesham, cum boscis, brueris et aliis pertinentiis, quam Ricardus
de Chittesham tenet. Ville de *Honeceteholne* et *Broford*, cum
boscis, brueris et aliis pertinentiis, quas Willelmus de Holne tenet.

Hameletæ de *Forde* et *Style*, cum bosco de *Hancombe* et bruerâ de *Dunneray*, quas Alianora Courteney tenet. Terræ de Elleworthe, cum boscis et brueris, quas Jacobus de Torthe tenet. Villæ de *Hankwelle* et *la Walles* cum boscis, brueris, et aliis pertinentiis, quas prior de Bath et prior de Cowyke tenent. Manerium de *Codecumbe*, cum boscis, brueris et aliis pertinentiis, quod Johannes de Moun et Symon de Raleigh tenent. Villa de *Quarmunces*, cum boscis, brueris et aliis pertinentiis, quas Willelmus de Monceans tenet. Villa de *Almonesworth* cum boscis, brueris, et aliis pertinentiis, quam Robertus filius Pagani tenet. Villa de *Exefordemony*, cum boscis, brueris et aliis pertinentiis, quam abbas de Neth tenet. Villa de *Begger-Quarme*, cum boscis, quam Willelmus de Kytenore tenet. Villa de *Wyneforde*, cum boscis, brueris et aliis pertinentiis, quam Ricardus de Ripariis et Stephanus Beumunde tenent. Hameleta de *Wydecumbe*, cum boscis, brueris et pertinentiis, quam Idonea de Kael tenet. Hameleta de Hoo, cum boscis, brueris et pertinentiis, quam Johannes de Hoo tenet. Hameleta de Tettebroke, cum boscis, brueris et pertinentiis, quam Thomas de Bokehegh tenet. Villa de *Exton*, et Villa *Haukbrugge*, et Villa de *Langacre*, cum boscis, brueris, et pertinentiis, quas Johannes Herun, Ricardus Durante, Adam Hustelegh, et heredes Galfridi de Scolonde et Eorde de Feynes tenent. Villa de *Wydepole*, cum boscis, brueris, et pertinentiis, quam abatissa de Wylton et Ricardus le Kynge tenent. Hameleta de *Brutenesworthey*, cum boscis, brueris et pertinentiis, quam . . . . de Tyntent tenet. Hameleta de *Westway*, cum boscis, brueris, et pertinentiis, quam Johannes de Sparkeford tenet. Hameleta de *Loscumbe*, cum boscis, brueris, et pertinentiis, quam Robertus de Boloyne tenet. Hameleta de *Estasway*, cum boscis, brueris et pertinentiis, quam Rogerus Beupel tenet. Hameletæ de *Telchete* et de *la Merse*, cum boscis, brueris et pertinentiis, quas prior de Taunton tenet. Villa de *Dilverton*, cum boscis, brueris et pertinentiis, quam Hawys de Pyne et Thomas de Saleye tenent. Hameletæ de *Hawkewell*, cum boscis et pertinentiis, quam Rogerus de Hawkewell tenet. Prioratus de *Barlich*, cum boscis, brueris, et pertinentiis suis, quem prior de Barlich tenet. In cujus rei testimonium sigilla juratorum huic perambulationi sunt appensa.*

* From the Episcopal Registers at Wells, as copied in Phelps's 'History of Somerset,' vol i., p. 46.

APPENDIX B

SUPERSTITION IN WEST SOMERSET

'THE schoolmaster is abroad.' This is an expression very common in the mouths of those people who believe that the reign of Ignorance is nearly at an end, and that Education is advancing with such rapid strides, that ere long few, or none, of the ancient beliefs and superstitions will be left in any corner of England, and in this belief they are probably right. Who among the rising generation will put any faith in the powers of the evil eye, of the 'conjurer,' of the witch? But there are still many old, ay, and middle-aged folk too, whose schooling days—such as they were—are over, and who have not come under the levelling influence of the Board School, nor know the benefits of Higher Education. These still believe in magic and 'curious arts,' and no amount of argument will convince them but that there is something in the fearful and wonderful tales, sights, and omens which they have heard, seen, or felt among their native hills. Did they know Shakespeare, they would doubtless exclaim with Hamlet: 'There are more things in heaven and earth, Horatio, than are dreamt of in our philosophy.' But they do not; proud are they if they have an elementary knowledge of the three R's—as they call reading, writing, and arithmetic. With them, indeed, the schoolmaster *is* abroad—in a sense the very reverse of that usually understood.

I have endeavoured, in the text, to give a general idea of some of the principal superstitions that prevail about Exmoor and the hill-country of West Somerset. Many more, however, might be cited; and it may be interesting to add here a few instances that have recently come under my notice, as well as sundry other scraps of folklore derived from other sources.

Mention has already been made of an assault case, heard before the magistrates of a town really beyond the limits of our hill-country, and, therefore, more remarkable than if it had occurred further west. I refer to the incident of a woman falling upon the neighbour by whom she had been 'overlooked.' Some may question in what manner such summary vengeance would break the spell. It appears that if blood be drawn,* the 'evil eye' loses its power, and it was doubtless with this intent that the bewitched lady took the law into her own hands. This drawing of blood, indeed, is a charm against the influence of all witchcraft, and many are the devices resorted to by the unsophisticated peasant who believes himself, or herself, 'ill-wished.' A favourite one is to place a nail or other sharp piece of metal in the witch's path, or about her house. Unfortunately, in the case above mentioned, the unsympathetic justices believed not in the evil eye, and marked their indifference to this time-honoured superstition by inflicting a fine on the aggressor.

In church, should she venture there, the witch at once stands revealed. *Stands*, literally, for she cannot kneel, try as she may, and the 'eastward position' is not for her. With her *back* to the altar, she must throughout the service maintain an erect position, for even the power to incline at the Sacred Name in the Creed is denied her.

Anyone may acquire the dubious pleasure of possessing the power of 'overlooking.' No steaming caldron or dried toads, no snakes' skins, nightshade, and other nastinesses are necessary. The 'treatment' is of the simplest. You have but to say the Lord's Prayer backwards, and walk, 'hind-side afore,' thrice round the church, and the trick is done. Try it, and see how the pig of your cantankerous neighbour fares when you look upon him, how the creditor thrives who has pressed you unduly, or whether the gossip next door, who threatened to have 'the law of you,' can meet your eye. If they do not all look sick and sorry there must

---

* ' I'll have a bout with the
Devil or Devil's dam ; I'll conjure thee,
Blood will I draw on thee; thou art a witch.'
  Talbot to La Pucelle: Shakespeare's ' Henry VI.'

' Till *drawing blood* o' the dames like Witches
They're forthwith cur'd of their Capriches.'
      Butler's ' Hudibras.'
And *vide* Brand's ' Popular Antiquities,' p. 596, Ed. 1877.

be something wrong in the manner of your carrying out my instructions.

I have lately met with an astonishing instance of belief in witchcraft. I say astonishing, because the scene is a village under the Quantocks, and within a few hundred yards of the matter-of-fact railway, the voice of whose iron steed is usually sufficient to frighten away superstition for evermore. Here there dwells an aged dame, as harmless a creature as can be found in the country. Nevertheless she is. credited, not only with the evil eye, but, O horror! with the power of turning herself into a black dog, in which form she was met a short time since, during the twilight hour, in a neighbouring lane. For these all-sufficient reasons the poor old soul was, for a while, unable to obtain the services of a nurse during an illness from which she is only now recovering.

Some witches harry their victims, not only at home, but when they—the victims—'take their walks abroad.' One poor fellow, who set out on a tramp of some fifteen miles, was so oppressed by the presence of a witch, and, like the wedding guest in the ' Ancient Mariner,' did so fear her 'glittering eye,' that he was obliged, as he said, to run all the way. And yet those he met on his flying path could see nothing. How devoutly he must have wished for the re-introduction of the stake, the ducking-stool and such like gentle remedies for ridding the world of witchcraft! Another man I hear of as suffering in a still more singular manner. He would wander in circles about the house, until he finally sunk upon the ground in such strong convulsions that it took several to hold him.

Great as are the powers of the wise woman, it is not always pleasant to be her husband. For apparently she controls his actions *wherever* he may chance to be. There was one Giles (this is not his real name, that I must not disclose) who was base—and bold —enough to desert his *bewitching* better half. For a while Mrs. Giles bore his absence with a fortitude born, perhaps, of no very great love for her partner. Then she suddenly took it into her head to have him home. She did not telegraph, she did not even write; but one day the errant husband was seen by the astonished villagers hurrying towards his deserted home. *And his footsteps were marked with blood!* The witch-wife had compelled his return in such haste that not only the soles of his boots but those of his *feet* were worn out.

From time immemorial the hare has been the animal whose form the witch most loves to assume. A man was very ill. Against the garden wall just opposite his window, day after day, crouched a hare. Why poor puss should not have been allowed to remain I cannot say, but an idea got abroad that one old *Sally* was somehow connected with the animal's watch, and the man's friends applied to the owner of the sporting right for permission to shoot her. This was refused ; and a dog was then procured, who soon chased puss from her form. She soon returned, however, though it was noticed that 'her scut was down.' What this signified I do not know. The fact of her having again taken up her position opposite the sick man's window was of course sufficient to convince the rustics that 'there wus zummut in it,' and one, braver than the rest, at last struck her a blow on the head. She then fled ; and was seen no more, but, strange to say, the suspected dame was encountered just after *bleeding about the head.* What could be plainer ?

Associated with the witch is the 'evil man,' by which name the wizard appears to be known in West Somerset. He is not so much *en évidence* as the witch, but is still not to be despised, as the following incidents will show. At a farm with which I am very familiar it is customary to work in wet weather in a large barn. One inclement day four men were engaged there, three of them ordinary individuals, but the fourth was, like the Heathen Chinee, conversant with

' Ways that are dark, and tricks that are vain.'

Dinner-hour came, and, emboldened, perhaps, by cider, the most frivolous of the uninitiated trio challenged the wizard to a specimen of his dark doings. The evil one at first declined, but presently, wearied with his comrade's importunity, solemnly took a mote (*i.e.*, a reed used for thatching), and, holding it vertically, raised it slowly from the ground. Presently the spectators found his face rising above the level of their own, and, looking down, lo ! his feet were lifted from the floor. Slowly, slowly this terrible personage ascended towards the cobwebby rafters, until his feet dangled, as might those of a victim of Lynch-law, over the heads of the awestruck rustics. This was too much, and, regardless of the *bathos*, one of the trembling three seized the ascending necromancer by the heels, and he was dragged back to terra firma. But the importunate youth had fled, and arrived, pale and in cold perspiration, at the house of my informant, to whom he poured forth the tale. The latter hastened to the spot, and, after interrogating the others separately, and finding that their versions agreed, was, as he told me, nonplussed. Nor was this the last feat of the 'evil man.' Being dismissed by his master, behold ! within a few days a *calf* was seen on the roof of the barn, a spot inaccessible even to bipeds without a ladder. Of course he had been ' spirited' there by the revengeful wizard, and very gingerly indeed—for might not magic be in it?— was the animal delivered from its unwonted position, and the labourers departed to their work more than ever convinced of the miraculous powers of their former companion.

The conjurer, too, still exists, and some of them attach great value to certain books (in manuscript), inscribed with mysterious and cabalistic figures. An acquaintance of mine was requested by one of these gentlemen to select and touch a numeral in his particular tome, which was, though with no belief, done. The conjurer remarked, ' That's a lucky number ; you'll come to no harm.' And, as a matter of fact, the years that have since elapsed have seen my old friend escape the various accidents that have overtaken his fellows, and he is as well preserved as the most hale octogenarian in West Somerset.

But what happens to the scoffer? Both conjurer and book were once derided by a toper at the inn at Stogumber. Whether he had kept his spirits up by pouring spirits down (as Tom Hood says) to such an extent that he knew not his head from his heels, is, perhaps, uncertain ; but he *says* that on his homeward way he encountered in the road an enormous stone, which something compelled him to carry groaning home. The weight was so terrible that he could scarce reach his destination, and when the incubus at last fell from his shoulder his relief was only to be measured by the woe of that last *mauvais quart d'heure.*

But stronger, perhaps, than belief in either witch or wizard is the belief in 'death-tokens.' Nor can one altogether be surprised at simple folk indulging in superstition about incidents so strange, so inexplicable that even the scepticism of the educated is not unfrequently shaken. Here is an instance. I was but the other day talking to a worthy yeoman and churchwarden who avows his utter disbelief in the supernatural, but who yet related an incident which though it did not affect *his* strong mind, might very well confirm the superstitious notions of his weaker brother. He was sitting with some friends at breakfast in full view of the front door, when the knocker rapped sharply thrice. He is perfectly sure that no one could have touched it without detection. One of the company remarked, 'Oh! I expect *that* is my uncle.' Strangely enough, a death had occurred in the family, not the uncle of the speaker, but my friend's aunt. Hence knockings are much dreaded, whether at the door or on the bed's head. Almost as fearsome is the 'cock's shrill clarion' at midnight, a bird entering a room or persistently haunting the window-sill. I am on intimate terms with the member of a family whose fatal bird is the robin, which has several times heralded the approaching dissolution of a son or daughter of the house. The old gossips, too, can tell from the tone of the church-bell whether it portends death, and the man or woman who encounters a white leaf on his or her beanstalk is certainly marked by the destroyer. Just before writing the above, I was in a cottage at no great distance from Watchet. The woman told me that she remembers her father dying shortly after noticing this sign of death in the garden.

A farmer riding home from Taunton Market noticed a white rook among the sable flock settling over a field. When he reached home there were symptoms of uneasiness among his cattle, and that night the dogs barked so vociferously that he had to get up and quiet them. In the morning he was dead.

With the ancient Greeks, the natives of West Somerset seem to believe that 'a dream, too, is from Zeus,' and Miss King recommends a man never to go to sleep in the neighbourhood of Exmoor, for to dream, *inter alia*, of eggs, copper money or a *surpliced clergyman*, is significant of great misfortune, if of nothing more.

As for bees, our West-country friends know as much of their movements as the Roman poet, and far more what those movements portend. How astonished Virgil would be to be told that to pay for bees in money brings ill-luck; that a young swarm re-entering the hive at once means death in the house, while the death of the buzzing insects *en masse* is still more indicative that the sands are running low!

With regard to the gruesome custom of spirit-watching on Midsummer's Eve, it appears that other churches, besides the one mentioned in the text, are favoured with a company eager to pry into the mysteries of futurity. In the *Argosy* for January, 1870, the authoress above mentioned relates how a father lost his reason when his daughter's phantom remained within the building. Into some churches every soul in the parish has been seen to go, including, even, the parson and clerk ; and it does not seem a *sine quâ non* that those who issue from its portals must have an illness, though those who remain will assuredly die.

But Midsummer Eve has pleasanter and more amusing—albeit, to the parties concerned, sufficiently nerve-shaking—customs than that of watching for those about to die. The amorous god is at hand to-night, and young men and maidens are on the tiptoe of expectation. *Place aux dames.* It is bright moonlight, and rosy-cheeked Chloe stands in the churchyard with something clutched tight in her hand. It is not a love-letter, or even a lock of her young man's hair, but something connected rather with the terrors of a halter than the joys of an altar—in other words, hemp-seed.

This she tosses over her shoulders, and with tremulous lips—is it laughter or dread?—exclaims :

> ' Hemp-seed I scatter,
> Hemp-seed I sow ;
> He that is my true love
> Come after me and mow.'*

Presently she casts a fearful glance behind, and there is her lover, scythe in hand, in pursuit. Then she incontinently takes to her heels. No second glance is permitted, or the phantom will overtake her and ungallantly cut her legs with his scythe.

On Midsummer Eve, too, she may discover the initials of her future lord, by placing beneath her bed a basin filled with water, where float the letters of the alphabet face downwards. If the fates be propitious, the morning light will reveal two or three which—presumably with Cupid's assistance—have turned over during the night—the first letters of the Christian name and surname of the husband that is to be.

---

* Gay, in his ' Pastorals,' alludes to this custom in the following lines .
> ' At eve, last Midsummer, no sleep I sought,
> But to the field a bag of hemp seed brought ;
> I scattered round the seed on every side,
> And three times in a trembling accent cried .
> "This hemp-seed with my virgin hand I sow,
> Who shall my true love be, the crop to mow ?" '

Another method for ascertaining the personal appearance of her true love is to lay the table for supper, open all the doors, and wait till the clock strikes twelve. As midnight chimes, a shadowy figure enters, and with very unspiritual appetite attacks the supper and disappears. I believe this privilege is common to both Chloe and Colin, and the young man and the maiden will often share the ghostly vigil together. The supper is then partaken of by two ghosts—a female and a male.

Twelve hours later Chloe may, if she list, know the year of her marriage. Midsummer Day dawns, and at noon let her take a wedding-ring, tie it to one of her hairs, and suspend it in a glass of water. The clock again strikes twelve, and ere the last stroke has died away 'the ring will have tinkled against the glass as many times as there will be years before she will be a wife.' Whether the gentleman can by the same simple means determine the period of his celibate existence, I know not.

One of the most beautiful of Easter customs still survives. Young men have not yet ceased, on the Resurrection morning, to climb the nearest hilltop to see the sun flash over the dark ridge of Quantock, or the more distant line of Mendip. The sight of the newly arisen luminary on this particular morning is to them an augury of good luck, as it was to the white-robed Druid in the ages that are past. Early in the century Dunkery, probably because it is the highest land in Somerset, was favoured above all surrounding hills, and its sides, says Miss King, 'were covered with young men, who seemed to come from every quarter of the compass, and to be pressing up towards the Beacon.'

Twelfth Day is another time when superstition reigns supreme. The lady above cited, who, as long resident among the rustics of West Somerset, is no mean authority, states that on Twelfth Day, *i.e.*, old Christmas Day, each farmer is supposed to double the allowance of fodder. Should he omit this duty, disaster in various forms will infallibly overtake him, as witness the story of the penurious housewife who once deprived the cattle of the extra provender allotted by her more liberal lord. What was the result? Blighted were the crops; barren were the hens; the cows kicked over the milk-pails; her daughter lost her sweetheart, and she herself met with an accident and broke her right arm.

On the eve of Twelfth Day, too, though not in many places, the

20—2

orchard is visited by Farmer, Mrs. Farmer, and every hind and maidservant on the farm. Hot spiced cider is handed round, sometimes with apples floating therein. A sort of incantation is then indulged in, something to this effect :

> ' Health to thee, good apple-tree !
> May you bear hats full,
> Caps full, three bushel-bags full !'*

and the fruitful trees are then toasted, and afterwards treated to a libation of the liquor.

And here our notice of superstition in West Somerset must end. Although much is ridiculous, most is interesting, especially when we remember how surely folklore is dying, withered by the breath of education. The above must only be taken as a sample of Western superstitions ; several other instances might be adduced to prove that here, under the shadow of the hills, the beliefs—harmless for the most part—of our forefathers have not yet ' perished out of the land.'

---

* This song was known as the ' Watsail,' the old Saxon *waes hael*, *i.e.*, wassail. ' Watsail : a drinking song sung on Twelfth Day Eve, throwing toast to the apple-trees in order to have a fruitful year, which seems to be a relic of the heathen sacrifice to Pomona.' Glossary to the Exmoor Dialect—*Vide* Brand's ' Popular Antiquities,' p. 16

APPENDIX C

INSCRIBED STONE ON WINSFORD HILL

THE antiquary referred to on p. 91, Professor Rhys, has, as was feared, been unable, up to the present, to visit this stone. A drawing, however, has been submitted to him, and the reading he gives of the first word of the inscription practically coincides with my own. The following is an extract from his letter :

'I take the inscription to be of the Romano-British type, which I have been in the habit of associating in Wales and Cornwall with the fifth and sixth centuries. I am not sure, without seeing the stone itself, as to the correct reading, but I should say that, according to your facsimile, the first name should read *Curataci*. The next letters I can make nothing of, unless they are the imperfect remains of FILIVS—that is to say, *filius*. This is, however, a mere guess.'

These stones are not uncommon in Wales and Cornwall, and I know of three in Devon, the Nabarr, Sabine and Nepranus Stones at Tavistock, and there is, I think, another in the neighbourhood of Modbury. A fifth lately, at Fardel, near Ivybridge, has been removed to the British Museum. But this stone on Winsford Hill is, so far as I am aware, the only specimen of its kind in Somerset.

ELEVATIONS OF THE PRINCIPAL HILLS IN WEST SOMERSET

DERIVED PARTLY FROM THE RECENTLY ISSUED ORDNANCE MAPS AND PARTLY SUPPLIED BY THE ORDNANCE SURVEY OFFICE, SOUTHAMPTON, FEB. 26, 1890.

NAME.	POINT WHERE ELEVATION TAKEN.	ALTITUDE IN FEET.
Alderman's Barrow (Exmoor)	Highest on Ordnance Sheet	1,457
Bendle's Barrows (Exmoor)	„ „ „	1,521
*Croydon Hill	Trigonometrical station	1,256
Danesborough (Quantocks)	Highest on Ordnance Sheet	1,094
*Dunkery Beacon (Exmoor)	Trigonometrical station	1,707
*Elworthy Barrows (Brendon Hills)	Highest recorded height near Trigonometrical station	1,283
Fire Beacon (Quantocks)	Highest on Ordnance Sheet	1,019
Hurley Beacon (Quantocks)	„ „ „	1,120
Lucott Hill (Exmoor)	„ „ „	1,519
*Span Head (Exmoor)	Trigonometrical station	1,619
*Willsneck (Quantocks)	Highest recorded height near Trigonometrical station	1,261
*Wiveliscombe Barrow (Brendon Hills)	„ „	1,283

* Supplied by the Ordnance Survey Office. Of the Trigonometrical stations they write 'These are presumably on the highest points of the hills, though that fact has not definitely been determined.'

INDEX

The reference in the second column is to the division on the map; e.g , Bratton Court, G2.

BILLING AND SONS, PRINTERS, GUILDFORD.

Lightning Source UK Ltd.
Milton Keynes UK
UKHW020634150321
380371UK00008B/859